Using Technology for Problem Solving in Middle and High School Mathematics

Investigations Using Scientific and Graphing Calculators, Spreadsheets, and The Geometer's Sketchpad®

Kenneth P. Goldberg
New York University

Upper Saddle River, New Jersey
Columbus, Ohio

KH

Library of Congress Cataloging-in-Publication Data

Goldberg, Kenneth P.
Using technology for problem solving in middle and high school mathematics: investigations using scientific and graphing calculators, spreadsheets, and Geometer's Sketchpad / Kenneth P. Goldberg.
p.cm.
Includes bibliographical references and index.
ISBN 0-13-118181-5
1. Mathematics—Study and teaching (Middle school) 2. Mathematics—Study and teaching (Secondary) 3. Calculators. 4. Computer-assisted instruction. 5. Educational technology. 6. Problem solving. I. Title.

QA20.C34G65 2007 2006043821
510.71′2—dc22

Vice President and Publisher: Jeffery W. Johnston
Executive Editor: Linda Ashe Bishop
Associate Editor: Meredith Sarver
Production Editor: Alexandrina Benedicto Wolf
Production Coordination: Carlisle Publishing Services
Design Coordinator: Diane C. Lorenzo
Cover Designer: Aaron Dixon
Cover image: Fotosearch
Production Manager: Pamela D. Bennett
Director of Marketing: David Gesell
Senior Marketing Manager: Darcy Betts Prybella
Marketing Assistant: Brian Mounts

This book was set in Times by Carlisle Publishing Services. It was printed and bound by Command Web. The cover was printed by Command Web.

Pearson Education Ltd.
Pearson Education Singapore Pte. Ltd.
Pearson Education Canada, Ltd.
Pearson Education—Japan
Pearson Education Australia Pty. Limited
Pearson Education North Asia Ltd.
Pearson Educatión de Mexico, S.A. de C.V.
Pearson Education Malaysia Pte. Ltd.

10 9 8 7 6 5 4 3 2 1
ISBN: 0-13-118181-5

6/23/06

To my wife Jeanne, who brings love and adventure into my life
and without whose patience and support I could never have completed this book.
To my three wonderful children,
Timothy, Rebecca, and Andrew,
who make life exciting and worthwhile on a daily and sometimes even hourly basis.

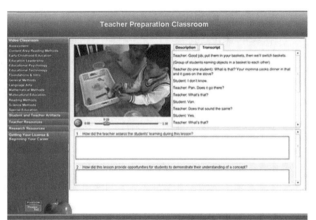

Contents

Preface vii

Introduction x

PART ONE The Scientific Calculator: Research Results on the Classroom Use of the Scientific Calculator 1

Investigation 1 Ancient Egyptian Mathematics and Unit Fractions 4
- Related Readings 7
- Activity Sheet 1.1 8

Investigation 2 Recursively Defined Functions and the Limit of an Infinite Sequence 9
- Related Readings 15
- Activity Sheet 2.1 16
- Activity Sheet 2.2 17
- Activity Sheet 2.3 18

Investigation 3 The Effect of Successive Percentage Increases and Decreases on the Price of an Item 19
- Related Readings 23
- Activity Sheet 3.1 24
- Activity Sheet 3.2 25

Investigation 4 Fixed Points and Converging Sequences 26
- Related Readings 31
- Activity Sheet 4.1 32
- Activity Sheet 4.2 33
- Activity Sheet 4.3 34

PART TWO The Graphing Calculator: Research Results on the Classroom Use of the Graphing Calculator 35

Investigation 5 The Formula for the Sum of an Infinite Geometric Series 37
- Related Readings 41
- Activity Sheet 5.1 42
- Activity Sheet 5.2 43

Investigation 6 The Units Digits of Perfect Squares: Histograms and Relative Frequency Tables 44
- Related Readings 47
- Activity Sheet 6.1 49
- Activity Sheet 6.2 50
- Activity Sheet 6.3 51

Investigation 7 **Probability and the Concept of Fairness: A Simple Program** 52

Related Readings 55
Activity Sheet 7.1 56
Activity Sheet 7.2 57
Activity Sheet 7.3 58
Activity Sheet 7.4 59

Investigation 8 **Examining the Trajectory of an Object in Motion Using Graphs and Tables of Values** 60

Related Readings 63
Activity Sheet 8.1 64
Activity Sheet 8.2 65

Investigation 9 **A Visual Inspection of the Real Roots of a Polynomial Function** 66

Related Readings 70
Activity Sheet 9.1 72
Activity Sheet 9.2 73

Investigation 10 **The Relationship between the Coefficients of a First or Second Degree Function and the Behavior of Its Graph** 74

Related Readings 79

Investigation 11 **A Visual Discovery of Trigonometric Identities and Formulas** 81

Related Readings 84
Activity Sheet 11.1 86
Activity Sheet 11.2 87

Investigation 12 **Exploring Derivatives Using Both Algebraic and Visual Representations** 88

Related Readings 90
Activity Sheet 12.1 91
Activity Sheet 12.2 92
Activity Sheet 12.3 93

Investigation 13 **Converging and Diverging Infinite Series and Special Mathematical Constants** 94

Related Readings 99
Activity Sheet 13.1 100
Activity Sheet 13.2 101

Investigation 14 **The Use of Linear and Nonlinear Regression for Curve Fitting and Making Predictions** 102

Related Readings 105
Activity Sheet 14.1 106
Activity Sheet 14.2 108

Investigation 15 Exponential Growth and Exponential Regression 110
Related Readings 113
Activity Sheet 15.1 114
Activity Sheet 15.2 115
Activity Sheet 15.3 116

Investigation 16 Generalized Fibonacci Sequences Using Matrices 117
Related Readings 120
Activity Sheet 16.1 122
Activity Sheet 16.2 123

PART THREE Dynamic Geometry Software: Research Results and Effective Classroom Practice 125

Investigation 17 Relating the Properties of Quadrilaterals to the Properties of Their Diagonals and Creating a Book of Shapes 127
Related Readings 130
Activity Sheet 17.1 131

Investigation 18 Inscribed Quadrilaterals 132
Related Readings 135
Activity Sheet 18.1 136

Investigation 19 The Sum of the Perpendicular Distances from an Interior Point of a Regular Polygon to Its Sides 137
Related Readings 140
Activity Sheet 19.1 141

Investigation 20 Perimeter and Area Relationships on a Line Segment 142
Related Readings 145
Activity Sheet 20.1 146

Investigation 21 Area Relationships between Inscribed and Circumscribed Circles of Regular Polygons 147
Related Readings 149
Activity Sheet 21.1 150
Activity Sheet 21.2 151

Investigation 22 The Product of the Segments of Intersecting Chords in a Circle 152
Related Readings 153
Activity Sheet 22.1 154

Investigation 23 The Geometric Solution of a Minimization Problem Using Reflection of a Point Across a Line Segment 155

Related Readings 157
Activity Sheet 23.1 158

Solutions 160

Index 177

Preface

Twenty-five or thirty years ago computers and hand-held calculators were things you read about in science fiction books and that only "nerds" owned and knew how to use. How times have changed. Now most people have computers both at home and at the office; hand-held calculators are commonly available with features we couldn't even have imagined; and we couldn't get along without either of these devices at home or at work.

Still, computers and calculators are often used on an ad hoc, improvised basis in mathematics classes rather than in a consistent, well-planned way, moving from simple to more sophisticated technology and mathematical understanding. Teachers who want to use technology as a tool for effective mathematics teaching, and to integrate its use into their classroom practices, must use whatever technology activities their textbooks contain, or search out activities independently and try to mold them into a coherent course.

Any teacher, however, needs an idea of the ultimate goal of an entire course, and an instructional strategy into which individual lessons and activities fit logically and sequentially. And so mathematics teachers need an overall plan for how to use technology as a regular part of instruction and for what objectives. This book is intended to help teachers do just that.

Problem Solving: The Focus of the Text

This book deals with *problem solving* and the skills this term encompasses, including *mathematical reasoning, communication, pattern recognition, conjecture*, and the development of a *mathematical proof* or a *convincing mathematical argument*. Problem solving underlies much of mathematics and how it is used. In fact, problem solving is the first process standard listed in the National Council of Teachers of Mathematics' *Principles and Standards for School Mathematics* (NCTM, 2000). According to the *Standards*, instructional programs from pre-kindergarten through grade 12 should enable all students to

- build new mathematical knowledge through problem solving;
- solve problems that arise in mathematics and in other contexts;
- apply and adapt a variety of appropriate strategies to solve problems;
- monitor and reflect on the process of mathematical problem solving.

Standards: Guidelines for Creating and Using Problem-Solving Investigations

In "Recommendations and Guidelines for Using Technology in the Mathematics Classroom" (pp. xii–xix) we use the National Council of Teachers of Mathematics' *Principles and Standards for School Mathematics* (referred to as the *Standards*) to create guidelines for the creation and use of technology-enhanced problem-solving investigations. We also use the recommendations of other professional associations and groups.

Inclusive: Four Types of Instructional Technology

This book provides a five-step model and numerous sample investigations that help students become better problem solvers using four types of instructional technology: the scientific calculator, the graphing calculator, spreadsheet software, and *The Geometer's Sketchpad®* software.

Many companies sell hand-held scientific and graphing calculators for home and classroom use. But Texas Instruments has consistently produced calculators that are most appropriate for classroom use and have the features teachers and students need. Consequently, the calculators discussed and illustrated in this book are those produced by Texas Instruments.

The scientific calculators illustrated in this text are the *TI Explorer Plus*, the *TI-34 II*, and the *TI-30X*. The graphing calculators demonstrated in the text are the *TI-83* and *TI-84*. All the investigations, however, with minor modifications, can be carried out using calculators from any other company.

For computer use in mathematics instruction this book emphasizes spreadsheet software, such as, but not limited to, Microsoft *Excel®* and *The Geometer's Sketchpad®* by Key Curriculum

Press (for doing dynamic geometry). The reasons that we focus on these two pieces of software are given below.

Spreadsheets

Several years before graphing calculators were commonly available, mathematics teachers used spreadsheet software for developing tables of values and corresponding graphs. Spreadsheets are easy to use and can generate tables of values and corresponding graphs or plots for many different functions. Furthermore, most computers now come with spreadsheet software, so spreadsheets are already available for teacher and student use in most computer labs at no additional expense.

The Geometer's Sketchpad® Software

Like the graphing calculator several years ago, Dynamic Geometry® software today is a fairly new addition to mathematics education technology. Many teachers have heard about this software, have attended conference presentations about it, or seen demonstrations of its use; but few are really aware of how it can enliven mathematics instruction and help students learn problem solving in a structured way.

The Geometer's Sketchpad® focuses on Euclidean geometry, an area of mathematics that calculators and spreadsheets do not. Furthermore, students at both the middle and high school level can use the software in tandem with the three other instructional technologies. Finally, newer versions include many features of the graphing calculator, making it even more versatile today than when it was first developed.

The Investigations: Function, Organization, and Goals

This text presents numerous detailed investigations, illustrating how to apply learning ideas in the classroom. This material is divided into three consistent and supportive but independent parts (The Scientific Calculator, The Graphing Calculator, and Dynamic Geometry Software), which can be used jointly or individually. Spreadsheet software is not treated separately, but is integrated into the first two parts of the book as either an alternative or a supplement to the scientific or graphing calculator.

Each part begins with a research overview on the use and effectiveness of that particular type of technology in mathematics education. It is followed by fully developed classroom investigations that show how to engage students' interest, to use the technology appropriately and effectively, and to develop problem-solving skills.

Each investigation comprises several useful sections.

- **Planning Matrices** identify the *NCTM Standards* and *Mathematical Skills and Concepts* that are covered and practiced in the investigation; the *Calculator Keys and Features* that are introduced and used in the investigation; and the *Materials* that will be needed in the investigation, including any activity and solution sheets. The *NCTM Standards* include only the content standards since those standards vary in their objectives from grade level to grade level. The related process standards are not listed since they are the same for all grade levels; these are integrated into each investigation.
- **Classroom Implementation.** This section always begins with *Background Information for the Teacher*. Then it presents a five-step model for implementing the investigation:
  Step 1 Introducing the problem-solving scenario.
  Step 2 Investigating the problem.
  Step 3 Developing a mathematical conjecture.
  Step 4 Testing the conjecture.
  Step 5 Developing either a mathematical proof or a convincing mathematical argument.
- **Follow-Up Activities** for in-class or homework use that continue and extend the basic investigation.
- A **Graphing Calculator Modification** for the scientific calculator investigations. This section is for teachers who use the graphing calculator as a scientific calculator at the middle school or junior high school level.

- A **Spreadsheet Modification** is included in investigations for which a spreadsheet can be used instead of, or in addition to, the scientific or graphing calculator.
- **Reflections for the Teacher** point out questions a teacher might want to ask during or after the investigation. They also identify mathematical or educational issues pertaining to the investigation that a teacher should be aware of.
- **Related Readings** consist of articles, books, and websites related to the mathematics and/or the pedagogy of the investigation.
- **Activity and Solution Sheets** for use in the investigation. Activity sheets appear at the end of each investigation, but all the solution sheets are in the back of the book. This makes it easier to assign the activity sheets for homework without the solutions being too readily available.

The goal here is *not* to provide you with all the calculator and computer classroom activities you will ever need as a teacher. No book could do that, nor could any book give just the right activities for your mode of teaching, your students' abilities and interests, and your school's curriculum. Only you can make those determinations.

Rather, this book tries to help you better understand what the research says are ways to effectively and successfully use technology as an ongoing part of mathematics teaching and learning; to show how instructional technology can make the mathematics classroom more engaging and participatory; and to demonstrate how technology can supplement regular classroom instruction and help students develop their problem-solving skills and all other required mathematical understandings.

My hope is that this text will help you plan how *you* can use technology regularly in *your* teaching. The problem-solving investigations and the five-step model of classroom implementation on which they are based can be the starting point for that planning.

I want to express my sincere thanks to my editors, Linda Bishop, Ben Stephen, and Meredith Sarver; they have made wonderful suggestions relating to the organization, format, and readability of this text. I would also like to express my gratitude to the reviewers who ensured that the mathematics and the pedagogy of the text would be realistic and useful. They are: Robert Berry, Old Dominion University; Linda Bolte, Eastern Washington University; Janet Bowers, San Diego State University; Roger Day, Illinois State University; Karen Hollebrands, North Carolina State University; Robert M. Horton, Clemson University; Laura Brinker Kent, University of South Carolina; Michael Mikusa, Kent State University; John Olive, The University of Georgia; John Wilkins, California State University, Dominquez Hills; and Melvin Wilson, Virginia Tech.

Introduction

RECOMMENDATIONS AND GUIDELINES FOR USING TECHNOLOGY IN THE MATHEMATICS CLASSROOM

To Enhance the Teaching, Learning, and Doing of Mathematics

Before you read this book, ask yourself—how do you feel about using technology in the mathematics classroom? Some of you might feel confident in your mathematical and technological capabilities, while others may feel quite the opposite. Throughout this text, you will examine research and standards documents that underscore the importance of integrating technology with mathematics instruction. No matter what your skill level, this text will help you integrate the use of technology with mathematics instruction. To help you do so, the text provides 23 sample investigations that use technology to enhance the teaching, learning, and doing of mathematics.

So why use technology when teaching mathematics? The National Council of Teachers of Mathematics document *Principles and Standards for School Mathematics*[*] (NCTM, 2000, p. 24) states that

> "Electronic technologies—calculators and computers—are essential tools for teaching, learning, and doing mathematics. . . . They can support investigation by students in every area of mathematics, including geometry, statistics, algebra, measurement, and number. When technological tools are available, students can focus on decision making, reflection, reasoning, and problem solving."

The *Standards* also state, in the section titled *A Vision for School Mathematics* (p. 3):

> Teachers help students make, refine, and explore conjectures on the basis of evidence and use a variety of reasoning and proof techniques to confirm or disprove these conjectures. Alone or in groups and with access to technology, they work productively and reflectively, with the skilled guidance of their teachers. Orally and in writing, students communicate their ideas and results effectively. They value mathematics and engage actively in learning it.

To Explore and Visualize Mathematics Concepts

The NCTM is not the only professional association that recommends the use of technology to enhance mathematics instruction. The American Mathematical Association of Two-Year Colleges (AMATYC) also supports the use of technology as a regular part of mathematics instruction. Their "rationale" for a position statement notes that teaching students how to visualize and explore mathematics concepts provides a solid educational foundation for further personal, academic, and professional growth: "The appropriate use of technology plays a key role in this instruction and in the teaching of appropriate problem-solving skills" (*AMATYC Position Statement on the Instructional Use of Technology in Mathematics*, http://www.amatyc.org/documents/Guidelines-Position/Tech-Use.htm).

To Support Problem Solving and Promote Mathematics Understanding

Similarly, the Committee on Undergraduate Programs in Mathematics (CUPM) of the Mathematical Association of America (MAA) recommends that "departments, programs and all courses in the mathematical sciences . . . use computer technology to support problem solving and to promote understanding." Specifically, the recommendation states that

---

[*]Reprinted with permission from *Principles and Standards for School Mathematics*, copyright 2000, by the National Council of Teachers of Mathematics. All rights reserved.

At every level of the curriculum, some courses should incorporate activities that will help all students progress in learning to use technology:

- Appropriately and effectively as a tool for solving problems;
- As an aid to understanding mathematical ideas.

To Take Advantage of Technology and Incorporate Multiple Mathematics Representations

Useful guidelines are also provided in the journal *Contemporary Issues in Technology and Teacher Education* in an article titled "Promoting Appropriate Uses of Mathematics in Mathematics Teacher Preparation" (Volume 1, Issue 1). This article was written by faculty from the Center for Technology and Teacher Education who, according to its website (http://www.teacherlink.org), are "a cross-disciplinary group of faculty working together in the Curry School of Education at the University of Virginia."

According to this article the primary guidelines for the instructional use of technology are to: (i) introduce technology in context; (ii) address worthwhile mathematics with appropriate pedagogy; (iii) take advantage of technology; (iv) connect mathematics topics; and (v) incorporate multiple representations.

To Experiment with Mathematics Concepts to Deepen Mathematical Understanding

Finally, we cannot omit a set of guidelines provided by Evan Glazer in his article "Creating Technology-Enhanced Mathematics Investigations" (Volume 1, Number 3, Spring 2003 issue of *On-Math*). National Council of Teachers of Mathematics (http://www.nctm.org).

In this article Glazer first describes technology-enhanced mathematics investigations (TEMIs) as activities that enable students to experiment with mathematical concepts and visualize multiple representations. TEMIs generally promote learning experiences that would be difficult or impossible without the appropriate technology. Glazer then provides guidelines for the design of TEMIs.

To Encourage and Enhance the Study and Understanding of Mathematics

In thinking about these recommendations and guidelines we should remember that the purpose of technology in the mathematics classroom is primarily to encourage and enhance the study and understanding of mathematics. Therefore, just pulling the calculator out of the closet once in a while to play games, or going to the computer lab a few times during the year, is not "an essential part of the [classroom] environment" as meant by the *Standards* when it refers to technology.

Using technology, however, can and should be fun. Students should become familiar and comfortable with calculators and computers, and should learn to use them as naturally in the mathematics classroom as in the home to balance a checkbook or write a letter. So let's not take that fun and excitement away from our students; rather we should use it as a very important means to help them see mathematics as more than just memorizing algorithms and applying formulas.

Following are guidelines for the development and implementation of technology-enhanced problem-solving investigations. These guidelines have been distilled from many sources, including the ones listed above. Keep them in mind as you read through (and use) the investigations in this book and as you develop your own technology-enhanced problem-solving investigations.

Guidelines for the Development of Technology-Enhanced Problem-Solving Investigations in Mathematics

1. The activity should have clearly defined mathematical objectives embedded in a problem-solving situation.
2. The activity should begin with an interesting problem or question that will grab the students' interest and motivate them to become involved in the investigation.
3. The activity should be one in which technology enables students to investigate the situation more easily or efficiently than they could without the technology.

4. Although the activity should primarily develop mathematical understanding, it should also enable the students, whenever possible, to became skilled in the use of the technology as well.
5. Activities should distinguish clearly between using technology to show that patterns, relationships, or formulas hold in a finite number of cases; and using mathematical techniques to show that these patterns, relationships, or formulas hold all the time. Consequently, whenever possible, students should follow the conjectures they develop from their technology-enhanced investigations with a mathematical justification of some type. Depending on the students' mathematical knowledge and maturity, they can develop either formal mathematical proofs or convincing mathematical arguments.
6. Whenever possible, provide follow-up questions to the initial problem. Students then can use what they have learned in a different context, or they can take what they have learned and generalize it.

Investigations in This Text

These guidelines are incorporated into the five-step problem-solving model upon which all the investigations are based. This five-step model consists of:

1. Introducing the problem-solving scenario;
2. Investigating the problem;
3. Developing a mathematical conjecture;
4. Empirically testing the conjecture; and
5. Whenever possible, developing either a mathematical proof or a convincing mathematical argument.

Notice the last step. It is always the teacher who, as the person most knowledgeable about students' mathematical capabilities, determines whether they can understand a formal proof of the conjectures they have made and empirically verified; or whether a less formal convincing mathematical argument is more appropriate.

Even where we provide a culminating proof as part of an investigation, the proof is intended for you, the teacher, and not necessarily the students, unless you feel that the students can understand it. You know your students best, so you must make this important decision.

PART ONE

The Scientific Calculator

Research Results on the Classroom Use of the Scientific Calculator

1 Ancient Egyptian Mathematics and Unit Fractions

2 Recursively Defined Functions and the Limit of an Infinite Sequence

3 The Effect of Successive Percentage Increases and Decreases on the Price of an Item

4 Fixed Points and Converging Sequences

BACKGROUND AND OVERVIEW

On December 4, 1997, Heidi Pomerantz of Rice University presented a paper, "The Role of Calculators in Math Education," to a Superintendents Forum in Dallas, Texas, as part of a project funded by the National Science Foundation for the improvement of mathematics and science teaching. In this document, Ms. Pomerantz lists and debunks five commonly held myths about the use of calculators as tools for mathematics instruction.

Essentially these myths are: (i) Calculators are a crutch for lazy students; (ii) calculators do all the work so students are not stimulated or challenged; (iii) calculators are unnecessary since people did fine in school for many years without them; (iv) the use of calculators hinders the learning of basic math facts and skills; and, (v) if students become dependent on calculators then they will be lost without them.

Ms. Pomerantz counters these myths by arguing that mathematics is more than simple memorization and "skill and drill." Rather, she notes that, "At its heart, mathematics embodies logic and reasoning, problem solving and number sense, and a search for order. It involves discovery, pattern recognition, applications, concepts, construction of relationships, reasoning from data, problem solving, and abstract thinking."

The message Ms. Pomerantz conveys is that using technology to solve math problems actually *enhances* mathematical learning, allowing teachers and students to focus more on the "whys" of mathematics rather than the "hows" (Pomerantz, Heidi. "The Role of Calculators in Math Education," http://education.ti.com/educationportal/sites/US/nonProductSingle/research_therole.html).

The literature concerning the debate on the use of calculators in the mathematics classroom reveals that disagreements continue because the opposing camps are focusing on two different aspects of learning and doing mathematics. The supporters of full calculator use worry most about the non-computational and non-algorithmic aspects of mathematics such as problem solving, developing and proving conjectures, pattern recognition and use concept development, and real world applications. These individuals argue that these higher level capabilities are of paramount importance in the modern world and the modern workplace; the old standbys of basic skills development and algorithmic competency are simply not enough anymore. Supporters of full calculator use believe that textbooks, curricula, and classroom activities that promote these higher level skills are superior to those that do not and that the evaluation of mathematical understanding should focus on these capabilities.

The opponents of full calculator use argue that a student does not really know, and cannot correctly use mathematics without competency and efficiency in basic computational and algorithmic skills. These individuals believe that textbooks, curricula, or classroom activities that do not develop these basic skills before higher level learning takes place are "soft" and "fuzzy."

Research that shows the positive effects of classroom use of calculators on higher level skills and understandings, but ignores the development of basic skills and algorithmic capabilities, encourages the first group of individuals but does not impress the second group. Conversely, research that shows calculator use harms basic skills and algorithmic capabilities will appeal to those who oppose full calculator use no matter how beneficial it may be to the development of higher level skills and understandings.

We must therefore look at what research on calculator use shows about the development of both basic skills and algorithmic understanding *and* higher level skills and concepts. If calculator use in the classroom enhances the learning and understanding of higher level skills and concepts, we must be sure that it also either enhances, or at least does not negatively affect, development of basic skills and algorithmic understanding. Only then can both sides be satisfied that calculators are a beneficial tool in the mathematics classroom.

THE RESEARCH

In 1992 the National Council of Teachers of Mathematics (NCTM) published its annual yearbook, *Calculators in Mathematics Education*, which as usual focused on a topic of current interest and concern for mathematics education. Chapter 4 deals with research on calculators in mathematics education.

The authors of this chapter, Ray Hembree of Adrian College and Donald J. Dessart of the University of Tennessee, begin by saying that in 1984 they "began to study all the research that could be found on the effects of calculator use in precollege mathematics" because calculators at that time seemed to be having little impact on the mathematics curriculum, in spite of their great potential benefit.

Hembree and Dessart found that negative forces were countering the positive attitudes of mathematics educators toward the use of calculators, and that ". . . these forces seemed to evolve from concerns that the hand-held computing machine would displace students' skills with mental arithmetic and paper-and-pencil algorithms."

The authors conclude, therefore, that there needed to be "a rigorous, formal study of the overall body of research literature on calculator effects. Perhaps such an analysis would help resolve the controversy." (Reprinted with permission from *NCTM Yearbook*, copyright 1992 by the National Council of Teachers of Mathematics.)

Hembree and Dessart then discuss the results of this meta-analysis, which culminated in their publication of the article "Effects of Hand-held Calculators in Precollege Mathematics Education: A Meta-Analysis," published in 1986 in the *Journal for Research in Mathematics Education* (Vol. 17, No. 2, p. 96). This article looked at the results of 79 reports of experiments and relational investigations in which a treatment group of students used calculators for a specified period of time (usually around 30 school days) and were then tested in the areas of computation, concepts, and problem solving. In some studies the students who had used calculators in class were also allowed to use them on tests, while in others neither the treatment group nor the control group students used calculators on tests.

In their meta-analysis Hembree and Dessart found that, in general, calculator use appeared to improve both achievement and attitude for most students at most ability levels and in most grades, with no negative effects on computational development except at the fourth grade. Even at this grade level, however, the results were so dependent on the specific use of the calculator that additional research would be needed to see if this result was merely an aberration.

In particular, Hembree and Dessart (1986) had this to say about the relationship between calculator use in the classroom and student attitude.

> Students using calculators possess a better attitude toward mathematics and an especially better self-concept in mathematics than noncalculator students. This statement applies across all grades and ability levels. (Reprinted with permission from *JRME*, copyright 1986 by the National Council of Teachers of Mathematics.)

Aimee J. Ellington of Virginia Commonwealth University presents a more recent meta-analysis of research on the use of calculators. It focuses on 54 research studies conducted during the period 1983 to 2002 ("A Meta-Analysis of the Effects of Calculators on Students' Achievement and Attitude Levels in Precollege Mathematics Classes." *Journal for Research in Mathematics Education,* 2003, Vol. 34, No. 5, pp. 433–463).

The abstract at the beginning of the article provides an overview of the results of this meta-analysis. A portion is provided below.

> The findings of 54 research studies were integrated through meta-analysis to determine the effects of calculators on student achievement and attitude levels. . . . Results revealed that students' operational skills and problem-solving skills improved when calculators were an integral part of testing and instruction. The results for both skill types were mixed when calculators were not part of assessment, but in all cases, calculator use did not hinder the development of mathematical skills. Students using calculators had better attitudes toward mathematics than their non-calculator counterparts.

Ellington makes the following two points concerning how calculators should be used as a part of classroom practice, and for how long, if positive results are to be achieved:

- Students received the most benefit when calculators had a pedagogical role in the classroom and were not just available for drill and practice or checking work.
- In order to have a positive influence on students' operational skills, the findings suggest that calculator use during instruction should be long term (i.e., 9 or more weeks). (Reprinted with permission from *JRME*, copyright 2003 by the National Council of Teachers of Mathematics.)

Another researcher who has focused on the use of technology in mathematics instruction is Penelope H. Dunham of the Department of Mathematical Sciences at Muhlenberg College. In 1998 Dunham reviewed dozens of studies carried out on this topic since 1986 and found several trends:

- Students who use graphing calculators display better understanding of functions and graph concepts, improved problem solving, and higher scores on achievement tests for algebra and calculus skills.
- Students who learn paper-and-pencil skills in conjunction with technology-based instruction and are tested without calculators perform as well or better than students who do not use technology in instruction.
- Those (teachers) who support mastery first often view mathematics as computation rather than a process for patterning, reasoning, and problem solving. (Reprinted by permission from *Hand-Held Technology in Mathematics and Science Education: A Collection of Papers*, copyright 1998 by The Ohio State University.)

The research seems to show clearly and unambiguously that calculators, when used appropriately and as a component of good teaching, benefit students in *both* basic skills and algorithms *and* higher order skills and understandings. The calculator is a tool of mathematical investigation similar to the tools used in scientific investigation, such as a microscope or a telescope. It should be employed as a regular part of effective mathematics instruction.

INVESTIGATION 1

Ancient Egyptian Mathematics and Unit Fractions

PLANNING: GRADES 6–8

RELATED NCTM STANDARDS: Number & Operations

- Work flexibly with fractions, decimals, and percents to solve problems.
- Understand the meaning and effects of arithmetic operations with fractions, decimals, and integers.

RELATED NCTM STANDARDS: Algebra

- Represent, analyze, and generalize a variety of patterns with tables, graphs, words, and, when possible, symbolic rules.
- Use symbolic algebra to represent situations and to solve problems.

MATHEMATICAL SKILLS AND CONCEPTS

Recognize numerical patterns.

Represent numerical patterns algebraically.

Simplify algebraic expressions using symbolic manipulation.

Learn about the historical development of mathematics.

CALCULATOR KEYS AND FEATURES

The fraction key [/].

The fraction simplify key [Simp].

MATERIALS

Copies of Activity Sheet 1.1 and Solution Sheet 1.1 for each student.

CLASSROOM IMPLEMENTATION

Background Information for the Teacher

It's difficult to appreciate the power of algebraic notation and symbolic manipulation without knowing what mathematics was like before the development of this important technique. Historical activities such as the one in this investigation are one way to illustrate this power to students. Who knows; they might even pique your students' curiosity and start them reading about other interesting events and people in the history of mathematics.

Step 1–Introducing the Problem Solving Scenario

Explain to your students that while modern mathematics originated with the Greeks more than 2,000 years ago and Euclid's axiomatic geometry, many civilizations before that time used mathematics for such practical purposes as determining the annual harvest taxes, land sales, astronomical predictions, and the construction of roads, aqueducts, and other structures.

In ancient Egyptian civilization, in particular, mathematics reached a high level of understanding and application. Individuals who learned the skills of both mathematics and writing were highly respected and called "scribes." In fact, many tablets from this period of time have been found that show the mathematical problems that scribes practiced to learn arithmetic skills. One of the most fascinating of these skills was the use of fractions.

Tell your students that the only fractions in ancient Egyptian arithmetic aside from $\frac{2}{3}$, were the unit fractions: $\frac{1}{2}$, $\frac{1}{3}$, $\frac{1}{4}$, and so on. Of course, any fraction can be written as a sum of unit fractions, for example, $\frac{3}{5}$ can be expressed as $\frac{1}{5} + \frac{1}{5} + \frac{1}{5}$; so using only unit fractions at first glance does not seem to be a major limitation. However, certain arithmetic shortcuts we use today without even thinking about them were not available to these scribes. For example, $\frac{1}{3}$ and $\frac{1}{5}$ could not be added together to obtain $\frac{1}{3} + \frac{1}{5} = \frac{5}{15} + \frac{3}{15} = \frac{8}{15}$ since $\frac{8}{15}$ is not a unit fraction and therefore could not be expressed in their arithmetic.

On the other hand, some simplifications involving unit fractions were possible at this time, such as $\frac{1}{3} + \frac{1}{6} = \frac{1}{2}$, since all three fractions in this relationship are *unit* fractions. In fact, Egyptian scribes memorized such relationships so that they would know if a sum or difference of unit fractions could be replaced by a simpler but equivalent unit fraction. In this investigation students will be able to discover one of these unit fraction relationships; to prove it algebraically (which the Egyptians of that time could not do since they did not have algebraic representation); and to create their own ancient Egyptian unit fraction relationships.

Problem. To discover when the sum of two unit fractions with the second denominator twice the first is itself a unit fraction.

Step 2–Investigating the Problem

This investigation involves the addition of many pairs of unit fractions, so tell your students they may use some basic keys on their calculators to simplify the process. If the calculator they are using has the fraction key [/] and the fraction simplify key [Simp] (like the *Explorer Plus* or the *TI-34 II*), you can show them how to use these keys to add two unit fractions and then determine whether this sum can be expressed as a unit fraction. For example, the keystroke sequence shown below adds $\frac{1}{3} + \frac{1}{6}$ to give $\frac{3}{6}$; then pressing [Simp] [=] reduces $\frac{3}{6}$ to the equivalent unit fraction $\frac{1}{2}$.

On the other hand, using a similar keystroke sequence to add $\frac{1}{2}$ and $\frac{1}{4}$ gives $\frac{3}{4}$; and since pressing [Simp] [=] leaves this result unchanged, this sum cannot be represented as a unit fraction.

A calculator like the *TI-30Xa*, which has the fraction key [a b/c] instead of the [/] and [Simp] keys, automatically displays the result of combining fractions in reduced form. It shows immediately, as illustrated below, that $\frac{1}{3} + \frac{1}{6}$ can be represented as a unit fraction while $\frac{1}{2} + \frac{1}{4}$ cannot:

Step 3–Developing a Conjecture

Explain to your students that one simplification rule for unit fractions that the scribes used involves the sum of two unit fractions where the second denominator is twice the first, such as $\frac{1}{2} + \frac{1}{4}$ or $\frac{1}{3} + \frac{1}{6}$. Hand out copies of **Activity Sheet 1.1** and let your students work on it in small groups so they can share their work with each other. Encourage students to use the fraction keys on the calculators to perform the unit fraction computations, as you demonstrated.

Stop the group work after the students have completed Questions 1 and 2 to make sure everyone recognizes the pattern that appears and what it tells them. Then facilitate the answers to Questions 3 and 4 in which they use the pattern they found to conjecture the rules used by the scribes to simplify unit fraction sums of this type. Sample conjectures are provided on the solution sheet.

Step 4–Testing the Conjectures

Once the students have come up with their conjectures, give them a few unit fraction sums of this type that were not included on the Activity Sheet. Ask them first to use their conjectures to predict the results of the additions, and then to use their calculator's fraction keys to verify their predictions.

For example, you could give them the following sums:

$$\frac{1}{20} + \frac{1}{40} \quad \text{and} \quad \frac{1}{21} + \frac{1}{42}$$

From their conjectures, the first sum cannot be written as a unit fraction, since 40 is *not* divisible by 3; and the sum found on the calculator is $\frac{3}{40}$, which cannot be simplified to an equivalent unit fraction. The second sum, however, can be written as a unit fraction since 42 *is* divisible by 3. This is found on the calculator to be $\frac{1}{21} + \frac{1}{42} = \frac{3}{42} = \frac{1}{14}$.

Step 5–A Mathematical Proof

The two conjectures can now be easily proven using algebraic representation and simplification. You can either provide the proof or let your students do it themselves after you have set it up for them. Simply represent the two unit fractions by $\frac{1}{a}$ and $\frac{1}{2a}$ and then add them as shown below.

$$\frac{1}{a} + \frac{1}{2a} = \frac{2}{2a} + \frac{1}{2a} = \frac{3}{2a} = \frac{1}{(2a/3)}$$

This result will be a unit fraction if and only if the denominator $\frac{2a}{3}$ is a whole number, which will happen only if 3 divides evenly into $2a$, the larger of the two original denominators. Furthermore, the larger of the two original denominators divided by 3 will be the denominator of the result. This proves the conjectures.

FOLLOW-UP DISCUSSION AND ACTIVITIES

Let your students create their own "Ancient Egyptian Unit Fraction Rule" by setting up their own type of unit fraction sum or difference and then algebraically determining when the result itself will be a unit fraction. For example, suppose a student wants to look at the sum of two unit fractions where the second denominator is *three* times the first instead of *two* times the first, as in our original investigation. In this case the unit fractions would be of the form $\frac{1}{a}$ and $\frac{1}{3a}$ and the algebraic simplification would be:

$$\frac{1}{a} + \frac{1}{3a} = \frac{3}{3a} + \frac{1}{3a} = \frac{4}{3a} = \frac{1}{(3a/4)}$$

Clearly, the sum will be a unit fraction if and only if 4 divides evenly into the larger of the original two denominators ($3a$). The result of this division ($\frac{3a}{4}$) would then be the denominator of the answer. This result can be stated as follows:

> *Ken's Unit Fraction Rule:* Given any two unit fractions with the second denominator equal to 3 times the first denominator, the sum of these two unit fractions itself will be a unit fraction if and only if 4 divides evenly into the larger denominator. Furthermore, the result of this division will be the denominator of the sum.

Students can even use subtraction instead of addition. For example, suppose you want to look at the difference of two unit fractions where the second denominator is twice the first, such as $\frac{1}{2} - \frac{1}{4}$ or $\frac{1}{3} - \frac{1}{6}$. In this case they will make the interesting discovery that *every* such difference is a unit fraction. The conjecture and its proof are provided on the next page.

Conjecture: Given the difference between two unit fractions with the second denominator equal to twice the first denominator, the difference will always be a unit fraction, and this result will be equal to the smaller of the two fractions with which you began.

Proof: $\frac{1}{a} - \frac{1}{2a} = \frac{2}{2a} - \frac{1}{2a} = \frac{1}{2a}$, a unit fraction.

GRAPHING CALCULATOR MODIFICATION

The graphing calculator does not have special keys for entering and performing computations on fractions. It does, however, have a built-in function for converting a given number into its fractional equivalent. This function, [▸Frac], is selected and brought to the main screen by pressing [MATH] followed by [ENTER]. The result of this function is always expressed in reduced form, so it enables your students to carry out this activity quite easily.

To add two fractions and obtain the result in reduced form, simply enter the fractions using the ordinary division key [÷] and then convert the result to reduced fraction form. For example, the keystroke sequence to add ½ and ¼ and display the result in reduced form as ¾ is:

[1] [÷] [2] [+] [1] [÷] [4] [▸Frac] [ENTER]

Similarly, the keystroke sequence to add ⅓ and ⅙ and display the result in reduced form as ½ is:

[1] [÷] [3] [+] [1] [÷] [6] [▸Frac] [ENTER]

REFLECTIONS FOR THE TEACHER

1. Students often seem to think that all of today's mathematics magically appeared long ago; or that it was created by geniuses who did nothing all day except mathematics and with whom they have nothing in common. Students are surprised to discover that mathematics is continually changing and that mathematicians, just like them, have families, children, hobbies, and problems. This discovery can help students see the human side of math and that they themselves can become mathematicians or knowledgeable users of mathematics.

2. To connect your students' math class with their other classes, ask their English teacher about assigning your students to write a paper on a mathematician or mathematical topic in their English class. Instruct students to use web resources and the very readable books on the history of math provided in the following section.

RELATED READINGS

Berlinghoff, William P., and Gouvea, Fernando Q. *Math Through the Ages: A Gentle History for Teachers and Others.* Oxton House, Farmington, ME, 2002.

Dunham, William. *A Journey Through Genius: The Great Theorems of Mathematics.* Wiley, 1990.

NCTM. *Mathematical History: Activities, Puzzles, Stories, and Games.* 2nd Edition, 2002.

Smith, Sanderson. *Agnesi to Zeno: Over 100 Vignettes from the History of Math.* Key Curriculum Press, 1996.

ACTIVITY SHEET

1.1 Ancient Egyptian Mathematics and Unit Fractions

Shown below is a list of unit fraction sums in which the second denominator is always twice the first. Use the fraction keys on your calculator to add each pair. Determine which pairs of fractions have a unit fraction for their sum.

If the sum can be written as a unit fraction, write the answer in the space provided. If not, write NO. Then answer the questions that follow.

$1/2 + 1/4 =$ ________	$1/9 + 1/18 =$ ________
$1/3 + 1/6 =$ ________	$1/10 + 1/20 =$ ________
$1/4 + 1/8 =$ ________	$1/11 + 1/22 =$ ________
$1/5 + 1/10 =$ ________	$1/12 + 1/24 =$ ________
$1/6 + 1/12 =$ ________	$1/13 + 1/26 =$ ________
$1/7 + 1/14 =$ ________	$1/14 + 1/28 =$ ________
$1/8 + 1/16 =$ ________	$1/15 + 1/30 =$ ________

Question 1. Look at the pairs of unit fractions above for which the sum could be written as a unit fraction. Do you see any pattern in their occurrence?

Question 2. Find some numerical characteristic of the larger denominator for pairs of unit fractions that give a unit fraction sum.

Question 3. Based on what you have discovered in Question 2, state a conjecture about when the sum of two unit fractions, with the second denominator twice the first, can itself be written as a unit fraction.

Question 4. For those pairs of unit fractions whose sum can be written as a unit fraction, compare the denominator of the sum to the larger denominator of the two original numbers. Express what you discover as a conjecture.

INVESTIGATION 2

Recursively Defined Functions and the Limit of an Infinite Sequence

PLANNING: GRADES 6–8

RELATED NCTM STANDARDS: Algebra

- Represent, analyze, and generalize a variety of patterns with tables, graphs, words, and, when possible, symbolic rules.
- Model and solve contextualized problems using various representations, such as graphs, tables, and equations.

PLANNING: GRADES 9–12

RELATED NCTM STANDARDS: Algebra

- Generalize patterns using explicitly defined and recursively defined functions.
- Use symbolic expressions, including iterative and recursive forms, to represent relationships arising from various contexts.

MATHEMATICAL SKILLS AND CONCEPTS

Represent a real world situation involving an iterative process using a recursively defined function.

Identify the fixed point of an iterative process.

Use algebraic representation and symbolic representation to find the limit of an infinite sequence generated by an iterative process.

CALCULATOR KEYS AND FEATURES

Fix decimal display key [Fix].

Operation keys [OP1] and [OP2].

MATERIALS

Copies of Activity and Solution Sheets 2.1, 2.2, and 2.3 for each student.

CLASSROOM IMPLEMENTATION

Background Information for the Teacher

Students usually study functions using the closed form, such as $y = x$ or $y = x^2$, in which an explicit formula is given for y in terms of x and they simply enter a value for x and calculate the corresponding value of y. Another type of function, much more useful for iterative situations such as compound interest or loans, is the recursive formula.

In this activity we represent a real-life situation using an iterative function. This representation then leads us to a conjecture about the long-term consequences of an environmental policy, a numerical verification of this conjecture, and finally a convincing mathematical argument.

Problem. To discover the long-term effects on the number of trees in a forest of a cutting and planting process in which 20% of the trees are cut down at the end of each year and 100 new trees are planted.

Step 1–Introducing the Problem Solving Scenario

Your students will pretend to be forest rangers in charge of a national forest that currently has 1000 trees. A new policy of cutting and planting has just been approved: At the end of each year, 20% of the trees in the forest will be cut down and 100 new, fast-growing trees will be planted. Your students are to figure out the long-term effects of this environmental policy; that is, whether all the trees will eventually disappear from the forest, the forest will be overwhelmed with trees, or something between these two extremes.

Step 2–Investigating the Problem

We begin by predicting what will happen in the next few years. Create a table showing the year and the corresponding number of trees, beginning with your current 1000 trees in Year 1:

Year	1	2	3	4	5	6	7	...
Trees	1000							

At the end of Year 1, 20% of the 1000 trees (or 200 trees) are cut down and 100 new trees are planted. This means an overall decrease of 100 trees, giving 900 trees in Year 2.

Year	1	2	3	4	5	6	7	...
Trees	1000	900						

Similarly, at the end of Year 2, 20% of the 900 trees (or 180 trees) are cut down and 100 new trees are planted. This gives an overall decrease of 80 trees and a total in Year 3 of 820. Using similar calculations for Years 4 and 5 our chart now looks as follows:

Year	1	2	3	4	5	6	7	...
Trees	1000	900	820	756	704.8			

We now have a problem. In Year 4 we had 756 trees in our forest. Since 20% of 756 is $0.2 \times 756 = 151.2$, we need to cut down 151.2 trees before planting 100 new trees for an overall decrease of 51.2. But you can't cut down 151.2 trees because it doesn't make sense in the real world to cut down part of a tree. So we will use a special feature of our calculator to do all calculations with exact values (even when they are decimal), but display all results with a pre-set number of decimal places.

On all three of the calculators we're using, this feature is accessed using the [Fix] key. When you press [Fix] followed by an integer, the display switches to show numbers composed of an integer part and a decimal part with the specified number of places. In this format, you can enter values with any number of decimal places; but once the calculator performs a computation it will display the result with only the specified number of decimal places. To restore the calculator to its regular display mode simply press [Fix] followed by the decimal point [.]. On the *Explorer Plus* the format also returns to normal display when you press the *all clear* key [ON/AC].

In this problem, the results of our computations represent numbers of trees, so we want to display all these results as whole numbers with no decimal places. To do this we simply press [Fix] [0].

If you're using a calculator on which pressing the clear key restores the calculator to standard display, you must do all your calculations in [Fix] [0] mode without ever pressing [ON/AC].

We could now continue to fill in our table of values. It would be easier, however, if we could find a simple keystroke sequence that, pressed repeatedly, does all the computations for us automatically and displays, the results for our table one value at a time.

To find such a keystroke sequence, consider that if 20% of the trees in the forest are cut down each year, 80% of them remain. Therefore, instead of reducing the tree population by 20% and then increasing it by 100 each year, we can simply multiply the current number by 80% (or by 0.8) and add 100. A sequence that will do all this for us is:

[×] [.8] [+] [100] [=]

We can enter the initial tree population size, 1000, into our calculator and, in [Fix] [0] display mode, continually enter this sequence. Then we will get the next result for our table each time we press the [=] key. Doing this and filling in the table for the first 10 years we obtain:

Year	1	2	3	4	5	6	7	8	9	10
Trees	1000	900	820	756	705	664	631	605	584	567

These repeated calculations are even easier if you have a calculator, like the *Explorer Plus* or the *TI-34 II*, that has the two operation keys [OP1] and [OP2]. In that case, you can store the two arithmetic operations, "multiply by 0.8" and "add 100," in [OP1] and [OP2] respectively, as shown below.

[×] [.8] [OP1]
[+] [100] [OP2]

Then, all you have to do is enter the starting value 1000 and keep pressing [OP1] [OP2]. Each time you do this you'll obtain the next value for the table as shown below.

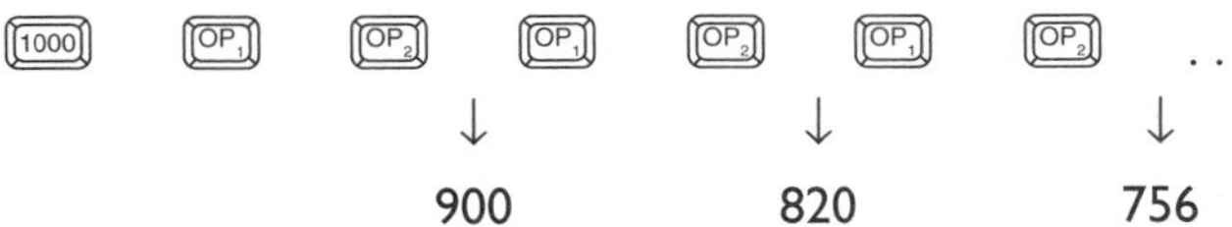

If you continue to use either of these keystroke sequences, eventually the number of trees in the forest reaches 500 and remains at that value from that time on. Of course, your students may think that 500 trees is too few for a forest, so suggest that they redo their table. Use the same cutting and planting values and the same calculator keystroke sequence as before, but this time assume that the starting tree population in Year 1 is 1500. Your students will soon discover that although it takes a few more years, the number of trees once again reaches 500 and remains at that value from that time on.

Year	1	2	3	4	5	6	7	8	9	10
Trees	1500	1300	1140	1012	910	828	762	710	668	634

Tell your students that you're really mad now and you're not going to let this forest end up with only 500 trees. To show that you can still control the situation, assume the forest begins with only 100 trees and see what happens then. Surprise, surprise! Once again the numbers appear to approach and then remain at 500, although this time they have to increase instead of decrease to reach that limiting value. Using either of the keystroke sequences given earlier, your table will look as follows:

Year	1	2	3	4	5	6	7	8	9	10
Trees	100	180	244	295	336	369	395	416	433	446

Step 3–Developing a Conjecture

Let your students know it's now time to accept the fact that however many trees you begin with, you will always obtain 500 as your limiting value as long as you follow the rule "cut down 20% and plant 100." Write these three values on the board as shown below and ask your students to tell you how they are related:

% cut	limit	planted
20%	500	100

Help them see that $20\% \times 500 = 100$. In other words, the limit value for this initial number of trees provides a balance, with the number of trees cut down exactly equal to the number of new trees planted. Once they notice this, ask them to state this observation as a conjecture about this cutting and planting process. Let them work on this in small groups of 3 or 4. After approximately 15 minutes ask the groups to share their conjectures with each other. One possible wording for such a conjecture is shown below.

Conjecture: In a cutting and planting situation like the one we are studying, the percent of trees cut down each year, multiplied by the limit value, will always be equal to the number of trees that are planted. Furthermore, the limit value is independent of the initial number of trees in the forest.

Step 4–Testing the Conjecture

Give each student a copy of **Activity Sheet 2.1,** which is similar to the problem just investigated except with different numbers. In this activity a conjecture is provided. The students will use this conjecture to predict what will happen in the new situation, and then verify the prediction using their calculators. Let them work on this activity sheet in small groups. Then either have one of the groups present their work to the rest of the class or review the questions in a whole class discussion.

Step 5–A Convincing Mathematical Argument

A good way to understand this type of situation is to look at the original problem in which 20% of the trees are cut down each year and 100 new trees are planted. We will examine why 500 is the limiting value of this particular cutting and planting process.

Notice that whenever the number of trees, T, is more than 500, the number you cut down ($0.2 \times T$) is greater than 100, the number you plant, and so the number of trees will be lower the following year. On the other hand, whenever T is less than 500, the number you cut down will be less than 100, so the number of trees will be greater the following year. Finally, at $T = 500$ trees, $0.2 \times 500 = 100$ and the number cut down is the same as the number planted, leaving the total unchanged at 500. So you either increase to 500, decrease to 500, or stay at 500 once you've reached it.

In this situation the value $T = 500$ is the limit of the sequences that are generated since they all get closer and closer to 500. It is also what we call a "fixed point" because once you are at 500 you remain fixed there. This limit value depends only on the cutting and planting numbers and not at all on the starting population of trees.

If, for example, you cut down 25% of the trees and planted 200 each year, the limiting value T would have to satisfy the relationship $0.25 \times T = 200$, which we could solve for $T = 800$. In other words, if you begin with more than 800 trees in this situation, you will have fewer trees each year with the number approaching 800 as a limit; if you begin with fewer than 800 trees, you will have more trees each year with the number approaching 800; and if you ever reach 800 you will remain there from that time on.

We could now present a formal proof using variables to represent the percent of trees cut down each year, the initial size of the forest, and the number of trees planted each year. But such a proof requires much symbolic manipulation, so it may be preferable to simply accept the numerical examples above as a convincing mathematical argument and leave it at that. If you feel, however, that your students can understand a formal proof go ahead and develop it as a whole class activity.

FOLLOW-UP DISCUSSION AND INVESTIGATIONS

Inform the class that the procedure you've been using to find the values for your table is called an iterative or recursive procedure and that it's simply another way of defining a function. Instead of giving the function in a closed form such as $y = x$ or $y = x^2$, an iterative or recursive formula gives a first value and then provides a procedure for getting from one value to the next. Point out that we use this type of procedure in the problem with the trees. We begin with 1000 trees, which we denote by U_1. Then we multiply the number of trees by 0.8 and add 100 to get the number of trees the following year, which we can write mathematically as $U_{K+1} = 0.8U_K + 100$.

Help your students understand that a closed formula for a function is obvious and useful in some situations; but in some situations, like our forest problem, the iterative or recursive form of the underlying function is better. Both forms, however, are perfectly correct and mathematically acceptable. Students will learn as they progress in mathematics how to decide which form is appropriate in any given situation.

Activity sheets are provided at the end of this investigation for two follow-up investigations. In **Activity Sheet 2.2** your students are given a limit value L and asked to find the percent of trees cut down each year and the number of trees planted each year that will give L as a limit no matter what the initial population size is. In **Activity Sheet 2.3** the students use the mathematics of the cutting and planting process to investigate a different situation: A patient is given a fixed dose of a drug each hour while, at the same time, a certain percent of the drug in the patient's body is lost. Let your students work in groups and then discuss their solutions. The context of Activity Sheet 2.3 is very different from that of previous problems that came before so you may need to help them get started on it.

GRAPHING CALCULATOR MODIFICATION

On the graphing calculator you select the number of decimal places to be displayed by pressing the [MODE] key; using the down arrow key to move the cursor to the second row (which begins with the word "Float"); using the right arrow key to move the cursor to the number of decimal places desired; and then pressing [ENTER]. To return to the default setting simply repeat this process and select "Float."

To automatically calculate the new number of trees in the forest for each year after you have set the display for 0 decimal places, first enter the initial number of trees, 1000, and press [ENTER]. Entering the keystroke sequence

[X] [.8] [+] [100] [ENTER]

gives the result after one year. Repeatedly pressing the [ENTER] key gives the results for subsequent years.

[1000]	[ENTER]	[X]	[.8]	[+]	[100]	[ENTER]	[ENTER]	[ENTER]	. . .
	↓					↓	↓	↓	
	1000					900	820	756	

At the high school level you can also use the sequence feature of the graphing calculator to develop and display a table of values for the number of trees in the forest each year and a corresponding scatterplot. Begin by pressing the [MODE] key and changing from standard function mode (Func) to sequence mode (Seq).

Now press [Y=] and set the values for the sequence you want in the original problem to

$$n\text{Min} = 1$$
$$\text{u}(n) = .8*\text{u}(n - 1) + 100$$
$$\text{u}(n\text{Min}) = 1000$$

To display a table showing the number of trees in the forest for each year, simply press [TBL SET]; select a starting value of 1 and an increment of 1; and then press [TABLE].

To display a scatterplot representing this sequence of values, press [WINDOW] and enter the following values.

nMin = 1	nMax = 50	
PlotStart = 1	PlotStep = 1	
Xmin = 0	Xmax = 50	Xscl = 5
Ymin = 0	Ymax = 1000	Yscl = 100

Now press GRAPH to see the scatterplot. It represents the number of trees each year converging toward a limit of 500.

SPREADSHEET MODIFICATION

You can also easily display a list of values for this problem, and a corresponding line graph, by using a computer spreadsheet program like Microsoft Excel. Begin by setting the column of the spreadsheet where you want the values to be shown (column A, for example) to display all of its values as integers with no decimal part. To do this, right click on the header for the column (here, the cell containing the letter *A*) and select "Format Cells". Under "Category" select "Number" and then select 0 for the number of decimal places to be displayed.

Now click on the first cell of this column, A1, and enter the starting size of the forest, 1000. Click on the next cell down, A2, and drag the cursor downward to select and highlight 10 consecutive cells in column A. In cell A2 enter the function " = .8*A1+100". The symbol A1 is obtained by clicking on cell A1 at the appropriate place in this expression.

Finally, press CTRL and ENTER at the same time. This repeats the function defined in cell A2 in all the other selected cells. In other words, each cell will be calculated as 0.8 multiplied by the value in the cell above it, plus 100. The number of trees in the forest for the first several years will now be displayed in column A as integer values with no decimal part.

To obtain a corresponding line graph, first select the cells by clicking on A1 and dragging the cursor down column A to highlight all the cells containing data. Now click on the chart wizard; select a line chart; click on the type of line chart you want to display; and then click on the word "Finish." You will obtain the graph in Figure 2.1, which shows clearly that the number of trees in the forest approaches the limiting value, 500.

REFLECTIONS FOR THE TEACHER

1. In the forest problem with which this investigation begins, the number of trees after several years seems to reach and remain at the limit value, 500. This is only because we have set the display to show 0 decimal places. If we were using an ordinary *floating decimal* display, the results would approach, but never really equal 500.

2. Cutting down 20% of the trees is the same as leaving 80% of the trees, which we use to develop the formula $U_{N+1} = 0.8*U_N + 100$. This fact may not be obvious to your students, so you should explain this slowly and give them time to think about it. You might also want to show this equivalence with a few numerical examples.

3. Emphasize to your students the two major differences between the iterative or recursive form and the closed form of a function. First, a closed form function is usually defined for either all real values of the variable (such as $y = x$ or $y = x^2$) or a large set of real numbers (such as $y = \sqrt{x}$ or $y = \log(x)$). A recursively defined function, on the other hand, is defined only on

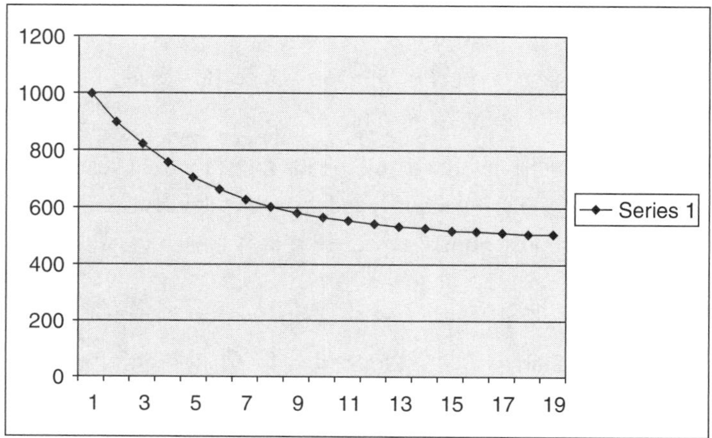

FIGURE 2.1

the positive integers and simply gives an infinite sequence with a first value U_1, a second value U_2, and so on. Second, you can evaluate a closed form function immediately for any number in its domain by simply plugging that value into the formula. But for a recursively defined function you have to evaluate the values of the function (or the corresponding sequence) one at a time, using the formula to go from one term of the sequence to the next.

4. In the first investigation as well as in Activity Sheets 2.1 and 2.2 we assume that we are working with objects (trees) that can take on only integer values. That's why we use the [Fix] [0] command to show the results of our calculations as whole numbers even though they may have decimal parts. In Activity Sheet 2.3 the variable is the amount of a drug in a patient's body. This certainly can be a non-integer value, so there is no need to display all results as integer values.

RELATED READINGS

Holley, Ann D. "A Question of Interest." *Two-Year College Mathematics Journal* (March 1978, Vol. 9, No. 2, pp. 81–83).

"The Next Billion." NCTM Illuminations web lesson (http://illuminations.nctm.org/index_d.aspx?id = 267).

"Using Algebra and Discrete Mathematics to Investigate Population Change in a Trout Pond." NCTM Illuminations web lesson (http://illuminations.nctm.org/index_o.aspx?id = 142).

Recursive functions are a staple of an area of mathematics called *discrete math*. Therefore, any discrete math textbook will contain numerous applications to which you can apply the methods of this investigation. Recursive functions are used to model and solve problems relating to mortgages and loans, population growth and decay, and drug dosages, among other applications.

ACTIVITY SHEET 2.1

Recursively Defined Functions and the Limit of an Infinite Sequence

Suppose we change the planting and harvesting procedure we investigated earlier: Now 15% of all the trees are harvested (cut down) and 120 new trees are planted each year. Use the conjecture stated below to answer the questions that follow about the long-term effects of this process.

> **Conjecture:** In a harvesting and planting process the percent cut down multiplied by the limit value will always be equal to the number that are planted; and the limit value is completely independent of the initial population value.

Question 1. Write an equation involving the percent of trees cut down each year, 15%; the limit value for the size of the forest, L; and the number of trees planted each year, 120.

Question 2. Solve the equation from Question 1 to find the limit value L for the ultimate size of the forest.

Question 3. Set the number of decimal places displayed on your calculator to 0. Start with a tree population size of 1000. Then use any of the calculator keystroke sequences presented in class to calculate the number of trees in the forest at the end of each year. Continue calculating for enough years to determine the limit value for this sequence. Is the result the same as the value of L you found in Question 2?

Question 4. Repeat the procedure from Question 3, but this time begin with a tree population of size 500. Do you again approach the value of L you found in Question 2?

Question 5. Repeat the procedure from Questions 3 and 4, but this time begin with a tree population of size L. What do you predict will happen? Do the calculations and see if your prediction was correct.

Recursively Defined Functions and the Limit of an Infinite Sequence

2.2 ACTIVITY SHEET

Suppose once again that you are a forest ranger responsible for a forest containing 500 trees. You have been asked to develop a yearly process that consists of cutting down $A\%$ of the trees and planting B new trees so that the forest will have a limiting population value of $L = 250$ trees.

Question 1. Find values of $A\%$ and B so that over time this forest, which currently has 500 trees, will get smaller and smaller and approach a limiting size of $L = 250$ trees.

Question 2. Create a table of values for the number of trees each year to verify that your values for $A\%$ and B in fact will give a limit of $L = 250$ trees. Remember to set your calculator to display 0 decimal places.

Question 3. Using the same values of $A\%$ and B as in Questions 1 and 2, show that the limit $L = 250$ does not depend on the starting size of the forest. Create a table of values for the number of trees each year starting with 100 trees. Show that this forest also tends toward $L = 250$ trees.

ACTIVITY SHEET 2.3

Recursively Defined Functions and the Limit of an Infinite Sequence

A patient in a hospital is given an initial dose of 200 cc of a certain drug. After one hour 75% of the drug has left the patient's body, but a new dose of 30 cc is injected. Assume that the patient is in the hospital for several days and this procedure is repeated every hour (75% of the drug leaves the body and 30 cc of the drug is injected). Investigate the amount of the drug that will be in the patient's body over time.

Question 1. The amount of the drug in the patient's body at any time is the equivalent of the number of trees in the forest in our previous investigations. What is the equivalent here for: (i) the initial size of the forest; (ii) the percent of trees cut down at the end of each year; and (iii) the number of new trees planted at the end of each year?

Question 2. Use the procedures we employed in the previous investigations to: (i) set up an equation to find the limit value L for the amount of the drug in the patient's body over time; (ii) solve this equation to find L; (iii) write down the keystroke sequence for finding the amount of drug in the patient's body from one hour to the next; and (iv) create a table of values to see if your value for L seems correct.

INVESTIGATION 3

The Effect of Successive Percentage Increases and Decreases on the Price of an Item

PLANNING: GRADES 6–8

RELATED NCTM STANDARDS: Number & Operations

- Work flexibly with fractions, decimals, and percents to solve problems.
- Understand the meaning and effects of arithmetic operations with fractions, decimals, and integers.

RELATED NCTM STANDARDS: Algebra

- Relate and compare different forms of representation for a relationship.
- Use symbolic algebra to represent situations and to solve problems, especially those that involve linear relationships.

MATHEMATICAL SKILLS AND CONCEPTS

Calculate successive percent discounts and increases on the price of an item.

Represent a percent discount or increase situation with an appropriate algebraic expression.

Use alternative symbolic representations of the same situation to solve a problem.

CALCULATOR KEYS AND FEATURES

The percent key [%].

The fix [Fix] key to set the number of decimal places to be displayed for arithmetic computations.

MATERIALS

Copies of Activity and Solution Sheets 3.1 and 3.2 for each student.

CLASSROOM IMPLEMENTATION

Background Information for the Teacher

Everyone likes to buy things at a discount. So the topic of percentage decreases is a natural one for problems involving percents and their calculation. Calculators compute efficiently and accurately (as long as we press the right buttons), so this topic also enables our students to go "behind the scenes" of successive discounts and increases and discuss the mathematics involved. It also allows us to show students that how you look at and approach an apparently difficult problem mathematically can sometimes make it much easier to understand and solve.

In this activity your students will use the percent key on their calculators to compute percentage increases and decreases from a starting value. The percent key may work a bit differently from calculator to calculator, so you should help your students understand how this key works and become proficient in its use.

For example, on the *Explorer Plus* and *TI-30Xa*, you enter a number and then press the [%] key to display immediately the decimal equivalent of that percent. To multiply a number by a given percent, divide it by that percent, add that percent of it to itself, or subtract that percent of it from itself, using the simple keystroke sequences shown below (with a starting value of 50 and a percentage change of 20%):

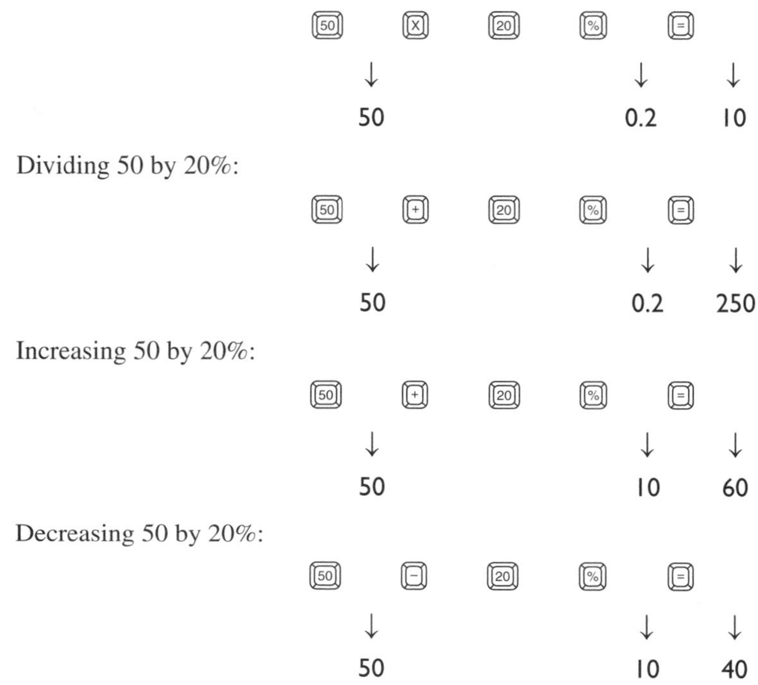

The *TI-34II*, however, displays the entire expression that is entered before evaluating it, including the display of the "%" symbol. So you have to enter a more exact expression for what you want the calculator to do. On this calculator the appropriate keystroke sequences for increasing and decreasing the number 50 by 20% of itself would be:

[50] [+] [20] [%] [×] [50] [=] (answer = 60)

and

[50] [−] [20] [%] [×] [50] [=] (answer = 40)

Step 1–Introducing the Problem Solving Scenario

Problem. Given two successive discounts on the price of an item, which sequence gives the lower final price: the smaller discount first and the larger second; or the larger first and the smaller second?

Announce to your students that you've been looking for an MP3 player, and you've spotted one at two local stores. The list price at both stores is the same, $100, but both stores have discounted this item twice because it has not been selling well.

You cannot recall the exact amounts of the two percentage discounts. You do remember, however, that the discounts were the same at both stores, but in the reverse order, with store #1 giving the small discount first and the larger one second and store #2 doing the opposite. Ask your students to find out whether you get a smaller final price if the larger percentage discount comes first or last. You have an activity sheet with some made-up percentage discounts that they can use.

Step 2–Investigating the Problem

Hand out **Activity Sheet 3.1** and let your students work on it for a while. Then ask them what they found and which store you should go to for your MP3 player. They will discover that the final price of the MP3 player does not depend on the order in which the two successive percentage discounts are applied.

Before continuing, ask your students if they could obtain the same price by simply adding the two successive discount percentages together and using this sum as one single discount. The first example on Activity Sheet 3.1 shows that this would not work. The sum of the two successive discounts of 10% and 15% would be 25%, which would give a final price of $75 for the $100 item. This is a different result from what they actually obtained.

Ask them why they think this happens. Explain that with successive discounts the second discount applies to the reduced price of the item after the first discount has been applied rather than to the original price. Consequently, successive discounts never give as large a savings as if you simply added the discount percentages together.

The result of Activity Sheet 3.1 shows that the final price of an item does not depend on which of two successive percentage discounts comes first or second. Ask your students if they think the order of the discounts would matter if a store gave three successive percentage discounts on an item. Then give them **Activity Sheet 3.2** to work on, either individually or in small groups.

Since there are six different possible orderings for three successive discounts, doing all six would take a great deal of time. So the activity simply asks each student to select two of the six possibilities and calculate the results for them. Assign orderings to each student or group to be sure that all six are done.

Step 3–Developing a Conjecture

When Activity Sheet 3.2 has been completed, list all six orderings on the board or overhead. Ask volunteers to tell you what they obtained as the final price for each ordering. Once again, your students will see that the ordering of the successive discounts had no effect of the final price of the item. Ask them now to state a conjecture on what they have found. A sample conjecture is shown below.

> **Conjecture:** When any number of successive percentage discounts are applied to the price of an item, the final price does not depend on the order in which the discounts were applied.

Step 4–Testing the Conjecture

The conjecture relates to *any* number of successive discounts, and your students have already seen that it holds for situations involving two and three successive discounts. So a good test is to try a situation involving four successive discounts. Ask your students to give you the starting price of an item, and different percentages for the four successive discounts. Ask half the class to find the final price of the item if the discounts are applied from smallest to largest; and the other half to find the final price if the discounts are applied from largest to smallest. Both results should be the same, supporting the truth of the conjecture.

Step 5–A Mathematical Proof

The proof of our conjecture provides a wonderful opportunity to show your students that there are often several ways to think about and represent a mathematical situation, which may make solving a difficult problem much simpler. Make this observation explicit if at all possible.

On the activity sheets students calculate the price of the item after each discount by finding the discount amount in dollars and cents and then subtracting this value from the previous price. They could represent this procedure algebraically, and then combine all the successive discounts; but the result would be cumbersome and require a great deal of algebra and symbolic manipulation to make sense. This proof demonstrates that you can find the new price after each individual discount in an equivalent but slightly different way, thereby simplifying and clarifying the algebraic representations and the symbolic manipulations.

Look at Example 1 of Activity Sheet 3.1. Point out to your students that another way to get the item's price after a discount of 10% is to simply multiply the original price of $100 by 90% to get $.90 \times \$100 = \$90$. The reason is that by discounting an item by 10% you are simply multiplying its price by the remaining 90%. Similarly, once you have the new price of $90, you can find the final price after a 15% discount by multiplying $90 by 85% to get $.85 \times \$90 = \$76.50$

(since discounting a price by 15% is the same as multiplying the previous price by the remainder, 85%). Combining both of these steps into one algebraic expression:

$$\begin{aligned}\text{Final Price} &= \$100 \times (1 - 0.10) \times (1 - 0.15)\\ &= \$100 \times (0.90) \times (0.85)\\ &= \$76.50\end{aligned}$$

In general, suppose you have an item that costs A and you want to discount its price by the N successive percentage discounts $d_1, d_2, d_3, d_4, \ldots, d_N$. Using the above reasoning, the final price of the item would be

$$\text{Final Price} = A \times (1 - d_1) \times (1 - d_2) \times (1 - d_3) \times (1 - d_4) \times \ldots \times (1 - d_N)$$

But multiplication is commutative, so the N terms in parentheses can be rearranged into any order without changing the result. Rearranging the order of these terms is equivalent to rearranging the order of the successive discounts, so the proof of the conjecture is complete.

FOLLOW-UP DISCUSSION AND INVESTIGATIONS

The results of this investigation can now be generalized or extended in two ways. First, you could discuss whether a similar result would be found with successive percentage increases in the price of an item rather than with successive percentage discounts. Alternatively, you could ask whether you would get a similar result if you had a combination of percentage increases and percentage discounts.

In both of these cases you can represent the final price of the item with an algebraic expression similar to the one above. But while a discount of d_1 gives a multiplicative factor of $(1 - d_1)$, a percentage increase of d_1 gives a multiplicative factor of $(1 + d_1)$. In either case, however, the commutativity of multiplication assures that the order of the discounts and increases will have no effect on the final result. After this mathematical analysis, your students can then work out an example of both types to verify that the mathematical result holds true in actual practice.

GRAPHING CALCULATOR MODIFICATION

The graphing calculator does not have a built-in percent function, so if your students perform this investigation on a graphing calculator they will have to do it a bit differently. Begin by reminding the students of the equivalence of a percent and its decimal equivalent. Point out that increasing (or decreasing) a number by a given percent just means multiplying that number by 1 plus (or minus) the decimal equivalent of that percent. For example, to increase the number 50 by 20% we simply calculate $50\,(1 + 0.2) = 50\,(1.2) = 60$; and to decrease the number 50 by 20% we simply calculate $50\,(1 - 0.2) = 50\,(0.8) = 40$.

You can now use this procedure to calculate percentage increases and decreases of a given number in any order quite easily. For example, the keystroke sequences below first increase then decrease the value of a $150 item by 20%; then they perform the same computations with the order reversed. As expected, the two results are the same.

Increase First:

Decrease First:

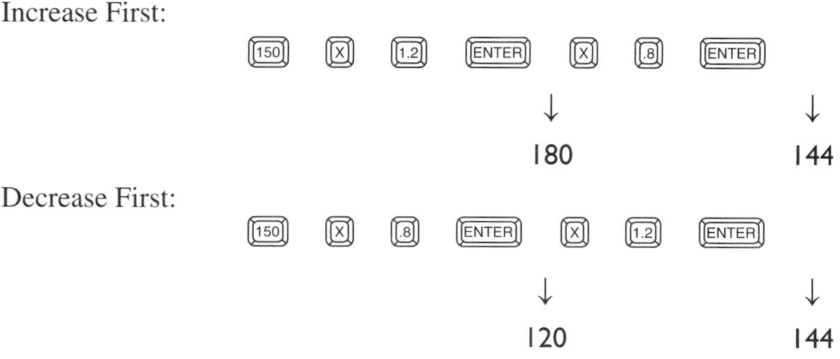

RELATED READINGS

Bennett, Albert B., and Nelson, L. Ted. "A Conceptual Model for Solving Percent Problems." *Mathematics Teaching in the Middle School* (NCTM, April 1994. Vol. 1, No. 1, pp. 20–25).

Lembke, Linda O., and Reys, Barbara J. "The Development of, and Interaction between, Intuitive and School-Taught Ideas about Percent." *Journal for Research in Mathematics Education* (NCTM, May 1994. Vol. 25, No. 23, pp. 237–59).

Metz, Mary Lou. "Mathematical Detective: Making Sense of Percents." *Mathematics Teaching in the Middle School* (NCTM, September 2003. Vol. 9, No. 1, pp. 44–45).

"So How Much Does It Cost?" *Figure This! Math Challenges for Families.* Math Challenge #17: Perplexing Percentages. www.figurethis.org/pdf/ch/challenges_17-19.pdf (NCTM, 2004).

ACTIVITY SHEET

3.1 The Effect of Successive Percentage Increases and Decreases on the Price of an item

An MP3 player is on sale at two different stores. The list price at both stores is $100, and both give the same two sequential discounts, but in reverse order. Below are three examples of what these discounts might be. In each example find the final price of the item in both stores and determine which sequence of discounts is better.

Example 1. Assume the two discounts are 10% and 15%. Perform the calculations below to determine which sequence of discounts gives the lowest final price for the item. We have started the calculations for you to get you started. Set your display to two decimal places using [Fix] [2] so your results look like they are in dollars and cents.

	Store #1	Store #2
Original Price	$100	$100
1st Discount	10% × $100 = $10	15% × $100 = $15
Reduced Price	$100 – $10 = $90	$100 – $15 = $85
2nd Discount	____________	____________
Final Price	________	________

Example 2. Assume the discounts are now 15% and 25%. Which sequence of discounts gives the lowest final price?

	Store #1	Store #2
Original Price	$100	$100
1st Discount	15% × $100 = $15	25% × $100 = $25
Reduced Price	$100 – $15 = $85	$100 – $25 = $75
2nd Discount	____________	____________
Final Price	________	________

Example 3. Just for fun let's change the original price of the item to $150 and assume the two discounts are 5% and 20%. Perform the calculations below and determine which sequence of discounts gives the lowest final price for the item.

	Store #1	Store #2
Original Price	$150	$150
1st Discount	____________	____________
Reduced Price	____________	____________
2nd Discount	____________	____________
Final Price	________	________

What do you think? Is it better to get the larger percentage discount first or second?

The Effect of Successive Percentage Increases and Decreases on the Price of an Item

ACTIVITY SHEET 3.2

A shoe store is discontinuing a line of expensive sneakers because the athlete they are named after has been traded to another team. The original price of these sneakers was $150, and the store has reduced the price with successive discounts of 10%, 20%, and 30%, but not necessarily in that order.

There are six different orderings in which these discounts could have been applied. These are shown below.

Possible Orderings of the Discounts

	#1	#2	#3	#4	#5	#6
1st Discount	10%	10%	20%	20%	30%	30%
2nd Discount	20%	30%	10%	30%	10%	20%
3rd Discount	30%	20%	30%	10%	20%	10%

Using Activity Sheet 3.1 as a guide, select any two of these orderings. Figure out what the final price of the item would be if the discounts were applied in each of the two orderings. Did the final price depend on the ordering or not?

INVESTIGATION 4

Fixed Points and Converging Sequences

PLANNING: GRADES 6–8

RELATED NCTM STANDARDS: Algebra

- Represent, analyze, and generalize a variety of patterns with tables, graphs, words, and, when possible, symbolic rules.
- Use symbolic algebra to represent situations and to solve problems, especially those that involve linear relationships.

PLANNING: GRADES 9–12

RELATED NCTM STANDARDS: Algebra

- Generalize patterns using explicitly defined and recursively defined functions.
- Use symbolic algebra to represent and explain mathematical relationships.
- Use symbolic expressions, including iterative and recursive forms, to represent relationships arising from various contexts.

MATHEMATICAL SKILLS AND CONCEPTS

Represent an iterative process mathematically.

Understand the concept of the limit of a sequence.

Understand the concept of a fixed point under a linear transformation and use algebraic representation and symbolic manipulation to find the value of the limit.

CALCULATOR KEYS AND FEATURES

The square root key [√].

The [Fix] key to set the number of decimal places displayed as the result of a computation.

The repeated operation keys [OP1] and [OP2] (if your calculator has them).

MATERIALS

Copies of Activity and Solution Sheets 4.1, 4.2, and 4.3 for each student.

CLASSROOM IMPLEMENTATION

Background Information for the Teacher

Critics had many concerns when hand-held calculators began to be used in classrooms. One was that students might use certain keys, such as the square root key, before they understood the mathematics that these keys represented. These critics believed that the teacher then would have to explain the mathematics involved before the students were ready, or tell the students to wait until a later math class to learn about these keys. In either case, they felt the students would become confused or disappointed.

It is not true that you cannot use a calculator key or feature until the student completely understands the corresponding mathematical function. In fact, you can use your students' natural curiosity about the calculator to introduce some aspects of a key and the mathematics behind it without going into explicit detail; and then turn this natural curiosity into an effective learning experience. That's exactly what we do with the square root key in this investigation.

Step 1–Introducing the Problem Solving Scenario

Point to the square root key [√] on your overhead calculator. Make sure your students understand that this key displays the square root of whatever number is in the display, and that its function performs the opposite operation of squaring a number. Take the square root of several numbers. Explain why taking the square root of a negative number gives an error message; why taking the square root of 0 gives 0; and why taking the square root of a positive number gives a positive number.

Problem. To discover what happens when you repeatedly take the square root of a positive number, and why this happens.

Step 2–Investigating the Problem

Give your students **Activity Sheet 4.1** to work on. In ordinary display mode your students may need to press the square root key as many as 15 or 20 times before they recognize what is happening. To speed up this activity and make its results more easily recognizable, suggest to your students that they use [Fix] [2] or [Fix] [3]; this displays results of all computations to only 2 or 3 decimal places.

Step 3–Developing a Conjecture

Let your students discuss what they've discovered with each other. It should be fairly obvious that repeatedly pressing the square root key with any positive value gives numbers that approach 1, which is the limit of this sequence of displayed values. The resulting conjecture might look something like the following.

> **Conjecture:** If you repeatedly take the square root of any positive number, the numbers you obtain will get closer and closer to 1.

Don't let your students stop with this result, however. Ask whether the sequence of numbers they obtained differed depending on whether the initial value was greater than or less than 1. Make the observation clearer by actually taking a starting value greater than 1 and listing the first six or seven values you obtain by pressing the square root key; and then do the same with a starting value less than 1. This demonstration should enable your students to modify their conjecture to state the actual values they obtain during this procedure:

> **Conjecture:** If you repeatedly take the square root of a value greater than 1, you obtain a sequence of values that are all greater than 1, but approach 1 as a limit. If you begin with a value less than 1, all the values you obtain are less than 1, but approach 1 as a limit. If you begin with 1, all the values you get will be exactly equal to 1.

Step 4–Testing the Conjecture

Have your students test this modified conjecture with a new number greater than 1 and a new number less than 1. Ask them to list the first six or seven values they obtain in each case. Have a few students write down the values they obtained on the board so everyone can see that all of them support the conjecture. Your ulterior purpose in having these values on the board, however, is to use them in a mathematical rationale for the truth of the conjecture.

Step 5–A Mathematical Proof

Use one of the sequences that begin with a value greater than 1 to make a column next to the list showing the distance of each number from 1. Show your students that each number in this list is less than half as far from 1 as the previous number was. Show that this same observation holds for all the lists that begin with a number greater than 1, providing a clear rationale for why all such sequences approach 1 if you keep pressing the square root key. This is illustrated in the sequence shown below that begins with 100.

The following algebraic inequality provides a mathematical proof of this observation. Remember that this algebraic proof is intended for you, the teacher, not your students, unless you think they have the algebraic maturity to understand it. In this inequality we assume $x > 1$ and that x and $\sqrt{x}$ are successive numbers in the sequence so that $1 - x$ and $1 - \sqrt{x}$ are their corresponding distances from 1.

$$1 - \sqrt{x} = \frac{(1 - \sqrt{x})(1 + \sqrt{x})}{1 + \sqrt{x}} = \frac{1 - x}{1 + \sqrt{x}} < \frac{1 - x}{1 + \sqrt{1}} = \frac{1 - x}{2}$$

Look at one of the sequences of numbers that begin with a value less than 1. You see that while successive numbers are not always less than half as far from 1 as the previous number was, nonetheless they do approach 1. In fact, if the first number entered into the display is x_0 with $0 < x_0 < 1$, then each number is less than $\frac{1}{1 + x_0}$ times the distance of the previous number from 1. For example, if we begin with $x_0 = 0.10$, each number is less than $\frac{1}{1 + 0.10} = \frac{1}{\frac{11}{10}} = \frac{10}{11} = 0.909090\ldots$ times the distance of the previous number from 1.

The proof of this observation is provided in the algebraic inequality shown below, where $0 < x < 1$ and x_0 is the first number in the sequence. Once again, this algebraic proof is provided for you, the teacher, and not your students.

$$1 - \sqrt{x} = \frac{(1 - \sqrt{x})(1 + \sqrt{x})}{1 + \sqrt{x}} = \frac{1 - x}{1 + \sqrt{x}} < \frac{1 - x}{1 + \sqrt{x_0}}$$

Illustrations of Sequences Obtained by Repeatedly Pressing [√]

First Number > 1		First Number < 1	
Value in Display	**Distance from 1**	**Value in Display**	**Distance from 1**
100.00	99.00	0.10	0.90
10.00	9.00	0.32	0.68
3.16	2.16	0.56	0.44
1.78	0.78	0.75	0.25
1.33	0.33	0.87	0.13
1.15	0.15	0.93	0.07
1.07	0.07	0.96	0.04

FOLLOW-UP DISCUSSION AND INVESTIGATIONS

Tell your students that you are going to give them another mathematical procedure that has the same two properties as the previous sequences: It will leave the number 1 fixed and unchanged; and at the same time take any positive number not equal to 1 and move it closer to, or shrink its distance from, 1. Say that this procedure will involve the operation of "averaging," or taking the arithmetic mean of two numbers. Then give them **Activity Sheet 4.2** to work on.

Your students should easily discover from this activity sheet that using the "averaging with 1" procedure with a positive starting value also gives a sequence of numbers that approach 1 as a limit. For middle school students, completing Activity Sheet 4.2 and discussing findings can end the investigation. For high school students, however, you can now generalize what was done in Activity Sheet 4.2. Point out that the "averaging with 1" procedure can be expressed in the following form, which takes any value x_N in the sequence and obtains from it the next value x_{N+1}:

$$x_{N+1} = \frac{x_N + 1}{2} = 0.5x_N + 0.5$$

In other words, averaging with 1 is nothing more than applying the linear function $y = 0.5x + 0.5$ to the current value in the sequence to get the next value. To verify this have your students calculate the sequence of values generated using this linear procedure with the starting values they used in Activity Sheet 4.2. The sequences produced by the "averaging with 1" procedure and this linear procedure should be identical. The calculator keystroke sequence using a starting value of 100, for example, would begin as follows.

If your calculator has the operation keys [OP1] and [OP2], the keystroke sequence is even easier. Simply store [*] [.5] as OP_1 and [+] [.5] as OP_2. The keystroke sequence will be

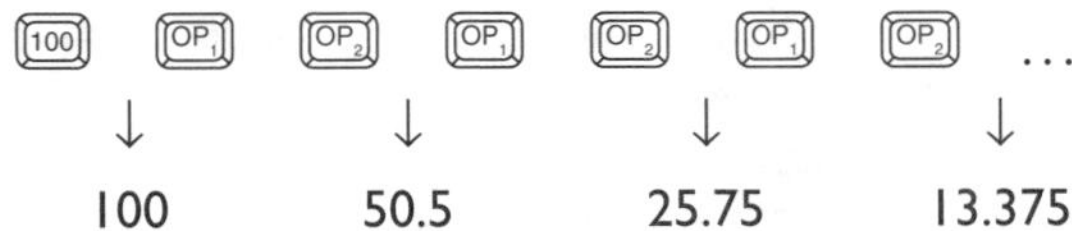

Now, does every linear procedure of the form $x_{N+1} = Ax_N + B$, beginning with a positive value, give rise to a sequence of numbers converging to a finite limit? If so, is there any simple way of predicting that limit? **Activity Sheet 4.3** lets your students investigate these questions. They should discover from Activity Sheet 4.3 that the sequence generated by a linear expression of the form $x_{N+1} = Ax_N + B$ will converge to a finite limit, which will be independent of the starting value of the sequence if $0 < A < 1$; but the sequence will diverge if $A \geq 1$.

The final piece of this investigation is to determine what the limit value is, when such a sequence converges. This is actually quite simple. If the generating expression is $x_{N+1} = Ax_N + B$ and the sequence does in fact approach a finite limit L, then both x_{N+1} and x_N will themselves approach L as N increases, and L should satisfy the relationship $L = AL + B$. We can then solve this equation to find the value of L as $L = \frac{B}{1 - A}$.

For example, in Activity Sheet 4.2 we had $A = B = 0.5$, which leads to $L = 0.5L + 0.5$. Solving this equation gives $L = 1$, which was exactly the limit we found. We can also use this procedure to verify that repeatedly pressing the [√] key gives a sequence with a limit of 1. Simply set $L = \sqrt{L}$ and solve to find $L = 1$.

GRAPHING CALCULATOR MODIFICATION

You can't simply enter a positive number into the display on the graphing calculator and then press the [√] key repeatedly. The graphing calculator requires that you enter the value whose square root you want *after* the √ symbol, not before. So you have to enter the initial value and store it in memory location X; enter the iterative expression [√] [X] [STO] [X]; and then press [ENTER] repeatedly. This is illustrated below with a starting value of 100.

[100] [STO] [X] [ENTER]

[√] [X] [)] [STO] [X] [ENTER] [ENTER] [ENTER] ...

The procedure is similar for finding successive iterations of a linear function. For example, to obtain the successive values of the linear function $y = 0.5x + 0.5$ when starting with 100, enter the following commands and then keep pressing [ENTER] as shown below.

[100] [STO] [X] [ENTER]

[X] [.5] [+] [.5] [ENTER] [ENTER] [ENTER] ...

SPREADSHEET MODIFICATION

To develop a sequence of values starting with 100 and then taking the square root repeatedly, simply follow the instructions on the next page. This will produce a sequence of values that approach the limit value 1.

- Enter the initial value, 100, into cell A1.
- Highlight cell A2 and several cells immediately below it by clicking on A2 and dragging the cursor down.
- Enter the formula "=SQRT (A1)" into cell A2 and press CTRL and ENTER at the same time. Note that the SQRT function is built-in in most spreadsheet programs and that you click on cell A1 to insert the symbol A1 into this formula.

To obtain a line graph representing this sequence of values simply highlight all the cells in column A containing the numbers in this sequence, click on the chart wizard, select line charts, click on the type of line chart you want, and then click on "Finish" to obtain the graph shown in Figure 4.1.

It's somewhat difficult to identify the limit of the values in our sequence as 1 from this line graph since the chart shows all the numbers in the sequence including the first number, 100. Redo the chart, but this time do not highlight the cells that contain either 100 or 10. You will get a line chart that much more clearly shows the limit of our sequence to be 1, as shown in Figure 4.2.

Similarly, we can use a spreadsheet to generate the sequence of values obtained by continually multiplying a starting value by 0.5 and then adding 0.5 to get the next value. Enter the initial value in cell A1 and enter the formula "= .5 *A1 + . 5" into cell A2. Then use the chart wizard to display the corresponding line graph.

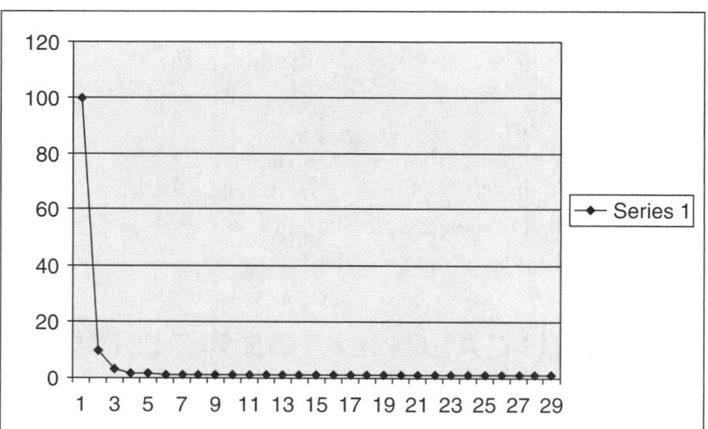

FIGURE 4.1

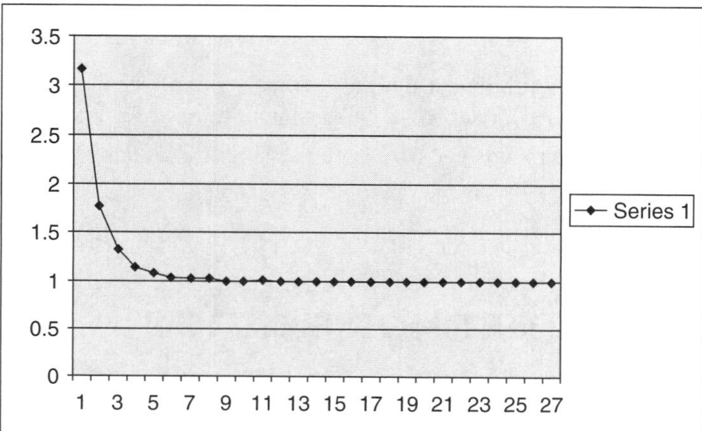

FIGURE 4.2

REFLECTIONS FOR THE TEACHER

There are many variations of this iterative procedure, some of which lead to interesting numbers as the limit. For example, the iterative procedure "take the inverse and then add 1," which can be expressed iteratively as $U_{N+1} = \frac{1}{U_N} + 1$, leads to the golden ratio $\frac{1 + \sqrt{5}}{2}$ as the limit. The keystroke sequence for repeatedly evaluating this iterative function with the starting value of 100 is as follows:

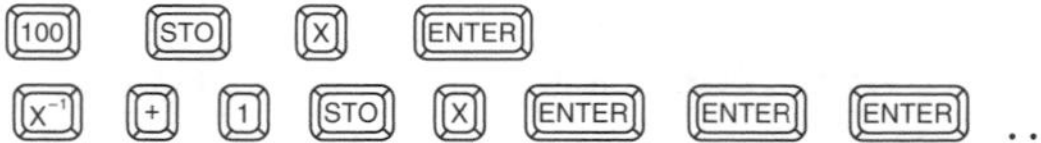

RELATED READINGS

Olson, Alton T. "Difference Equations." *Mathematics Teacher* (NCTM, October 1988, Vol. 81, No. 7, pp. 540–544).

Spence, Lawrence E. "The Difference Equation $X_N = aX_{N-1} + b$." *Mathematics Teacher* (NCTM, December 1990, Vol. 83, No. 9, pp. 709–713).

Walsh, Thomas P. "Exploring Difference Equations with Spreadsheets." *Learning and Leading with Technology* (September 1996, Vol. 24, No. 1, pp. 28–32).

ACTIVITY SHEET

4.1 Fixed Points and Converging Sequences

Step 1. Enter any positive number, integer or non-integer, large or small, into your calculator's display.

Step 2. Press the square root key [√].

Step 3. Press the square root key [√] again repeatedly until something interesting happens. (You may have to press this key 15 or even 20 times so be patient. Something interesting will eventually happen!)

Step 4. Note what happened above that was interesting. Then repeat the procedure, but this time begin with a different positive first number. Do this three or four times.

Step 5. Make a conjecture about the effects of repeatedly pressing the square root key after entering a positive number into the calculator's display.

Fixed Points and Converging Sequences

4.2 ACTIVITY SHEET

In class we discovered that repeatedly applying the square root function to a positive number has the following properties: If you begin with a number greater than 1, all the numbers you get are greater than 1 and approach 1 as a limit; if you begin with a number less than 1, all the numbers you get are less than 1 and approach 1 as a limit; and if you begin with 1, you simply keep getting 1 over and over again.

In this activity you will determine whether the "averaging with 1" function, taking a number x and averaging it with 1 by calculating $\frac{x+1}{2}$, has these same three properties.

Step 1. Start with a number $x > 1$ and repeatedly average it with 1. Do the numbers you obtain approach 1 as a limit? Try a different starting value and see if the same thing happens.

Step 2. Start with a positive number $x < 1$ and repeatedly average it with 1. Do the numbers you obtain approach 1 as a limit? Try a different starting value and see if the same thing happens.

Step 3. Start with 1 and keep averaging it with itself. Do you keep getting 1 as a result?

ACTIVITY SHEET

4.3 Fixed Points and Converging Sequences

Step 1. For the linear expression $y = Ax + B$, select a value for A that is between 0 and 1 ($0 < A < 1$) and any value for B; select a starting value for your sequence; and then calculate the first 10 or so values of the sequence given by the relationship $x_{N+1} = \mathrm{A}x_N + \mathrm{B}$. Does this sequence seem to be approaching a limit? If so, what is this limit?

Step 2. Repeat the process using the same values of A and B as in Step 1, but use a different starting value for your sequence. Do you get a result similar to what you obtained in Step 1? Try it again with the same values for A and B but a different starting value. Do you still get a similar result?

Step 3. Repeat Steps 1 and 2, but select a value of A that is first equal to 1 ($A = 1$) and then greater than 1 ($A > 1$). Contrast the result with what you found when you assumed $0 < A < 1$.

Step 4. State what you have found above as a new conjecture about using a linear expression to generate a sequence of numbers.

PART TWO

The Graphing Calculator
Research Results on the Classroom Use of the Graphing Calculator

5 The Formula for the Sum of an Infinite Geometric Series

6 Histograms and Relative Frequency Tables

7 Probability and the Concept of Fairness

8 Examining the Trajectory of an Object in Motion

9 A Visual Inspection of the Real Roots of a Polynomial Function

10 The Relationship between the Coefficients of a First or Second Degree Function

11 A Visual Discovery of Trigonometric Identities and Formulas

12 Exploring Derivatives Using Both Algebraic and Visual Representations

13 Converging and Diverging Infinite Series and Special Mathematical Constants

14 The Use of Linear and Nonlinear Regression for Curve Fitting and Making Predictions

15 Exponential Growth and Exponential Regression

16 Generalized Fibonacci Sequences Using Matrices

BACKGROUND AND OVERVIEW

At the beginning of Part One of this text we presented research results on the use of the scientific calculator as a classroom instructional tool. The scientific calculator was leaps and bounds beyond the original four-function calculator in terms of its mathematical features and capabilities; but the graphing calculator is an entirely new device and could more realistically be called a hand-held computer rather than a handheld calculator.

As yet there is not as much research on the classroom use of graphing calculators as there is on the use of four-function and scientific calculators. Nevertheless, we can draw some very clear and useful conclusions. Following is a brief overview of some of this research.

THE RESEARCH

One of the most comprehensive reports on this topic is "Handheld Graphing Technology at the Secondary Level: Research Findings and Implications for Classroom Practice," prepared through a grant from Texas Instruments to Michigan State University and published in 2002. This compilation and synthesis of 43 studies is selected from over 180 on the topic. It focuses on a number of important issues relating to the use of graphing technology including teacher knowledge and beliefs, student use, the relationship of the technology to student achievement, and the influence of technology on diverse student populations. Some of the conclusions of this report are shown below.

- The research indicates that students who used handheld graphing technology with curriculum materials supporting its use had a better understanding of functions, variables, solving algebra problems in applied contexts, and interpreting graphs than those who did not use the technology.
- Students who spent more time using handheld graphing technology showed greater gains than students who had access to the technology for brief interventions or short periods of time.
- Simply providing teachers with information about how the technology functions is not likely to result in effective integration in the classroom. Substantial professional development and support is necessary for teachers to make informed decisions about how to best use handheld technology in their classrooms.
- Students with access to handheld graphing technology engaged in problem solving and investigations more often and were more flexible in their solution strategies than students without access.
- Integrating, not simply adding, the use of handheld graphing technology within the context of the mathematics being studied can help students develop essential understandings about the nature, use, and limits of the tool, and promote deeper understanding of the mathematical concepts involved.

Another overview of research on the use of the graphing calculator is a paper by Penelope H. Dunham, presented at a June, 1998 Eisenhower National Clearinghouse (ENC) Technology and NCTM Standards 2000 Conference in Arlington, Virginia. (This paper was later included in E. Laughbaum (Ed.), *Hand-Held Technology in Mathematics and Science Education: A Collection of Papers*, pp. 39–47.) Dunham says the following about research on the use of graphing calculators.

> In the dozen years since graphing calculators were introduced in 1986, we have seen a steady flow of research on graphing calculators in mathematics classrooms . . . . The consensus of the reviews is that students who use graphing calculators display better understanding of function and graph concepts, improved problem solving, and higher scores on achievement tests for algebra and calculus skills.
>
> Moreover, several studies indicate that graphing technology may have even greater benefits for some special populations—in effect, leveling the "playing field" for women, nontraditional college students, and students with less spatial visualization ability.
>
> The reviews also point to positive changes in classroom dynamics and pedagogy. Reprinted with permission from *Hand-Held Technology in Mathematics and Science Education: A Collection of Papers,* copyright 1998 by The Ohio State University.

In the final analysis, the mathematics teacher decides how, when, and for what purpose graphing calculators are used in the mathematics classroom. So we will end by looking at an article from the April 2000 issue of the online journal *Issues in the Undergraduate Mathematics Preparation of School Teachers* (http://www.k12prep.math.ttu.edu/journal/technology/volume.shtml). "The Evolution of a Graphing Calculator Course for Preservice Mathematics Teachers," by Kathleen Cage Mittag of the University of Texas at San Antonio and Sharon E. Taylor of Georgia Southern University, examines the training of new mathematics teachers to use graphing calculator technology. In the section titled "Why," the authors demonstrate the need for such a course as well as why particular components should be included.

> A search of the literature for curricular ideas for this course found no curriculum that would meet the needs of the students. As the course evolved, ideas also appeared in research articles that validated the teaching methods being used.
>
> The teaching strategy of using activity-based learning, cooperative groups, and classroom exercises mirrored the ACE cycle (activities, class discussions, and exercises) advocated by Asiala, Brown, Devries, Dubinsky, Mathews, and Thomas.
>
> Over the years, the course has undergone some changes, but the underlying ideas of classroom activities, cooperative learning, and the careful integration of technology, pedagogy, and content have not changed and have eventually come to be an established and accepted practice of teaching undergraduate mathematics.

Mittag and Taylor conclude that the most appropriate and effective way to teach preservice teachers how to integrate technology into mathematics instruction is exactly the philosophy that mathematics teachers should have in using graphing technology with junior high and high school students: Use activity-based learning, cooperative group activities, class discussions, and learning the features of the technology as it is applied to the investigation of mathematical situations and the solution of mathematical problems.

This is the guiding philosophy of this text and the basis for the investigations included in it. Always remember this as you read and use these investigations with your own students, and when you integrate technology into your own mathematics teaching.

The Formula for the Sum of an Infinite Geometric Series

PLANNING: GRADES 9–12

RELATED NCTM STANDARDS: Algebra

- Generalize patterns using explicitly defined and recursively defined functions.
- Use symbolic algebra to represent and explain mathematical relationships.
- Use symbolic expressions, including iterative and recursive forms, to represent relationships arising from various contexts.
- Draw reasonable conclusions about a situation being modeled.

MATHEMATICAL SKILLS AND CONCEPTS

Recognize an infinite geometric series and identify the first term and the common ratio.

Develop the formula for the sum of an infinite geometric series in terms of the first term and the common ratio and apply this formula to specific examples.

CALCULATOR KEYS AND FEATURES

LIST

Seq(

CumSum

MATERIALS

Several transparent plastic cups on which you have written the numerals 1, 2, 3, and so on using a magic marker.

A pitcher of colored water (blue or red dyes are easy for the students to see).

Copies of Activity and Solution Sheets 5.1 and 5.2 for each student.

CLASSROOM IMPLEMENTATION

Background Information for the Teacher

This investigation begins with an interesting classroom activity using plastic cups of water that leads naturally to the development of an infinite geometric series. Students learn how to use the *List* capabilities of the graphing calculator to approximate the sum of such a series.

Then they create a conjecture for a formula to find the exact sum of such a series. This conjecture is first empirically tested using the graphing calculator and then proven mathematically.

Step1–Introducing the Problem Solving Scenario

Bring to class several transparent plastic cups on which you've written the numerals 1, 2, 3, and so on using a magic marker; and a pitcher of colored water (blue or red dyes are easy to see). Take cup #1, fill it with the colored water almost to the top, and place it on a desk or table so it can be seen by the entire class. Tell your students to assume there are 32 ounces of water in this cup, and write "32" on the board.

Take cup #2, pour half the water from cup #1 into cup #2, and place both cups next to each other on the desk. Ask the class how much water is now in each cup. Obviously the answer is 16 ounces since each has half of the original 32 ounces. On the board, after the number 32, write "= 16 + 16" to give the equation "32 = 16 + 16".

Now take cup #3 and empty half of cup #2 into it. Then place all three cups next to each other and ask the students how many ounces are in each cup. There should be 16 ounces in cup #1, 8 ounces in cup #2, and 8 ounces in cup #3. Rewrite the equation on the board to represent this as "32 = 16 + 8 + 8". Repeat this procedure until you have a total of eight cups in a row and the corresponding equation

$$32 = 16 + 8 + 4 + 2 + 1 + \tfrac{1}{2} + \tfrac{1}{4} + \tfrac{1}{4}$$

Point out to the students that if it were physically possible to continue this procedure forever you would have a never-ending sum of values on the right side of the equation. Each number would be half the previous number and the equation would look like the following, where the three dots at the end indicate that the sum continues forever:

$$32 = 16 + 8 + 4 + 2 + 1 + \tfrac{1}{2} + \tfrac{1}{4} + \tfrac{1}{8} + \tfrac{1}{16} + \ldots$$

Explain that the equals sign in this expression means that if you keep adding additional terms one by one to the first term of the series on the right side, 16, the "partial sums" you obtain will approach 32.

To show the class that this in fact happens, demonstrate how to use the *List* features of the graphing calculator by placing the first 50 terms of this infinite sum into the calculator's list L_1 and then the first 50 partial sums into list L_2. Simply follow these steps on your TI Viewscreen or Presenter:

Step 1. Press the LIST key.

Step 2. Use the right arrow key to move to the word OPS.

Step 3. Select "seq(" to bring this command to the home screen.

Step 4. Complete the command that follows, then press ENTER. This will calculate the first 50 terms of the sequence and automatically place them into list L_1: Seq (16(1/2)^x, x,0,49)→L_1.

Step 5. Once again press LIST and move to OPS.

Step 6. This time select "cumSum" to bring this command to the home screen.

Step 7. Complete the command that follows, then press ENTER. This will calculate the first 50 partial sums of the sequence and place these partial sums into list L_2: cumSum (L_1)→L_2.

Problem. To find a formula for the sum of an infinite series in which each term is the same constant multiple of the term that came before it.

If you now press STAT followed by ENTER you can see that list L_1 contains the first 50 terms of the sequence and list L_2 contains the first 50 partial sums. Scrolling down list L_2 shows that the partial sums are approaching 32; and when they get close enough the calculator displays the values as 32 although this is not perfectly accurate. These partial sums support the equation shown above in which the sum of this infinite series appears to be 32.

Step2–Investigating the Problem

Explain to your students that the infinite series you've been investigating is an example of a "geometric" series in which each term is some constant multiple of the previous term; and that the common multiplier is represented by the letter r and called the "common ratio" because it represents the ratio of successive terms. In this geometric series the common ratio is $r = \tfrac{1}{2}$ because each term of the series is one half the previous term.

In this activity your students will discover a formula for the sum of any infinite geometric series. They will do this by completing a few activity sheets, using their calculators to do the computations, and their heads to do the thinking. Then put them into small groups and give them **Activity Sheet 5.1** to work on.

Step 3–Developing a Conjecture

After all the groups have completed Activity Sheet 5.1 ask for volunteers to answer the two questions and explain their reasoning. Then ask the class to help you state, as a conjecture, what they now think they know about the sum of an infinite geometric series with a constant ratio of $\frac{1}{2}$. The conjecture should read something like this.

> **Conjecture:** Given an infinite geometric series with a constant ratio of $r = \frac{1}{2}$, the sum of the series will be equal to twice the first term of the series.

Step 4–Testing the Conjecture

Write the following infinite geometric series on the board.

$$\frac{1}{2} + \frac{1}{4} + \frac{1}{8} + \frac{1}{16} + \frac{1}{32} + \ldots$$

Ask your students to use their conjecture to predict the sum of this infinite geometric series with constant ratio of $r = \frac{1}{2}$. They should predict that the sum will be twice the first term, or $2 \times \frac{1}{2} = 1$.

Although the students could verify this prediction using the *List* commands on their graphing calculators, as they did in Activity Sheet 5.1, for fun you are going to help them show it in a different way. Walk over to one side of the classroom, then turn to face the other side.

Ask your class to assume that the room is exactly one unit long, whatever that unit might be. Walk half the distance to the other side of the room and ask how far you have walked. Help them realize it is $\frac{1}{2}$ of whatever unit of measurement you are using. Now walk half the remaining distance to the other side of the room and ask what this new distance is. Since it is half of the $\frac{1}{2}$ that is remaining, the distance should be $\frac{1}{4}$. Continue this a few more times, covering distances of $\frac{1}{8}$, $\frac{1}{16}$, and $\frac{1}{32}$.

Now go to the board and write the mathematical representation of the distances you have just traveled:

$$\frac{1}{2} + \frac{1}{4} + \frac{1}{8} + \frac{1}{16} + \frac{1}{32}$$

Ask how this expression would be written if you had kept walking toward the other side of the room forever, always covering half of the remaining distance. This should lead to:

$$\frac{1}{2} + \frac{1}{4} + \frac{1}{8} + \frac{1}{16} + \frac{1}{32} + \ldots$$

Point out that this process would bring you as close as desired to the other side of the room, which you assumed was 1 unit away from your starting point. So the sum of this infinite geometric series should be, as predicted, 1:

$$1 = \frac{1}{2} + \frac{1}{4} + \frac{1}{8} + \frac{1}{16} + \frac{1}{32} + \ldots$$

Step 5–A Mathematical Proof

Let S represent the sum of an infinite geometric series with constant ratio $\frac{1}{2}$ and first term A. Then S can be written as

$$S = A + \frac{A}{2} + \frac{A}{4} + \frac{A}{8} + \frac{A}{16} + \frac{A}{32} + \ldots$$

Multiply both sides of this equation by $\frac{1}{2}$ and place the result under the original series, lining up similar terms:

$$S = A + \frac{A}{2} + \frac{A}{4} + \frac{A}{8} + \frac{A}{16} + \frac{A}{32} + \ldots$$

$$\frac{1}{2}S = \qquad \frac{A}{2} + \frac{A}{4} + \frac{A}{8} + \frac{A}{16} + \frac{A}{32} + \ldots$$

Subtracting the second equation from the first gives:

$$\tfrac{1}{2} S = A$$

and multiplying both sides by 2 gives $S = 2A$. In other words, the sum of the infinite geometric series, S, is equal to twice the first term of the series, $2A$. This completes the proof. (See the "Reflections for the Teacher" section for some comments on this proof.)

FOLLOW-UP DISCUSSION AND INVESTIGATIONS

All the infinite geometric series investigated so for have had a constant ratio of ½. However, this constant ratio could have been any other positive fraction, such as ⅓ or ¼. In **Activity Sheet 5.2** your students extend what they've learned above to these other possible values for r, first creating conjectures and then proving their conjectures mathematically.

Following, for your information, is the development of the general formula for the sum of an infinite series with first term A and common ratio r, $0 < r < 1$. If you feel your students can understand this development you can share it with them. Show that for r = ½, ⅓, and ¼ this general formula gives exactly the same result they found in Activity Sheets 5.1 and 5.2.

Let $S = A + rA + r^2A + r^3A + r^4A + \ldots$ be an infinite geometric series with first term A and constant ratio r, $0 < r < 1$. Multiplying both sides of this equality by r and lining up the similar terms, we find:

$$\begin{aligned} S &= A + rA + r^2A + r^3A + r^4A + \ldots \\ rS &= \phantom{A + {}} rA + r^2A + r^3A + r^4A + \ldots \end{aligned}$$

Subtracting the second equation from the first and solving for S then gives:

$$S(1 - r) = A \quad \text{or} \quad S = \left(\frac{1}{1 - r}\right)A$$

SPREADSHEET MODIFICATION

Let's see how we might examine the original infinite geometric sum in this investigation, $16 + 8 + 4 + 2 + 1 + \tfrac{1}{2} + \tfrac{1}{4} + \tfrac{1}{8} + \tfrac{1}{16} + \ldots$, using a spreadsheet.

First, open a new spreadsheet. Enter the first 30 individual terms of this series in column A and the corresponding first 30 partial sums in column C so as to leave a bit of space between the two columns.

Place the first number, 16, in cell A1. Highlight cell A2 and drag the cursor down to select all the cells in column A down to A30. Now enter the formula "=. 5*A1" into cell A2 (remember, simply click on cell A1 to get the symbol A1 in this formula) and then press the [CTRL] and [ENTER] keys at the same time. Each cell will display a value that is 0.5 times the value in the cell directly above it, giving us the first 30 terms of the infinite series in cells A1 through A30.

Now enter the first value, 16, into cell C1. Then click on cell C2 and highlight all the cells below C2 down to C30 by dragging the cursor down. Enter the formula "=C1+A2" into cell C2 (just click on cells C1 and A2 to get these symbols in the formula) and press the [CTRL] and [ENTER] keys at the same time. The first 30 partial sums of the infinite series will appear in cells C1 through C30, showing very clearly that these partial sums approach 32 as a limit.

If you want to, highlight cells C1 through C30, click on the chart wizard, select a line graph, and click on [Finish] to obtain the visual display in Figure 5.1 that shows the partial sums approaching the limiting value of 32.

REFLECTIONS FOR THE TEACHER

1. In this investigation we look only at infinite geometric series for which the constant ratio r is positive and less than 1. If r were greater than or equal to 1, the terms of the series would either

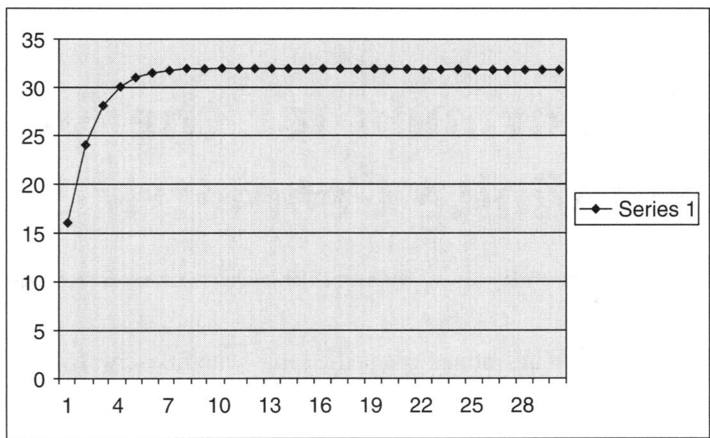

FIGURE 5.1

remain constant or increase in size. In either case the sequence of partial sums would increase without bound; consequently the series would be what we call *divergent.*

2. The proofs in this investigation involve arithmetic operations and manipulations with infinite series. These are valid for finite sums, but we have no guarantee they will work equally correctly with infinite sums. These operations and manipulations do work correctly in this investigation. But in general you have to be careful when you try to use mathematical operations that work for finite sums with infinite sums. To learn more about this you could read an introductory text on the development of infinite series and their properties.

RELATED READINGS

Erickson, Dianne. "A Problem Based Approach to Mathematics Instruction." *On-Math* (the online journal of the NCTM, http://www.nctm.org, Spring 2003, Vol. 1, No. 3).

Fletcher, Aylwin. "Decimals and Progressions: I Geometric Progressions." *Mathematics Teaching* (September 1979, No. 88, pp. 52–55).

Maor, Eli. *To Infinity and Beyond: A Cultural History of the Infinite.* (Princeton University Press, 1991).

Martinez, Joseph G.R. "Thinking and Writing Mathematically: 'Achilles and the Tortoise' as an Algebraic Word Problem." *Mathematics Teacher* (NCTM, April 2001, Vol. 94, No. 4, pp. 248–252).

Morris, Richard. *Achilles in the Quantum Universe: The Definitive History of Infinity.* (Souvenir Press, Ltd., 1998).

ACTIVITY SHEET

5.1 The Formula for the Sum of an Infinite Geometric Series

In class we found that the infinite geometric series with first term 16 and constant ratio $r = \frac{1}{2}$,

$$16 + 8 + 4 + 2 + 1 + \frac{1}{2} + \frac{1}{4} + \frac{1}{8} + \frac{1}{16} + \ldots$$

has a sum of 32, exactly twice the first term. In light of this result, does *any* infinite geometric series with a constant ratio of $\frac{1}{2}$ have a sum equal to twice its first term? That is what you will determine in this activity.

Question 1. Predict the sums of the following two infinite geometric sequences, each with a constant ratio of $\frac{1}{2}$.

$$40 + 20 + 10 + 5 + \frac{5}{2} + \frac{5}{4} + \frac{5}{8} + \ldots$$

$$100 + 50 + 25 + \frac{25}{2} + \frac{25}{4} + \frac{25}{8} + \ldots$$

Question 2. Find the first 50 partial sums of each series on your calculator to verify your predictions.

The Formula for the Sum of an Infinite Geometric Series

5.2 ACTIVITY SHEET

Question 1. For the following infinite geometric series with constant ratio $r = 1/3$, use your calculator to find the first 50 partial sums. Then use these partial sums to guess the sum of the infinite series. (Hint: The sum is a whole number.)

$$S = 30 + 10 + 10/3 + 10/9 + 10/27 + \dots$$

Question 2. Write a conjecture for the sum of an infinite geometric series with constant ratio $r = 1/3$ as a function of the first term of the series.

Question 3. Prove your conjecture the same way we proved our conjecture for the case $r = 1/2$.

Question 4. Repeat Questions 1, 2, and 3 for the sum of an infinite geometric series with $r = 1/4$. Start with the following infinite series:

$$S = 36 + 9 + 9/4 + 9/16 + 9/64 + \dots$$

INVESTIGATION 6

The Units Digits of Perfect Squares: Histograms and Relative Frequency Tables

PLANNING: GRADES 6–8

RELATED NCTM STANDARDS: Data Analysis & Probability

- Select, create, and use appropriate graphical representations of data, including histograms, box plots, and scatterplots.

PLANNING: GRADES 9–12

RELATED NCTM STANDARDS: Number & Operations

- Use number theory arguments to justify relationships involving whole numbers.

RELATED NCTM STANDARDS: Data Analysis & Probability

- Understand histograms, parallel box plots, and scatterplots and use them to display data.

MATHEMATICAL SKILLS AND CONCEPTS

Identifying patterns in the squares, cubes, and fourth powers of the positive integers.

Writing or understanding and modifying a program designed to perform a desired algorithmic procedure.

Understanding and using a histogram to represent the relative frequency of occurrence of a specified mathematical result.

Representing a positive integer in expanded form in terms of its digits and algebraically manipulating this representation to analyze the results of such operations.

CALCULATOR KEYS AND FEATURES

PRGM and associated programming features

fPart

STAT

Histogram

MATERIALS

Copies of Activity and Solution Sheets 6.1, 6.2, and 6.3 for each student.

CLASSROOM IMPLEMENTATION

Background Information for the Teacher

This investigation begins with a very simple question: "Which digits from 0 to 9 can occur as the units digit of a perfect square, and which cannot; and of those that can, which occur more often and which less often?" This question provides an interesting and mathematically rich investigation that is easy to understand for grades 6–8, yet rich enough in its use of both mathematics and graphing calculator technology for grades 9–12.

Step 1–Introducing the Problem Solving Scenario

Write a large number 2 on an 8½ by 11 inch sheet of paper. Draw a circle around the number and a line through it, like the no smoking signs you see in public places. Place the paper face down on your desk. Now ask your students to give you three different numbers between 1 and 9 and then three different numbers between 10 and 99. Write these numbers on the board, and next to each number write its corresponding square.

Now circle the units digit of each of these squares and ask your students what all of these units digits have in common. Give them a chance to think about it and suggest possible answers. Then take the piece of paper from your desk, turn it over, and show it to them. Say, "None of these perfect squares has a 2 as its units digit." How did you know this was going to happen? Was it just a lucky guess? Can you foretell the future? No, it's just a matter of mathematics, and at the end of this investigation the students will know not only why this happened, but much more about perfect squares as well.

Problem. Which digits from 0 to 9 can and cannot occur as the units digit of a perfect square; and for those that can, which occur more often and which less often?

Step 2–Investigating the Problem

Hand out **Activity Sheet 6.1**. When the students have completed it, have them report on what they found. They should find that they obtain the same results in all three columns of this chart.

Step 3–Developing a Conjecture

The chart in Activity Sheet 6.1 shows that the same digits occur with the same percentages whether you look at the set of perfect squares from 1^2 to 10^2, or from 1^2 to 20^2, or from 1^2 to 30^2. The natural conjecture these observations lead to is:

> **Conjecture:** For *all* perfect squares from 1^2 on, only the digits 0, 1, 4, 5, 6, and 9 can occur as the units digit. Furthermore, the digits 0 and 5 each occur 10% of the time while the digits 1, 4, 6, and 9 each occur 20% of the time.

Step 4–Testing the Conjecture

To test this conjecture numerically, a large number of squares should be used, such as 1^2 to 100^2 or even 1^2 to 500^2. Doing all of this computation and then calculating the corresponding frequencies and percentages is relatively simple in theory; but extremely cumbersome in practice and prone to error if it is done by hand. This is exactly the kind of work, however, for which a programmable calculator is perfectly suited.

We will use a simple program that calculates the squares from 1^2 up to any desired stopping point N^2; determines the frequency of occurrence of the digits that appear in the units place of the results; and then converts these frequencies to corresponding relative frequencies and draws a histogram of the results.

This program, called *UNITS*, is shown below. Your students may find it difficult to enter this program into their calculators by hand, so you might prefer to enter it into your own calculator and then transfer it to your students' calculators using a link cable. Demonstrate its use with $N = 10$, 20, and 30 to verify the results obtained in Activity Sheet 6.1. Use the TRACE feature after each histogram is complete to display the relative frequency of occurrence of each digit from 0 to 9. Then press STAT ENTER to display the actual frequencies and relative frequencies in lists L_2 and L_3. Now have your students perform the same procedure, this time testing the conjecture by using values $N = 100$, 200, and 300.

```
PROGRAM:UNITS
:ClrHome
:ClrList L1,L2,L3
:For(X,1,10)
:X − 1 → L1(X)
:0 → L2(X)
:End
:Disp "WHAT IS N"
:Input N
:For(X,1,N)
:(fPart(X²/10)) × 10 → A
:L2(A + 1) + 1 → L2(A + 1)
:End
:L2/N → L3
:0→Xmin : 10→Xmax
:1→Xscl
: −.1→Ymin :.3→Ymax
:Plot1(Histogram, L1,L3
:DispGraph
:Stop
```

Step 5–A Mathematical Proof

Let N represent an arbitrary positive integer. Then N can be written as

$$N = a_0 + 10a_1 + 100a_2 + 1000a_3 + \ldots$$

where the a_i are digits from 0 to 9. Squaring N we find

$$N^2 = a_0^2 + 20a_0a_1 + 100a_1^2 + \ldots$$

Clearly none of the terms of this expression after the first contribute anything to the units digit of the sum. Therefore, the units digit of N^2 must be the same as the units digit of a_0^2, which, since a_0 must be a digit from 0 through 9, can only take on the values 0, 1, 4, 5, 6, or 9 (as we found in our first class investigation). Furthermore, each group of 10 successive positive integers has the digits 0 through 9 in their units positions, so the relative frequency of the occurrence of these digits must be the same as the relative frequency you obtain from the integers 1 through 10. This completes the proof of the conjecture.

FOLLOW-UP DISCUSSION AND INVESTIGATIONS

You can give a number of simple-to-state, interesting, and simple-to-investigate follow-up questions to your students depending on the time available and their level of mathematical understanding. Three of these are shown below. The first two are appropriate for all students, and the third is at a somewhat higher level of mathematical ability.

Follow-up Investigation 1–Your students found above that the perfect squares of the positive numbers have only six of the ten digits from 0 to 9 (0, 1, 4, 5, 6, and 9), or 60% of them, as the units digit. Furthermore, these six digits have differing percentages of occurrence, with some occurring 10% of the time and others 20%. The students could reasonably ask whether, in the units digit of perfect cubes, even fewer of the digits 0 through 9 can occur and with even more widely varying percentages of occurrence. **Activity Sheet 6.2** leads your students through this investigation. As the corresponding solution sheet shows, however, all the digits from 0 to 9 unexpectedly do occur as the units digit of a perfect cube, and each of them occurs 10% of the time.

Follow-up Investigation 2–This follow-up question can be used in place of the previous one or after it. Ask your students to determine, based on the classroom investigation of perfect squares, which digits (0 through 9) can occur as the units digit in positive integers raised to the fourth power, and what the percentages of occurrence of these digits are. Then let them test their predictions using a very slightly modified version of the *UNITS* program.

Activity Sheet 6.3 takes them through this investigation. The corresponding solution sheet shows the result, how they can develop it, and how they would test it.

Follow-up Investigation 3–In the set of all positive integers there are 100 possibilities for the last two digits of these numbers: 00 (e.g., 100) up through 99 (e.g., 5199). In this investigation your students can use an approach similar to that of our original investigation to determine which of these 100 possibilities can actually occur as the *last two digits* of a perfect square.

Remind them that if the general form for a positive integer is

$$N = a_0 + 10a_1 + 100a_2 + 1000a_3 + \dots$$

then the general form of its square will be

$$N^2 = a_0^2 + 20a_0a_1 + 100a_1^2 + \dots$$

Clearly only the first two terms, given by

$$a_0^2 + 20a_0a_1$$

can contribute to the last two digits of the square since every other term is being multiplied by 100. Ask your students to evaluate this expression, $a_0^2 + 20a_0a_1$, for all possible combinations of a_0 and a_1 as these two numbers each take on the values 0 through 9. Then they can make a list of all the numbers between 00 and 99 that can occur as the last two digits in a perfect square. They will find that only 22 of these numbers can occur, and that 20 of them occur 4% of the time each while the other two each occur 10% of the time.

Finally, your students can create a new program based on *UNITS* that will develop a frequency and relative frequency count of how often each number between 00 and 99 occurs. For example, they can examine the set of perfect squares from 1^2 through 500^2 and compare this result to what they predicted was going to happen.

REFLECTIONS FOR THE TEACHER

1. Many teachers feel that writing a program, or even simply understanding the logic of a program and being able to modify it in some desired way, is good practice in logical thinking and really understanding what an algorithmic process is. In the follow-up investigations described above your students were asked to modify the original program *UNITS*. If your students are graphing calculator savvy and can write simple programs, they could write a program to accomplish what *UNITS* does instead of using the prewritten program.

2. The number theory investigations presented above are numerical in the sense that, aside from the use of histograms to display percentage of occurrence of the various digits of numbers, the identification and analysis of the patterns that occur use numbers. Most number theory, however, at all levels, is now conducted visually. The set of all positive integers is displayed as pixels on a screen, with darkened or colored pixels corresponding to numbers that possess a certain specified property. Then we can see if any interesting visual pattern emerges. A few web sites that use such a visual approach to number theory investigations are listed in the *Related Readings* section below.

RELATED READINGS

Litwiller, Bonnie H., and Duncan, David R. "Patterns in Powers." *School Science and Mathematics* (May–June 1974, Vol. 74, No. 5, pp. 398–402).

Shoemaker, Richard W. "Patterns in Powers of Digits." *Mathematics Teacher* (NCTM, April 1988, Vol. 81, No. 4, pp. 294–298).

Whitin, David. "Patterns with Square Numbers." *Arithmetic Teacher* (NCTM, December 1979, Vol. 27, No. 4, pp. 38–39).

"Number Spirals." Placing the consecutive non-negative integers on a ribbon with zero at the center and rolling the ribbon around and around displays many numerical patterns and relationships (http://numberspiral.com).

"Prime Spiral." Arranging the natural numbers in a square grid in a certain way color codes the primes, resulting in a spiral pattern (http://mathworld.wolfram.com/PrimeSpiral.html).

"The Prime Village." A java applet website that allows you to specify the types of primes you want to investigate and then automatically displays the results. It's easy to pick out visual patterns. Click the phrase "Instructions in English" on the screen for an automatic translation from French to English (http://platon.lacitec.on.ca/~dmorin/applets/village/index.html).

The Units Digits of Perfect Squares: Histograms and Relative Frequency Tables

6.1 ACTIVITY SHEET

Square the positive integers from 1 to 10. Then count how often each digit from 0 to 9 occurs as the units digit of these squares, and enter the percent of time each digit occurs into the appropriate column of the chart below. Then extend your results to go from 1 to 20; and finally extend your results to go from 1 to 30. Compare the columns. Find anything interesting?

Possible Units Digits	Rel. Freq. 1 to 10	Rel. Freq. 1 to 20	Rel. Freq. 1 to 30
0			
1			
2			
3			
4			
5			
6			
7			
8			
9			

ACTIVITY SHEET

6.2 The Units Digits of Perfect Squares: Histograms and Relative Frequency Tables

From our investigation in class we discovered that only six of the digits from 0 to 9 (0, 1, 4, 5, 6, and 9) could occur as the units digit of a perfect square, and that they did so with varying percentages of occurrence.

In this activity you will make a similar investigation about the digits that occur as the units digit of perfect cubes of the form A^3.

Step 1. Cube each of the positive integers from 1 to 10, and list their units digits and the percentage of time each digit occurs. Then do the same for the cubes of 1 to 20, and also for the cubes of 1 to 30.

Step 2. Based on your results in Step 1, create a conjecture about which digits can and cannot occur as the units digit of a perfect cube and how often each digit will occur.

Step 3. In the *UNITS* program, change the line ":(fPart(X^2/10)) $\times$ 10 $\rightarrow$ A" to ":(fPart(X^3/10)) $\times$ 10 $\rightarrow$ A". Now run the program for $N = 100$, 200, and 300 and see if your conjecture holds up under this test.

The Units Digits of Perfect Squares: Histograms and Relative Frequency Tables

6.3 ACTIVITY SHEET

From our investigation in class we discovered that only six of the digits from 0 to 9 (0, 1, 4, 5, 6, and 9) could occur as the units digit of a perfect square, and that they did so with varying percentages of occurrence.

In this activity you will use these results to investigate which digits occur as the units digit of the fourth powers of the positive integers numbers of the form A^4.

Step 1. Recalling that $A^4 = (A^2)^2$ and which digits occur as the units digit of a perfect square and their relative frequency of occurrence, algebraically predict which digits can and cannot occur as the units digit of a fourth power and their corresponding relative frequencies. Express this result as a conjecture about the units digits of the fourth powers of all positive integers.

Step 2. In the *UNITS* program change the line ":(fPart(X^2/10)) × 10 → A" to ":(fPart(X^4/10)) × 10 → A" and ".3 → Ymax" to ".5 → Ymax". Now run the program for $N = 100$ and 200 and see if your conjecture holds up under this test.

INVESTIGATION 7

Probability and the Concept of Fairness: A Simple Program

PLANNING: GRADES 6–8

RELATED NCTM STANDARDS: Data Analysis & Probability

- Use proportionality and a basic understanding of probability to make and test conjectures about the results of experiments and simulations.

PLANNING: GRADES 9–12

RELATED NCTM STANDARDS: Data Analysis & Probability

- Use simulations to explore the variability of sample statistics from a known population and to construct sampling distributions.
- Understand how sample statistics reflect the values of population parameters, and use sampling distributions as the basis for informal inference.

MATHEMATICAL SKILLS AND CONCEPTS

Apply the concepts of equally likely and unlikely in a real world experiment.

Understand the relationship between the probability of an event in a real world situation and that event's relative frequency of occurrence and use this relationship to make predictions.

Develop a mathematical simulation to represent a real world situation.

Calculate empirical probabilities through the development of a chart and simple counting.

Write and run simple programs to estimate probabilities of events in real world experiments.

CALCULATOR KEYS AND FEATURES

PRGM

min(

max(

abs(

MATERIALS

A pair of dice for each pair of students.

Copies of Activity and Solution Sheets 7.1 through 7.4 for each student.

CLASSROOM IMPLEMENTATION

Background Information for the Teacher

Programming may be one of the most useful yet most underutilized features of the graphing calculator. Sometimes you wish the calculator had a certain feature that it doesn't come with. Wouldn't it be nice if you could add this feature to your machine? Often you can add this feature through a short and simple program.

The newer TI graphing calculators do have "flash technology" that enables you to download and install applications (called "APPS") on your calculator. But programming gives you more flexibility and allows you to use your calculator in ways that the APPS cannot.

In this investigation we develop a program that simulates a game. Then we develop a conjecture based on the evidence obtained as to whether the game is fair for the opposing players, A and B. We then help our students to understand the mathematics that underlies this game and determine mathematically whether it is fair.

Step 1–Introducing the Problem Solving Scenario

Tell your students that they are going to play a two-person game using a pair of dice and that the rules of the game are very simple. The two people playing the game are called A and B. They each roll one die and if the difference between the two dice is 0, 1, or 2, Player A wins $1; while if the difference is 3, 4, or 5, Player B wins $1. The students will try to discover whether this is a fair game for both players.

Problem. To determine whether or not this is a fair game in the sense that both players have an equal chance to win every time the game is played.

Step 2–Investigating the Problem

Divide your class into pairs. Select one student in each pair to be Player A and the other to be Player B. Give each pair of students two dice and give each student a copy of **Activity Sheet 7.1**. Put a transparency on the overhead projector with a chart showing two columns headed "A Wins" and "B Wins." As each pair of students completes Activity Sheet 7.1, one of them is to come up and list the number of times, in their 30 trials, that each player won.

Once all the results are listed, discuss the data with your students. There will be variability, but usually Player A will have won more often than Player B, in many cases twice as often. Add up all the times A won and all the times B won and compare these totals, since everyone was playing the game the same way with similar equipment. These totals should really make it clear that A won more often than B, perhaps even twice as often.

Step 3–Developing a Conjecture

Discuss with your class the question of whether or not this game is fair to both players; that is, whether in general it is equally likely in any one trial that A and B would win. From the data that has been collected it is clearly not fair and in fact favors Player A for some reason. Help your students to express this as a conjecture, such as the following.

> **Conjecture:** In the game we have been playing, Player A and Player B do not have an equal chance of winning. In fact, this game favors Player A, perhaps by as much as a ratio of 2 to 1.

Step 4–Testing the Conjecture

To test this conjecture, you are going to write a graphing calculator program that simulates this game. Now you can see what happens if several hundred or even a thousand games were to be played without actually using the dice and keeping track of the results by hand.

You can use the program as a whole-class demonstration; show the students the program steps so they can see how the program was created and copy it into their own calculators; or use the graphing calculator cable link to transfer the program from your calculator to your students' calculators. A simple and very direct version of this program is shown below. You can change the number of trials by replacing the number 50 in the third line with any other positive integer. Every time you run this program the calculator screen will display the number of times Player A won followed by the number of times Player B won.

```
PROGRAM: GAME1
:ClrHome
:0→A:0→B
:For (X, 1, 50, 1)
:randInt (1, 6) →C
:randInt (1, 6) →D
:abs(C−D) →E
:If E≤2
:A+1→A
:If E>2
:B+1→B
:End
:Disp A, B
```

Running this simulation several times will reinforce the validity of our conjecture. Change the 50 to 500 or even to 1000 to see what happens in a really large number of games. The results of these 500 or 1000 trials should convince your students even more strongly of the truth of their conjecture.

Step 5–A Mathematical Proof

To investigate this problem mathematically, hand out copies of **Activity Sheet 7.2** to your students. This activity sheet provides a chart with rows and columns representing the results of rolling the two dice. At the intersection of each row and column, your students are to write the letter A if that combination of die results would make Player A the winner, or B if it would make Player B the winner. For example, we would put the letter A where row 3 meets with column 5 since the difference of 3 and 5 is 2 and this value makes Player A the winner.

At the bottom of the chart your students will record how many of the 36 possible outcomes let A win and how many let B win in both fractional and percentage form. The results are shown on the accompanying solution sheet.

The numerical results show that Player A has twice the probability of winning the game as Player B. This provides mathematical proof of our conjecture.

FOLLOW-UP DISCUSSION AND INVESTIGATIONS

At the end of this investigation are two variations of the game. The first one, given in **Activity Sheet 7.3**, can be done by your students in class working in pairs. The second one, given in **Activity Sheet 7.4**, is to be done individually by your students as a homework assignment. In both activities the students investigate a slight variant of the game by simulating it with a calculator program; they develop a conjecture about the fairness of the game and then analyze the game mathematically using a chart, as we did above, to prove their conjecture.

If you want your students to get practice in programming you can have them write the programs themselves. Otherwise, use your calculator link to transfer the programs from your calculator to theirs. Both programs are simple modifications of the one given above, so the programming required is not too demanding. The programs and the answers to the questions are provided on the solution sheets at the end of the text.

REFLECTIONS FOR THE TEACHER

Students often regard the results of an experiment, especially if it is carried out many times, as equivalent to a proof. It's therefore important in this investigation that they understand why they are using the chart to mathematically prove their conjecture. If, in any of the activity sheets, students obtain a result in their small number of trials that is different from the result that is proven mathematically, inform your students that relying on experimental results could lead to erroneous conclusions.

Having your students modify the first program in Activity Sheets 7.2 and 7.3 and going over these modifications will be time well spent if you intend to use simulations in the future with students creating the programs themselves. Such programming is good practice in logical thinking and planning.

RELATED READINGS

Bright, George W. "Teaching Mathematics with Technology: Probability Simulations." *Arithmetic Teacher* (NCTM, May 1989, Vol. 36, No. 9, pp. 16–18).

Cromer, Fred E. "The Use of Simulation in Teaching Probability." *School Science and Mathematics* (October 1976, Vol. 76, No. 6, pp. 511–514).

Hoffman, Nathan. "Some New Ways of Solving a Coin Tossing Problem." *Two-Year College Mathematics Journal* (January 1978, Vol. 9, No. 1, pp. 6–10).

Lappan, Glenda, and Winter, M. J. "Probability Simulation in Middle School." *Mathematics Teacher* (NCTM, September 1980, Vol. 73, No. 6, pp. 446–449).

McClintock, Edwin, and Jiang, Zhonghong. "Spreadsheets: Powerful Tools for Probability Simulations." *Mathematics Teacher* (NCTM, October 1997, Vol. 90, No. 7, pp. 572–579).

Pratt, Dave. "Making Sense of the Total of Two Dice." *Journal for Research in Mathematics Education* (NCTM, 2000, Vol. 31, No. 5, pp. 602–625).

ACTIVITY SHEET

7.1 Probability and the Concept of Fairness: A Simple Program

This is a two-player game, with one player called A and the other B, and both players having a fair die. Both players roll their dice. If the difference between the two dice is equal to 0, 1, or 2, Player A gets $1. If the difference between the two dice is equal to 3, 4, or 5, Player B gets $1.

Is this a fair game? That is, do both players have an equal chance of winning in each game? Proceed as follows to try to answer this question.

Let one person in each pair be Player A and the other Player B. Play this game 30 times using your pair of dice. Keep track of who gets the $1 prize each time you play, and at the end of 30 plays see how much each player has earned. When you are done enter your results on one of the lines of the chart on the overhead sheet.

Stop when this is done. We will discuss what we've found before proceeding to the next part of this investigation.

Probability and the Concept of Fairness: A Simple Program

7.2 ACTIVITY SHEET

In the chart below fill in the letter A wherever the results of rolling the two dice would make A the winner, and B wherever B would be the winner. After the chart is complete, count how many results would favor A, how many would favor B, and fill in the blanks in the statements below the chart.

		Die 2					
		1	2	3	4	5	6
	1	–	–	–	–	–	–
	2	–	–	–	–	–	–
Die 1	3	–	–	–	–	–	–
	4	–	–	–	–	–	–
	5	–	–	–	–	–	–
	6	–	–	–	–	–	–

Player A wins in __________ out of the 36 results, or __________% of the time.

Player B wins in __________ out of the 36 results, or __________% of the time.

Based on these results, we would expect Player A to win approximately __________ as often as Player B.

ACTIVITY SHEET

7.3 Probability and the Concept of Fairness: A Simple Program

This game is similar to the one you've already played in class. This time, however, we look at the *maximum* of the two die faces to decide which player gets the $1 prize rather than the difference between the two die faces.

Player A wins if the maximum of the two faces is 1, 2, 3, or 5. Player B wins if the maximum of the two faces is 4 or 6.

Step 1. Either modify the program you used in the first game to fit this new situation or get the program from your teacher. Call this new program GAME2.

Step 2. Run the program and record how many times each player wins. Do this several times until you have a sense of whether the game is fair or not and, if not, whom it favors.

Step 3. Make a conjecture about the fairness of the game or whom it appears to favor and by how much.

Step 4. Use the chart below, as we did before, to list who would win under all 36 different possible outcomes. Then count the results and answer the questions below the chart. Remember, we are interested in the *maximum* of the two dice: Player A wins if it is 1, 2, 3, or 5, while Player B wins if it is 4 or 6.

		Die 2					
		1	2	3	4	5	6
	1						
	2						
Die 1	3						
	4						
	5						
	6						

Player A wins in __________ out of the 36 results, or __________% of the time.

Player B wins in __________ out of the 36 results, or __________% of the time.

Is the game fair? If not, whom does it favor? __________

Probability and the Concept of Fairness: A Simple Program 7.4

ACTIVITY SHEET

This game is similar to Game #2. This time, however, we are looking at the minimum of the two dice, not the maximum.

Player A wins if the minimum of the two dice is 1, 2, or 3, while Player B wins if the minimum of the two dice is 4, 5, or 6. Follow the directions below to investigate the game's fairness.

Step 1. Either modify the program you used in the first activity to fit this new situation or get the program from your teacher. Call this new program GAME2.

Step 2. Run the program and record the results you obtain for how many times each player wins. Do this several times until you have a sense of whether the game is fair or not and, if it is not, whom you think it favors.

Step 3. Make a conjecture about the fairness of the game or whom it appears to favor and by how much.

Step 4. Now use the chart below, as we did before, to list who would win under all 36 different possible outcomes. Then count the results and answer the questions below the chart.

		Die 2					
		1	2	3	4	5	6
	1						
	2						
Die 1	3						
	4						
	5						
	6						

Player A wins in __________ out of the 36 results, or __________% of the time.

Player B wins in __________ out of the 36 results, or __________% of the time.

Is the game fair? If not, whom does it favor? __________

INVESTIGATION 8

Examining the Trajectory of an Object in Motion Using Graphs and Tables of Values

PLANNING: GRADES 9–12

RELATED NCTM STANDARDS: Algebra

- Generalize patterns using explicitly defined and recursively defined functions.
- Use symbolic algebra to represent and explain mathematical relationships.
- Draw reasonable conclusions about a situation being modeled.

MATHEMATICAL SKILLS AND CONCEPTS

Represent a real world situation using a mathematical equation.

Use symbolic manipulation on an algebraic equation to solve a real world problem.

Use graphs and tables of values to investigate and better understand a real world problem situation.

CALCULATOR KEYS AND FEATURES

TBLSET	TABLE	WINDOW
GRAPH	TRACE	CALC

MATERIALS

Copies of Activity and Solution Sheets 8.1 and 8.2 for each student.

CLASSROOM IMPLEMENTATION

Background Information for the Teacher

Here we set up a straightforward problem to be investigated both numerically using a table of values and visually using a graph. We then ask the students, working in small groups, to discover what happens when certain aspects of the problem are changed and to speculate, based on common sense, what the results of these changes might be. The students then verify these speculations using the graphing and table generation features of the graphing calculator and, finally, prove them mathematically.

Step 1–Introducing the Problem Solving Scenario

Pose to your class the well-known problem of a person throwing an object into the air with a specified initial velocity. You will find the maximum height the object reaches and the time it takes for the object to reach this height and then come back down again. The statement of this problem is given below. Put it on an overhead transparency for the entire class to see.

> An object is thrown upward with an initial velocity of 32 feet per second. The equation relating the height of the object above ground y (in feet) to the time that has passed x (in seconds) is given by:
>
> $$y = 32x - 16x^2$$
>
> Use both the table generation and graphing features of your calculator to find: (i) the maximum height of the object; (ii) the time it takes the object to reach this maximum height; and (iii) the time it takes the object to come down again.

Start by discussing with your students what the two terms that make up this function represent in real life. Explain that the term $32x$ represents the distance that this object would travel straight up in x seconds if there were no force of gravity working against the initial velocity of 32 feet per second. Then mention that the term $16x^2$ represents the force of gravity and the negative sign indicates that this force is acting opposite to the initial velocity.

Problem. To discover how the three measurements we've made relating to the motion of this object change if the initial velocity is doubled or tripled, or if the force of gravity is reduced.

Work through this problem with your students. Let them suggest what to do if they are experienced with the table and graphing features of the calculator, or guide them if they are not. For the graphical solution use *TRACE* and *ZOOM* to estimate the solutions graphically; then verify the results using the *CALC* command. For the table solution start with the instant the object is thrown, $x = 0$, and use an increment of 1 second. Since the maximum occurs at an integer value ($x = 1$ second) this selection will let you find the answers quickly and easily. The answers are: (i) a maximum height of 16 feet; (ii) 1 second to reach this maximum height; and (iii) 1 additional second to come down again (for a total round-trip time of 2 seconds).

Up to this point the questions asked and the uses of the calculator have been fairly typical and straightforward. But now it's time for your students to start thinking about the situation and what would happen if one or more of the conditions were to be changed.

Step 2–Investigating the Problem

Ask your students what they would expect to happen if the object were thrown upwards with an initial velocity greater than 32 feet per second. Explain that in this case the force of gravity should take longer to overcome the initial velocity and start pulling the object back down to earth; so all three of your original measurements (time to go up, time to come down, and maximum height reached) should increase.

Now put your students into small groups and give each student a copy of **Activity Sheet 8.1.** In this activity the students multiply the initial velocity of the object by 2 and then by 3 and use these results to develop a conjecture about the effects of multiplying the initial velocity by a positive constant value K on the three measurements.

Step 3–Developing a Conjecture

Ask some of the groups to share their results and their conjecture with the class. Then ask the students how they might test (not prove yet, just test) this conjecture. Take a suggested value of K that has not yet been used, predict from the conjecture what the three measurements should be, and then use the calculator to verify the predictions.

Step4–Testing the Conjecture

Steps 1 and 2 of Activity Sheet 8.1 ask the students to multiply the initial velocity of the object by 2 and then by 3, so if your students assume that K needs to be an integer value as well (such as 4 or 5), that's fine for the first test of the conjecture. Explain, however, that there is no mathematical reason to limit the value of K in this way and then use a fractional value of K (such as $\frac{5}{2}$, for example) to test the conjecture as well.

Step 5–A Mathematical Proof

Rewrite the equation relating time passed to height above ground as shown below.

$$y = 32x - 16x^2 = 16x\,(2 - x)$$

In this form it's easy to see algebraically why the time in the original situation is 1 second to go up and come down, and why the maximum height is 16 feet. The height y must be 0 when the object is on the ground, so it is clear in the factored form of the function that $y = 0$ exactly when $x = 0$ or when $x = 2$. Since $x = 0$ represents the instant at which the object is released, $x = 2$ must be the instant when it hits the ground. Therefore it takes $x = 2$ seconds to make the entire trip up and down, and half that amount of time, 1 second, for each half of the journey.

Once we know that half the journey is completed at $x = 1$, we can simply substitute this value into the equation to obtain the maximum height, which is then found to be $y = 16(1)\,[2 - 1] =$ 16 feet. Now let's look at the general form of this equation when the initial velocity of 32 feet per second is multiplied by K to give an initial velocity of $32K$ feet per second.

$$y = 32Kx - 16x^2 = 16x\,(2K - x)$$

Solving for $y = 0$ gives $x = 0$ and $x = 2K$, so it takes $2K$ seconds to make the entire trip with K seconds to go up and K seconds to come down. So the part of the conjecture that says the time of travel is multiplied by K is proven. Furthermore, since it takes K seconds to reach a maximum height, simply substitute $x = K$ to find that the maximum height is $32K \times K - 16K^2 = 16K^2$, or K^2 times the original value.

FOLLOW-UP DISCUSSION AND INVESTIGATIONS

In the investigation above we looked at the effects of changing the initial upward velocity of the object. The other variable in the situation is the force of gravity acting downward to counteract this initial velocity. **Activity Sheet 8.2** leads the students through an investigation of this second variable similar to what they've done in Activity Sheet 8.1.

Before they begin work on the activity sheet, begin this follow-up investigation, with a discussion of what would happen to the three measurements they've been investigating if the force of gravity were to be reduced and why they think this would happen. The students should understand that if the force of gravity is weakened this downward acting force will take longer to counteract the upward initial velocity; therefore, both the time for the trip and the maximum height reached should increase.

SPREADSHEET MODIFICATION

You can use a spreadsheet in this investigation both to develop a table of values for the height of the object versus time and to create a corresponding line graph. You need to be careful however, with the values that you use since in the initial problem the object takes only 2 seconds to go up and come down again.

To display the time, in tenths of a second, in column A simply enter 0 into cell A1; click on cell A2 and drag down to highlight cells A2 through A21; enter the formula "=A1+.1" into cell A2; and press CTRL and ENTER at the same time. The values 0 through 2 will be displayed in cells A1 through A21, in increments of 0.1.

To display the corresponding heights in column B simply click on cell B1 and drag the cursor down to highlight cells B1 through B21; enter the formula "=32 × A1−16 × A1 × A1" into cell B1; and press CTRL and ENTER at the same time. The values for the height of the object will be displayed in cells B1 through B21; B21 = 0 shows that the object has returned to earth after A21 = 2.0 seconds, and B11 = 16 shows that the maximum height reached by the object is 16 feet after A11 = 1.0 seconds.

You can now obtain a graph of the heights by highlighting cells A1 through A21 and B1 through B21 all at the same time; clicking on the chart wizard; selecting the scatter plot of your choice; and clicking on "Finish." The graph will look like the one shown in Figure 8.1 where the units on the horizontal axis are in seconds and the units on the vertical axis are in feet.

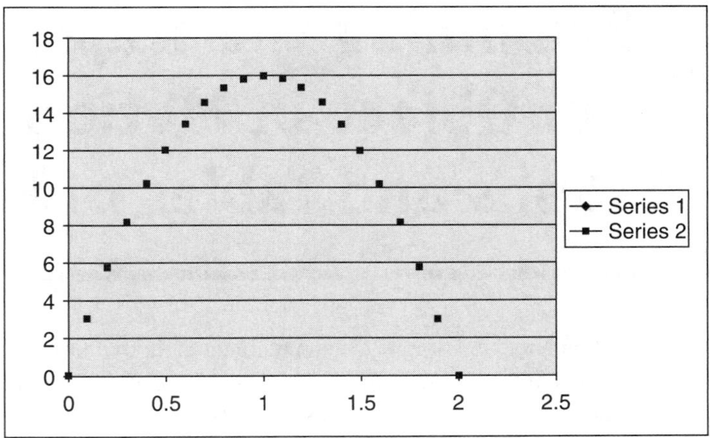

FIGURE 8.1

REFLECTIONS FOR THE TEACHER

The students should discuss what they *think* will happen when changes are made to the original problem before actually investigating using the calculator. Encourage them to use their common sense to think things through: If the experimental results are not what they expected they can either improve their understanding of the problem or they can examine how they represented the situation mathematically to discover any errors.

RELATED READINGS

Coutis, Peter. "Modelling the Projectile Motion of a Cricket Ball." *International Journal of Mathematical Education in Science and Technology* (November–December 1998, Vol. 29, No. 6, pp. 789–798).

Grant, Ruari A. "A Study of the Trajectories of Projectiles." *Physics Education* (September 1990, Vol. 25, No. 5, pp. 288–292).

Malone, Mark R. "Marshmallow Catapults." *CESI Science* (Spring 1996, Vol. 28, No. 4, pp. 10–12).

Nelson, Robert A., and Wilson, Mark E. "Mathematical Analysis of a Model Rocket Trajectory Part I: The Powered Phase." *Physics Teacher* (March 1976, Vol. 14, No. 3, pp. 150–161).

Svec, Michael T. "Effect of Micro-Computer Based Laboratory on Graphing Interpretation Skills and Understanding." *Research Report* (April 23, 1995, ERIC # ED383551).

ACTIVITY SHEET

8.1 Examining the Trajectory of an Object in Motion Using Graphs and Tables of Values

In class we investigated a situation in which an object is thrown upward with an initial velocity of 32 feet per second and eventually the force of gravity brings the object back down to Earth. The equation representing this situation was $y = 32x - 16x^2$ and we found that the object took 1 second to reach its maximum height of 16 feet and another 1 second to come back down.

Step 1. Suppose we double the initial velocity of the object from 32 to 64 feet per second, giving the new equation $y = 64x - 16x^2$. Do you expect that the time to reach a maximum height, the time to come down again, and the maximum height will now all be doubled as well? Make a guess, then use the graphing and table generation features of your calculator to see if your guess was correct.

Step 2. Suppose you triple the initial velocity of the object from 32 to 96 feet per second, giving the new equation $y = 96x - 16x^2$. Based on your results in Step 1, what change would you now expect in the time to go up, the time to come down, and the maximum height reached? Make a guess and then use your calculator to see if your guess was correct.

Step 3. Make a conjecture about the new time to go up, the time to come down, and the maximum height reached if the original initial velocity of 32 feet per second is multiplied by K to give an equation of the form $y = 32Kx - 16x^2$.

Examining the Trajectory of an Object in Motion Using Graphs and Tables of Values

8.2 ACTIVITY SHEET

In this investigation the initial velocity is still 32 feet per second. But we assume that the experiment is taking place on a planet with a weaker force of gravity than Earth. It seems reasonable that if gravity is weaker the time to go up and come down and the height reached should be greater. Let's see.

Step 1. Assume the force of gravity is halved (multiplied by 0.5) to give a corresponding equation $y = 32x - 8x^2$. Use your calculator to see what effect this has on the time for the object to go up and come down and its maximum height.

Step 2. Using what you found in Step 1 as a guide, what do you predict would happen to the time to go up, the time to come down, and the maximum height if you multiplied the force of gravity by $1/4$ to give the equation $y = 32x - 4x^2$? Make a prediction, then use your calculator to see if you were right.

Step 3. Make a conjecture about the effects on the time to go up, the time to come down, and the maximum height when the force of gravity is multiplied by $1/k$.

INVESTIGATION 9

A Visual Inspection of the Real Roots of a Polynomial Function

PLANNING: GRADES 9–12

RELATED NCTM STANDARDS: Algebra

- Analyze functions of one variable by investigating rates of change, intercepts, zeros, asymptotes, and local and global behavior.
- Understand and compare the properties of classes of functions, including exponential, polynomial, rational, logarithmic, and periodic functions.

MATHEMATICAL SKILLS AND CONCEPTS

Identify through visual inspection the number and type of real roots of a polynomial equation with real coefficients.

Recognize the relationship between the number of "turns" of a graph and the number of real roots of its corresponding equation.

CALCULATOR KEYS AND FEATURES

Y =

WINDOW

GRAPH

MATERIALS

Copies of Activity and Solution Sheets 9.1 and 9.2 for each student.

CLASSROOM IMPLEMENTATION

Background Information for the Teacher

As students grow mathematically more experienced and mature they start thinking of mathematical objects as members of families with similar properties and characteristics instead of as individuals. One topic for which this change of perspective is most important is that of functions and families of functions.

Instead of considering individual linear equations, for example, students begin to think about the family of all linear equations and what they have in common. This then leads to a graphical consideration of their slopes and y-intercepts, and an algebraic consideration of a general procedure for solving a linear equation. A similar shift occurs when students then move on to consider second degree equations, exponential equations, and logarithmic equations.

In this activity we use the graphing calculator to help our students discover some properties of the family of polynomial equations with real coefficients. Specifically, we examine properties of the real roots of such equations.

Step 1–Introducing the Problem Solving Scenario

Put the following two lists of polynomial functions on the board or overhead projector. Ask your students to use their graphing calculators to graph first the functions on List A, and then the functions on List B one at a time. Then try to identify the major visual difference between the two sets of graphs. Point out that the functions in List A are all of odd degree while those in List B are all of even degree, which is a symbolic difference. But what is the major difference between the *graphs* of the functions on the two lists?

List A	List B
$y = x$	$y = x^2$
$y = .05x^3 + 2$	$y = 0.1x^4 - 4$
$y = 0.001x^5 - 3$	$y = 0.001x^6 + 2$

Show your students that, as you move from left to right on the x axis, the graphs of the three odd-degree functions in List A all begin and end at opposite ends of the y axis (Figures 9.1a, 9.1b, and 9.1c), while the graphs of the even-degree functions in List B all begin and end at the same end (Figures 9.2a, 9.2b, and 9.2c).

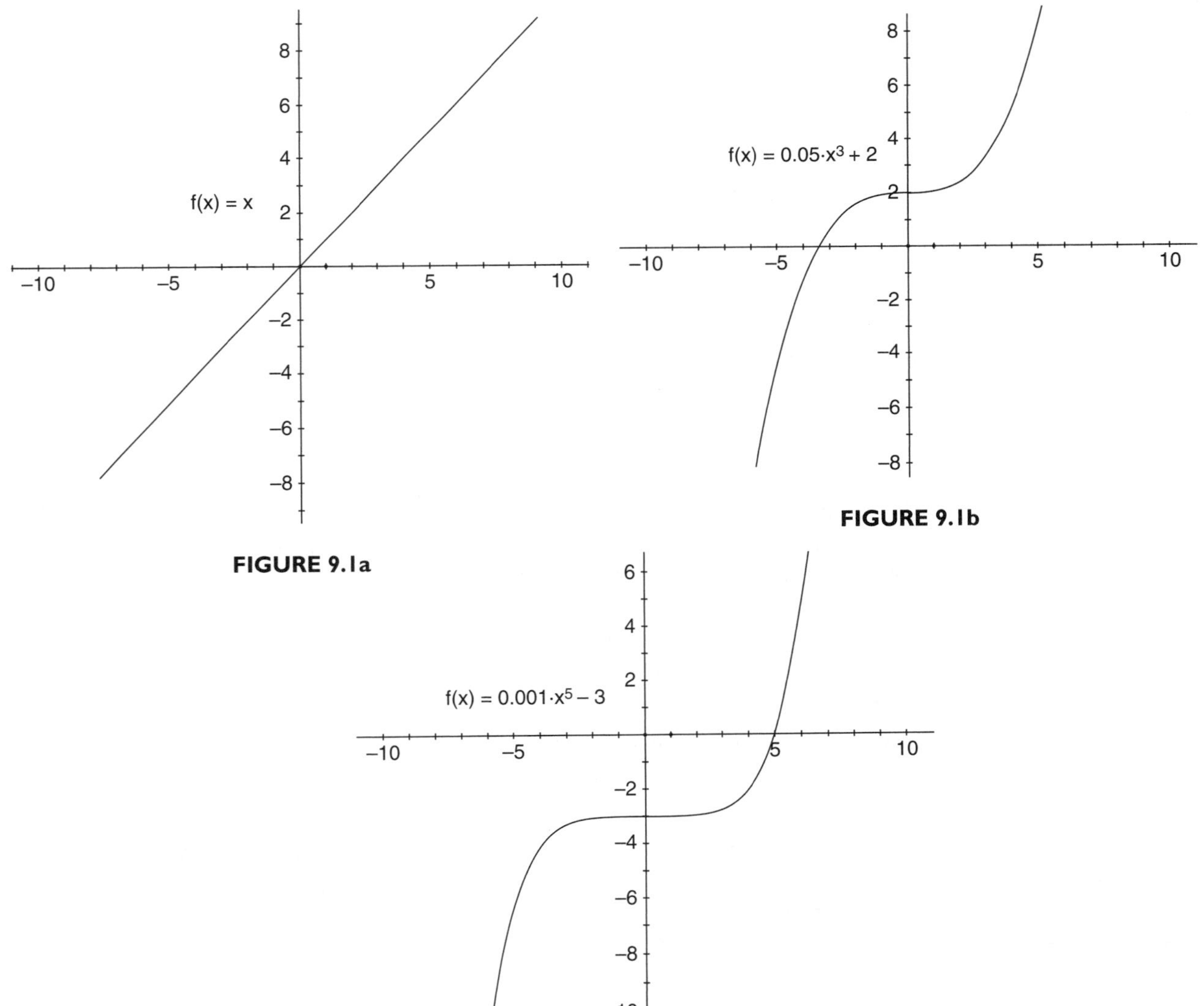

FIGURE 9.1a

FIGURE 9.1b

FIGURE 9.1c

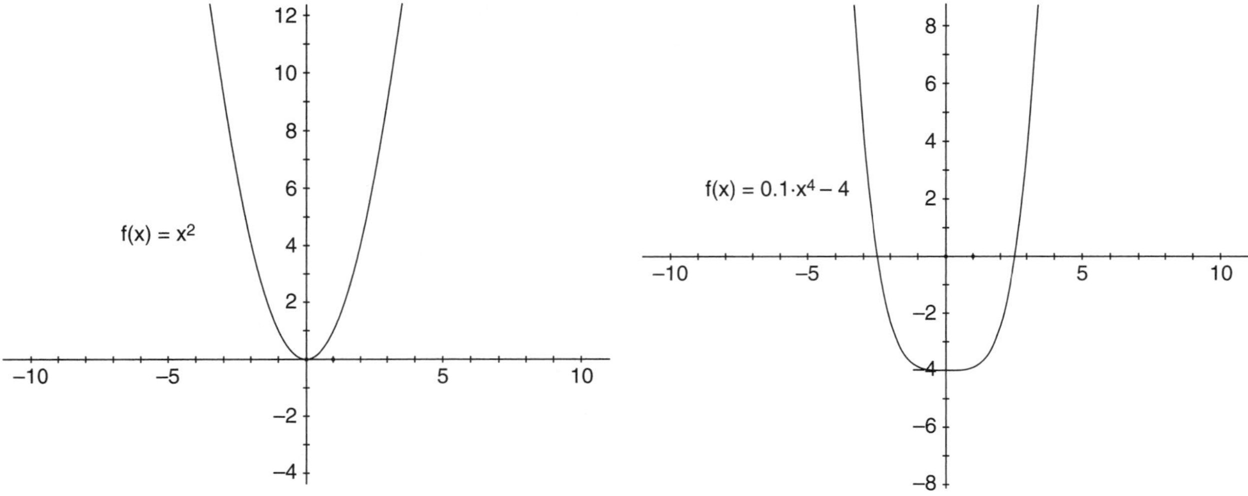

FIGURE 9.2a

FIGURE 9.2b

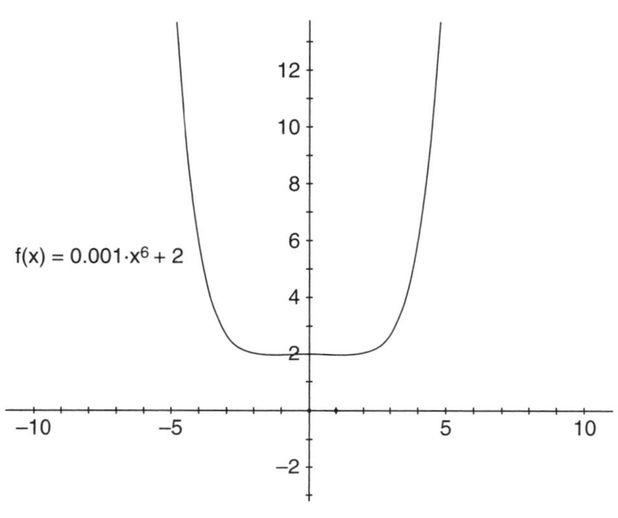

FIGURE 9.2c

Ask your students to give you some other odd- and even-degree polynomials with real coefficients, and graph them to see if this pattern continues. Point out to your students that all the odd-degree polynomials begin and end at opposite ends of the *y* axis, while all the even-degree polynomials begin and end at the same end.

Then write the following statement on the board and ask your students how they could use what they've just learned about the graphs of polynomial functions with real coefficients to give a convincing argument for its truth.

> Every odd-degree polynomial with real coefficients must have at least one real root, whereas a polynomial of even degree with real coefficients does not have to have any real roots.

Since the graph of a polynomial of odd degree begins and ends at opposite ends of the *y* axis, clearly it must intersect the *x* axis at least once; and since the graph of a polynomial of even degree begins and ends at the same end of the *y* axis, it could always remain either above or below the *x* axis and therefore does not have to possess any real roots. The functions in Lists A and B demonstrate these alternatives nicely.

Problem. To determine how many real roots a polynomial function with real coefficients can have.

Finally, tell your students you now want to use graphs to determine *how many real roots* a polynomial function with real coefficients can have.

Step 2–Investigating the Problem

The students should discover that a polynomial function of degree N with real coefficients can have at most N real roots. More importantly, even-degree polynomial functions of degree N with real coefficients can have anywhere from 0 to N real roots while odd-degree polynomial functions of degree N with real coefficients can have from 1 to N real roots.

Separate your students into small groups and give each student a copy of **Activity Sheet 9.1.** Students are to work on the activity sheets together and come up with a group answer to the questions that are posed. After they have sketched a graph of the given polynomial functions and completed the chart on the activity sheet, call them together to discuss their findings.

Step 3–Developing a Conjecture

Use the TI Viewscreen or the TI Presenter to discuss what the students found and how they completed the chart on the activity sheet. Now ask your students to make a conjecture, based on the completed chart, about the number of real roots of a polynomial function of degree N with real coefficients. The functions listed in Activity Sheet 9.1 might lead them to believe that an Nth degree polynomial function with real coefficients will always have N real roots. However, that's not quite correct.

Show the graph of the first degree polynomial function from the activity sheet, $y = 2x+1$, on the Viewscreen or Presenter. Then move it up and down by first increasing and then decreasing the constant term of the equation. Note to the class that this graph has exactly one real root no matter how much you raise or lower it since it still passes through the x axis exactly once.

Now graph $y = x^2$, a second degree polynomial function from the activity sheet. Add and then subtract the constant value 4 to show the students that such a second degree equation can have 0, 1, or 2 real roots.

Repeat this graphical inspection using a third degree function and a fourth degree function from the activity sheet. Then ask your students to complete the following conjecture.

> **Conjecture:** An *N*th degree polynomial function with real coefficients will have between ____________ and ____________ real roots if *N* is even; and between ____________ and ____________ real roots if *N* is odd.

The completed conjecture should look as follows:

> **Conjecture:** An *N*th degree polynomial function with real coefficients will have between <u>0</u> and <u>*N*</u> real roots if *N* is even; and between <u>*1*</u> and <u>*N*</u> real roots if *N* is odd.

Step 4–Testing the Conjecture

Test this conjecture together with your students. Select some additional polynomial functions with real coefficients, graph them, and note the number of times the graph passes through the x axis, giving a real root. Zoom out and change the values of the viewing window for graphs, if needed, to display clearly where and how often the graph crosses the x axis.

Step 5–A Convincing Argument and a Mathematical Proof

Visual inspection and manipulation of the functions from the activity sheet alone provide a reasonably convincing argument for the conjecture. For your information, however, here is a more formal proof that such a function cannot have more than N real roots. Show this to your students if you think they can understand it.

Let $P(x)$ be a polynomial function with real coefficients. Suppose $P(x)$ has more than N real roots. Denote these real roots by $r_1, r_2, r_3, \ldots, r_s$ with $S > N$. Then $P(x) = A(x - r_1)(x - r_2)\ldots(x - r_s)$ where A is some constant. But then $P(x)$ is of degree $S > N$, a contradiction.

FOLLOW-UP DISCUSSION AND INVESTIGATIONS

Now we will see if the students understand the visual interpretation of what was done in this investigation. Give them **Activity Sheet 9.2** to work on either individually or in small groups. Then let them use the Viewscreen or Presenter to demonstrate their findings.

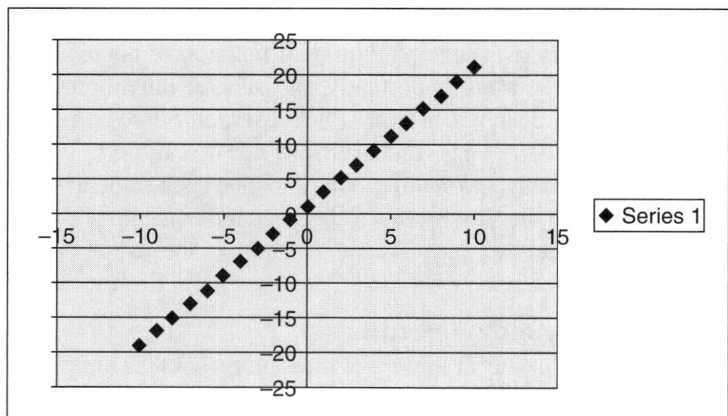

FIGURE 9.3

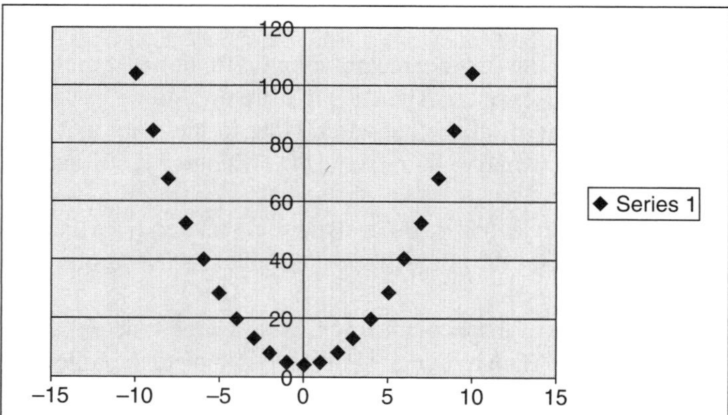

FIGURE 9.4

SPREADSHEET MODIFICATION

While it isn't as easy or as effective, you can graph the functions in this investigation using a spreadsheet instead of a graphing calculator. For example, to graph the linear function $y = 2x + 1$ you first enter the values –10 through 10 into cells A1 through A21; and then enter the corresponding function values into cells B1 through B21. This is accomplished in the following way.

Enter –10 into cell A1. Click on cell A2 and highlight all the cells in column A down to cell A21. Enter the formula "=A1+1" into cell A2, then press Ctrl and ENTER at the same time. Now click on cell B1 and highlight all the cells in this column down to B21. Enter the formula "=2*A1+1" into cell B1 and press Ctrl and ENTER at the same time. You now have the desired values in columns A and B.

To graph this data, highlight cells B1 to B21; click on the chart wizard; select an XY Scatter plot; and click on "Finish." This procedure can be used to graph any of the functions in this investigation. Figures 9.3 and 9.4 show the graphs for the functions $y = 2x + 1$ and $y = x^2 + 4$, respectively.

RELATED READINGS

Arcavi, Abraham, and Nachmias, Rafi. "What Is Your Family Name, Ms. Function? Exploring Families of Functions with a Non-Congenital Representation." *Journal of Computers in Mathematics and Science Teaching* (1993, Vol. 12, No. 3–4, pp. 315–329).

Buck, Judy Curran. "Building Connections Among Classes of Polynomial Functions." *Mathematics Teacher* (NCTM, October 2000, Vol. 93, No. 7, pp. 591–598).

Dugdale, Sharon, et al. "Visualizing Polynomial Functions: New Insights from an Old Method in a New Medium." *Journal of Computers in Mathematics and Science Teaching* (1992, Vol. 11, No. 2, pp. 123–141).

Duren, Phillip E. "Retaining a Problem-Solving Focus in the Technology Revolution." *Mathematics Teacher* (NCTM, October 1989, Vol. 28, No. 7, pp. 508–510).

Owens, John E. "Families of Parabolas." *Mathematics Teacher* (NCTM, September 1992, Vol. 85, No. 6, pp. 477–479).

Travers, Robert, and Kim, David. "Those Elusive Imaginary Zeros." *Mathematics Teacher* (NCTM, January 1982, Vol. 75, No. 1, pp. 62–64).

ACTIVITY SHEET

9.1 A Visual Inspection of the Real Roots of a Polynomial Function

Given below is a chart in which you are to record the results of the problems that follow. Answer each question and then fill in the appropriate row of the chart. The first row is already filled in, although you will want to do Question 1 yourself just to make sure that it is answered it correctly.

Degree of Polynomial Function	Maximum Number of Turns	Maximum Number of Real Roots
1	0	1
2		
3		
4		

Question 1. Graph the first degree function $y = 2x+1$. Record in the first row of the chart the number of times this curve turns (changes direction) and intersects the x axis and therefore has a real root.

Question 2. Repeat Question 1, this time graphing the second degree equations listed below. Record what you discover in the second row of the chart.

a. $y = x^2 + 4$ b. $y = x^2$ c. $y = x^2 - 4$

Question 3. Repeat Question 1, this time graphing the third degree equations listed below. Record what you discover in the third row of the chart.

a. $y = 0.1x^3 - 2.5x + 7$ b. $y = 0.1x^3 - 2.5x + 5$ c. $y = 0.1x^3 - 2.5x + 3$

Question 4. Repeat Question 1, this time graphing the fourth degree equations listed below. Record what you discover in the fourth row of the chart.

a. $y = 0.1x^4 + 0.6x^3 - 0.9x^2 - 5.4x + 10$
b. $y = 0.1x^4 + 0.6x^3 - 0.9x^2 - 5.4x + 8$
c. $y = 0.1x^4 + 0.6x^3 - 0.9x^2 - 5.4x + 4$

A Visual Inspection of the Real Roots of a Polynomial Function

9.2 ACTIVITY SHEET

Step 1. Graph the third degree polynomial function $y = (x)(x - 4)(x + 5) = x^3 + x^2 - 20x$. Clearly, this function has three real roots, $x = 0$, $x = 4$, and $x = -5$, and crosses the x axis only at these three points.

Step 2. Add positive constants to the equation in Step 1 to create third degree polynomial functions with real coefficients that have exactly 1 and exactly 2 real roots. Can you create a third degree polynomial function that has either 0 real roots or more than 3 real roots? Why or why not?

Step 3. Graph the fourth degree polynomial function $y = (x + 4)(x + 2)(x - 4)(x - 2) = x^4 - 20x^2 + 64$. Clearly, this function has four real roots, $x = -4$, $x = -2$, $x = 2$, and $x = 4$, and crosses the x axis only at these four points.

Step 4. Add positive and negative constants to the equation in Step 3 to create fourth degree polynomial functions with real coefficients that have exactly 0, exactly 2, and exactly 3 real roots. Why were you able to create a function with 0 real roots here when you could not do so in Step 2?

INVESTIGATION 10

The Relationship between the Coefficients of a First or Second Degree Function and the Behavior of Its Graph

PLANNING: GRADES 9–12

RELATED NCTM STANDARDS: Algebra

- Analyze functions of one variable by investigating rates of change, intercepts, zeros, asymptotes, and local and global behavior.
- Understand and compare the properties of classes of functions, including exponential, polynomial, rational, logarithmic, and periodic functions.

MATHEMATICAL SKILLS AND CONCEPTS

Understanding the relationship between the coefficients of a first or second degree function and its corresponding graph.

Solving a system of two linear equations in two unknowns algebraically.

Solving a system of two quadratic equations in two unknowns algebraically.

CALCULATOR KEYS AND FEATURES

Y=

WINDOW

GRAPH

CALC

MATERIALS

Viewscreen calculator with overhead projector and screen. Large sticky dots that you can get in any stationery store.

CLASSROOM IMPLEMENTATION

Background Information for the Teacher

When personal computers were relatively new, many wonderful, simple pieces of mathematical software were created. The one we are interested in for this investigation was called "Green Globs." It is currently available from *Sunburst Technology* (http://store.sunburst.com) in an expanded version called "Green Globs and Graphing Equations."

In the original computer game one or more green circles, or "globs," appeared in various places on an x, y-coordinate grid displayed on screen. The objective was to create a polynomial function that would pass through as many green globs as possible.

We can't match the color and sophistication of this game on the graphing calculator. But we can use its underlying idea to create a learning activity that not only helps our students better understand the relationship between the coefficients of a polynomial function and its graph, but provides a connection between algebra and trigonometry, as we will see in the next investigation.

This investigation differs from others in this text in that there is no conjecture to be developed, tested, and proved. Instead, it provides a pleasant change of pace and a "game" that develops solid mathematical understanding in a fun way.

Step 1–Introducing the Problem Solving Scenario

Use your Viewscreen to display the default x, y-coordinate window with x values going from –10 to +10, y values from –10 to +10, and both Xscl and Yscl equal to 1. Now press the [Y=] button and enter the function $y = 1x + 0$ as function y_1. Tell your students there is a reason for entering the function this way rather than in the form $y = x$ and to just bear with you for a bit. Then press [GRAPH] to graph this function, which is of course a straight line through the origin with a slope of +1 (Figure 10.1).

Press [Y=] again and enter $y_2 = 2x + 0$; then press [GRAPH] to show both lines on the screen at the same time. Set your calculator to "sequential" graphing mode so that y_1 is drawn before y_2. This enables you to tell which is which and to compare them as they are drawn (Figure 10.2).

Return to the [Y=] screen and change y_2 to $y_2 = 4x + 0$ and press [GRAPH]. Ask your students how the graph of $y = 1x + 0$ is changing as the coefficient of x, which began as 1, gets larger. Explain that as the coefficient increases, the corresponding line gets steeper, or it rises faster, or its slope gets bigger. Ask what the graph would look like if you changed y_2 to $y_2 = 10x + 0$; then make the change and press [GRAPH] to verify their prediction. End by asking what would happen to the graph if you made the coefficient of x negative; then illustrate by changing the equation for y_2 to $y_2 = -1x + 0$, $y_2 = -2x + 0$, and finally $y_2 = -5x + 0$ and graphing (Figures 10.3a, 10.3b, and 10.3c).

Repeat this series of questions and illustrations, once again with $y_1 = 1x + 0$, but this time change the value of the constant to create the second function y_2. Explain that the line rises as the constant value increases, while the line descends as the constant value decreases. (A straight

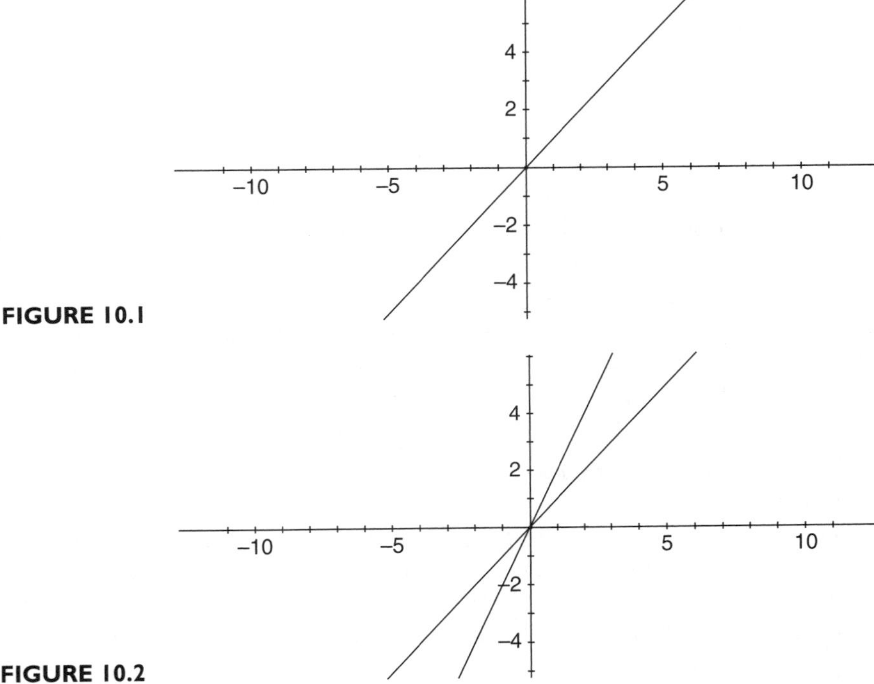

FIGURE 10.1

FIGURE 10.2

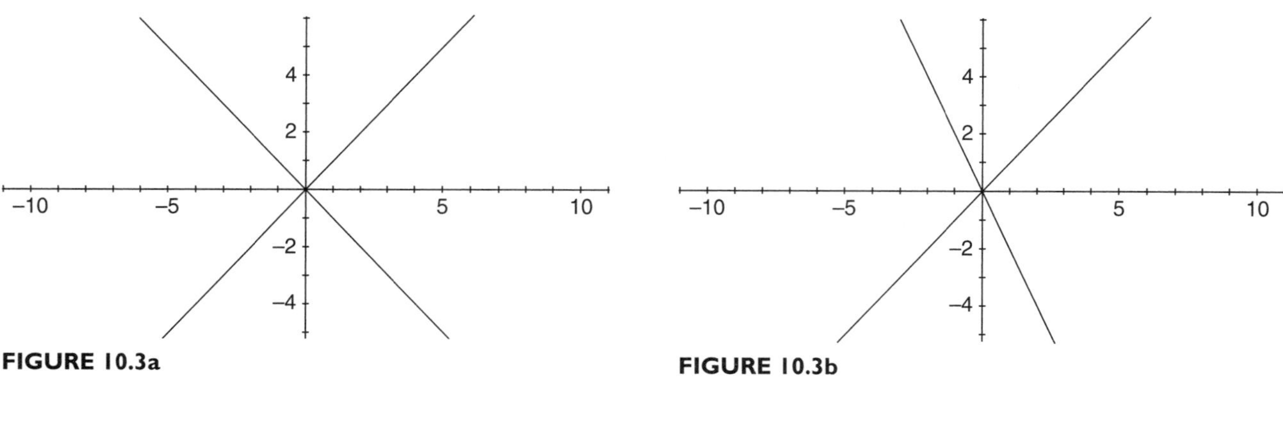

FIGURE 10.3a

FIGURE 10.3b

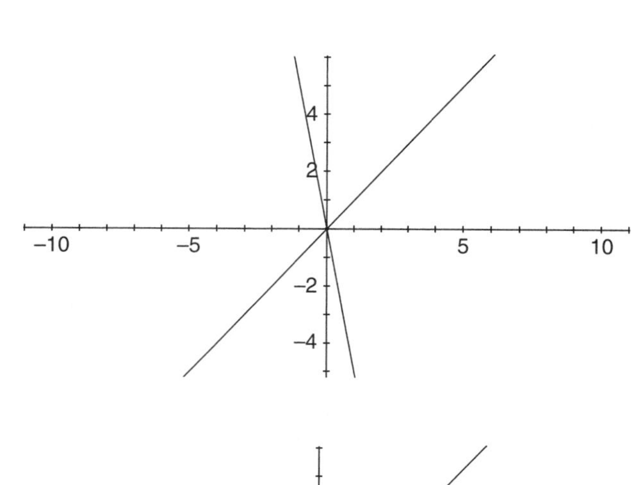

FIGURE 10.3c

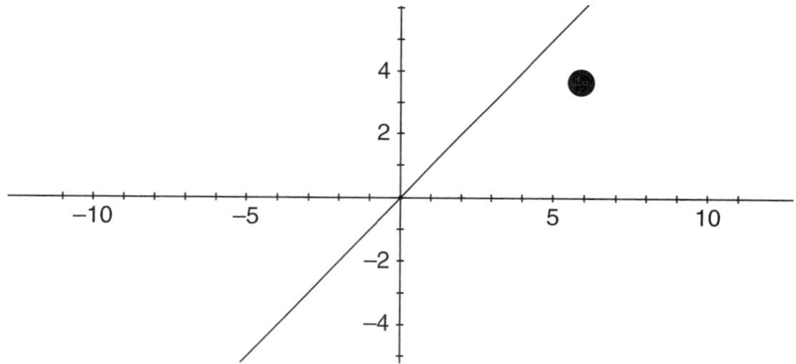

FIGURE 10.4

line extends infinitely in both directions, so some students may describe the movement of the line as going left instead of up; and going right instead of down. That's fine as well.) After you have finished this illustration, delete function y_2 so that only y_1 remains in the [Y=] screen.

Problem. By changing either or both of the coefficients of a linear function, make the graph of the function pass through a specified point in the plane.

Tell your students that you're now going to play a game that uses what they've just learned about the relationship between the coefficients of a linear function and its graph. Then place a large colored sticky dot (red, green, or blue are easy colors to see from a distance) on the overhead screen in the first quadrant of the x, y-coordinate grid, but *not* on the line that is showing, which is the graph of $y_1 = 1x + 0$ (Figure 10.4). This sticky dot is the target.

Step 2–Investigating the Problem

Explain that the aim of the game is to create a linear equation y_2 whose graph passes through the target. To do this they will start with the line corresponding to $y_1 = 1x + 0$; tell how they would move this line to make it go through the target; and then give the equation to enter as y_2 in your calculator to make this happen. Remind them that they can "move" the line in the display only by changing its slope (by changing the coefficient of x in the linear function) or moving it up or down (by changing the constant in the linear function).

Ask for a volunteer to give it a try. Have the student first tell you how they would "physically" move the line ("increase the steepness," "decrease the steepness," "make it go down from left to right," "move it up," "move it down," "move it to the left," or "move it to the right") before giving you the new function. Repeat how the student wants to "move" the line for the entire class to hear. Ask the class if the new function will do what the student wants it to do before pressing the [GRAPH] key.

If the graph of y_2 does not go through the target have the student explain why not and modify y_2, then graph it again. Allow other students to help, but let this student make the final decisions. Eventually the student will create a function y_2 for which the corresponding line goes through the target. After this is accomplished go into the [Y=] screen and deactivate y_2 so that it is not graphed. Then ask for another volunteer to create a different equation whose graph goes through the same target. Use y_3 for this new attempt.

Have the students discuss, using mathematical terminology, how they want to change the graph so they really begin to understand the relationship between the coefficients of the function and the visual characteristics of its corresponding graph. Don't let them just give a function without explaining what that function does, and don't let them simply guess the coordinates of the target and figure out the function algebraically.

After you have two different lines that pass through the target return to the [Y=] screen, deactivate y_1, and make sure y_2 and y_3 are active. Then press [GRAPH] to display the target and the two lines that go through it on the screen at the same time (Figure 10.5).

Ask the students how they would use the two lines to find the coordinates of the target. Explain that all they need to do is find the point of intersection of the lines. You can now lead them through this process by either using the [TRACE] key to move the cursor along one of the lines until it is very close to the point of intersection, or using the [CALC] key, or both.

When you have these coordinates, ask your students how they could find the coordinates of the target algebraically using the equations of the two lines that pass through it. Then let them help you write the two linear equations on the board and solve them to obtain their point of intersection, the position of the target. The graphical result and the algebraic result should be close to each other, thus verifying the result they found with the [TRACE] or [CALC] procedures. Now repeat the game, this time placing the sticky dot in one of the other quadrants to make the problem a bit harder.

Step 3–Extending the Game to Quadratic Functions

Repeat the development you used in leading up to the game with linear functions, but this time use quadratic functions of the form $y = Ax^2 + Bx + C$. Let $y_1 = 1x^2 + 0x + 0$ be the function you will use for purposes of comparison as you alter the coefficients to see what effect such alternations have on the shape and position of the graph. Use the function y_2 for the altered function. (If you prefer, put the quadratic function into the form $y = A(x - B)^2 + C$ and investigate the relationship between the coefficients A, B, and C and the shape and position of the corresponding parabola.)

Begin by changing the value of the coefficient A of the x^2 term. Explain that the graph becomes thinner as this coefficient increases while it becomes wider as this coefficient decreases toward 0 (Figure 10.6). Then show that making this coefficient negative causes the graph to open downward rather than upward (Figure 10.7).

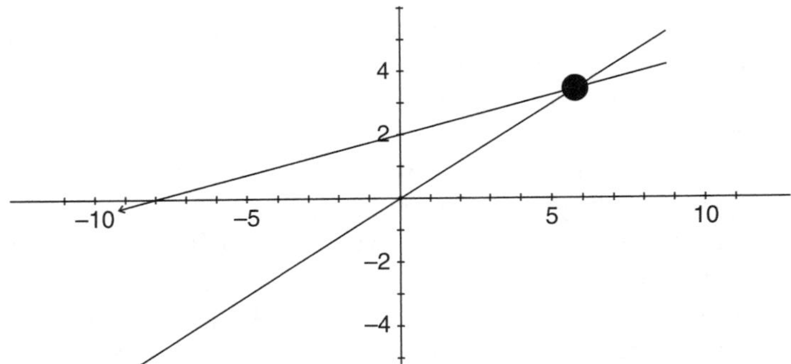

FIGURE 10.5

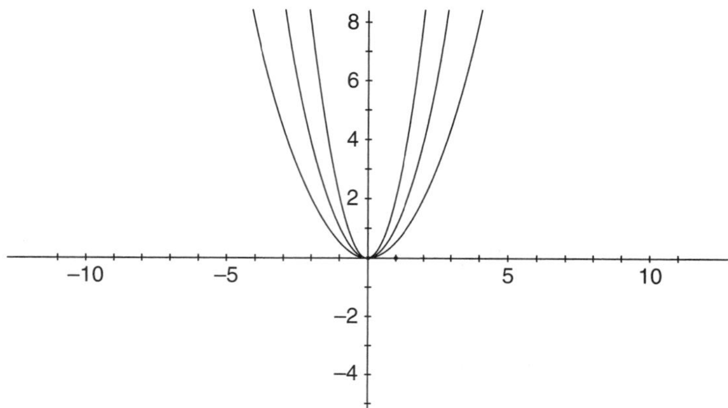

FIGURE 10.6

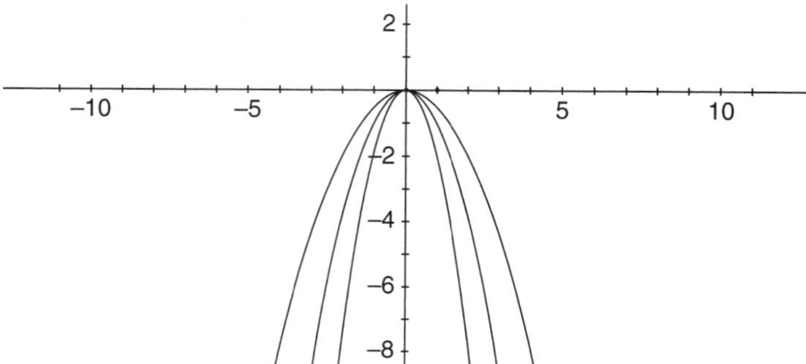

FIGURE 10.7

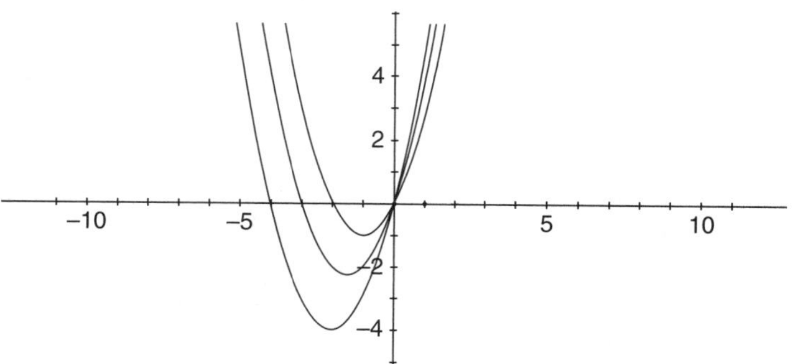

FIGURE 10.8

Now set the coefficient of x^2 back to 1 and vary the coefficient B of the x term instead. We find that as this coefficient takes on increasingly larger positive values, the graph moves further to the left and down (Figure 10.8); while as this coefficient takes on increasingly larger negative values, the graph moves further to the right and down (Figure 10.9).

Finally, set the coefficients of x^2 and x back to 1 and 0, respectively, and vary the value of the constant term C. As with the linear functions, changing the value of the constant term moves the graph in a vertical direction: larger values move the graph upward, and smaller values downward (Figure 10.10).

Play the game again, starting with the basic quadratic function $y_1 = 1x^2 + 0x + 0$. Let a student explain how they would move this parabolic graph to make it pass through the target (thinner or wider, to the left and down, to the right and down, or up or down); which coefficient they would change to move the graph in this way; and what values to use. Use these values to create a function y_2. Allow the student to continually modify the function, describing the purpose of each change, until they find a parabola that passes through the target.

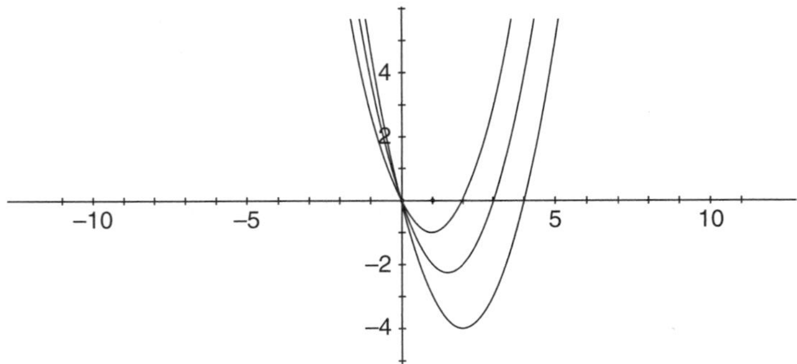

FIGURE 10.9

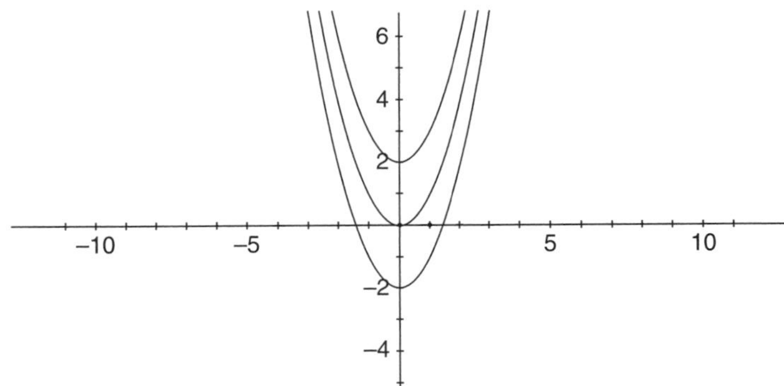

FIGURE 10.10

Now let another student find another quadratic function that passes through the glob. The student can use TRACE or CALC to find the coordinates of the target graphically; then solve the system of two quadratic equations to find the coordinates algebraically and compare with the previous result.

FOLLOW-UP DISCUSSION AND INVESTIGATIONS

As a follow-up activity ask your students to find a line and a parabola that both pass through the target. Solving the system of two equations provides good practice in substituting the linear equation into the quadratic to solve for the point of intersection.

A second follow-up activity is to place two sticky dots on the screen and ask your students to find a parabola that passes through both targets. This game is a bit harder than the others, but still a lot of fun, and involves a lot of good mathematical thinking.

REFLECTIONS FOR THE TEACHER

Using two parabolas or a line and a parabola to find the location of the target produces a graph in which the curves intersect in two points rather than one point. When using CALC to find the point of intersection, make sure that you place the cursor close to the point of intersection at the target when asked for an estimate. Similarly, when solving the system of two equations algebraically, you will obtain two solutions and must decide which one represents the target's position.

RELATED READINGS

Edwards, Laurie D. "A Comparison of Children's Learning in Two Interactive Computer Environments." *Journal of Mathematical Behavior* (March 1992, Vol. 11, No. 1, pp. 73–82).

Greenwood, James. "Name That Graph." *Mathematics Teacher* (NCTM, January 1995, Vol. 88, No. 1, pp. 8–11).

Mayes, Robert L. "The Effects of Using Software Tools on Mathematical Problem Solving in Secondary Schools." *School Science and Mathematics* (May–June 1992, Vol. 92, No. 5, pp. 243–248).

Newell, G. J., and MacFarlane, J. D. "A Computer Simulation Game to Teach Curve-Fitting." *Australian Mathematics Teacher* (June 1983, Vol. 39, No. 2, pp. 11–13).

INVESTIGATION

11

A Visual Discovery of Trigonometric Identities and Formulas

PLANNING: GRADES 9–12

RELATED NCTM STANDARDS: Algebra

- Understand and compare the properties of classes of functions, including exponential, polynomial, rational, logarithmic, and periodic functions.
- Understand the meaning of equivalent forms of expressions, equations, inequalities, and relations.
- Use symbolic algebra to represent and explain mathematical relationships.

MATHEMATICAL SKILLS AND CONCEPTS

Fitting a trigonometric function to a given graph by manipulating the coefficients of the function.

Understanding the algebraic and graphical meaning of a trigonometric identity to show that different representations of a trigonometric function are equivalent.

CALCULATOR KEYS AND FEATURES

Y=	WINDOW	SIN
COS	GRAPH	CALC
TRACE	TBLSET	TABLE

MATERIALS

Copies of Activity Sheets 11.1 and 11.2 for each student.

CLASSROOM IMPLEMENTATION

Background Information for the Teacher

In Investigations 9 and 10 we showed how a visual approach can make certain algebraic results and relationships clearer than would be possible using only algebraic methods. In this investigation we show, similarly, that some trigonometric expressions are more intuitively understood when introduced visually through graphing of trigonometric functions and manipulations of trigonometric curves.

This is not to say that a visual approach to these topics should replace an algebraic one; simply that each type of representation has its own strengths, and students should be able to employ either when appropriate.

Step 1–Introducing the Problem Solving Scenario

On your Viewscreen calculator press the [MODE] key and select degree mode for trigonometric calculations; then set your viewing window display to Xmin = 0°, Xmax = 360°, Xscl = 30°, Ymin = –2, Ymax = 2, and Yscl = 0.5. Now graph the functions $y_1 = \sin^2(x)$ and $y_2 = \cos^2(x)$ on the screen at the same time. The display should look as shown in Figure 11.1.

Point out the obvious symmetry displayed in these graphs and ask if anyone can describe the symmetry. Someone should say that there appears to be symmetry around (or above and below) a height of 0.5, just where the dot corresponding to Yscl = 0.5 appears. To make this symmetry more apparent graph the function $y_3 = 0.5$. Notice that this horizontal line passes right through the middle of the first two graphs (Figure 11.2).

Now ask if anyone can represent this visual symmetry algebraically using an equation. Help them, if necessary, by saying something like, "Notice that whenever the $\sin^2(x)$ curve is above the line $y = 0.5$, the $\cos^2(x)$ curve is below the line by exactly the same amount, and vice versa."

You want someone to state the algebraic representation of this observation, while you write it on the board:

$$\sin^2(x) - 0.5 = 0.5 - \cos^2(x)$$

Rearranging the terms of this equation, you obtain

$$\sin^2(x) + \cos^2(x) = 1$$

which is the most basic trigonometric identity, and usually the first one learned.

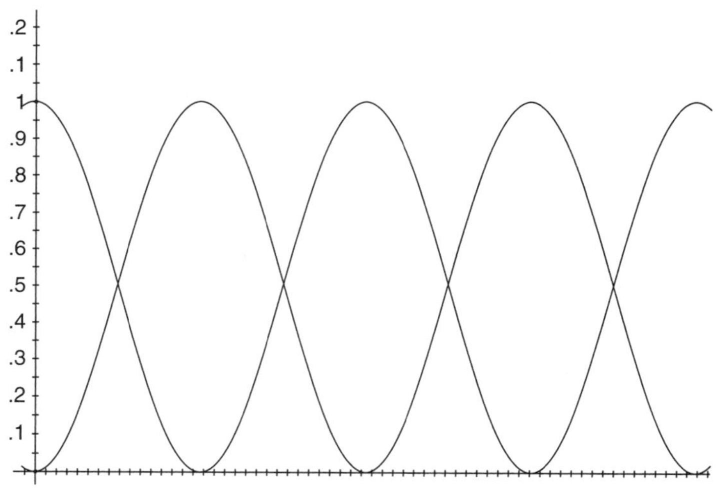

FIGURE 11.1

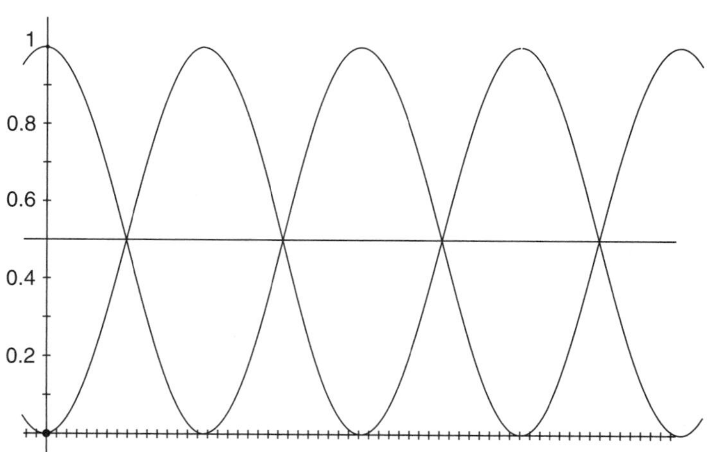

FIGURE 11.2

Explain to your students that they have now discovered through a visual observation of symmetry a trigonometric identity that is usually introduced using right triangles and the Pythagorean theorem. In this investigation they will continue to use a visual approach to trigonometry. Through this approach students will discover other identities and formulas that are usually introduced numerically.

Problem. To use a visual approach to discover trigonometric formulas and identities.

Step 2–Investigating the Problem

Remind your students of Investigation 10 in which they discovered the relationship between the coefficients of a first or second degree function and the shape and position of that function's graph. Then give them **Activity Sheet 11.1** to work on. The students can do the work themselves if you have enough class time, or you can go through it with them using the Viewscreen calculator for whole class viewing. Either way, your students should discover and understand the following relationships between the coefficients of the general sine function and the properties of the corresponding graph.

For the General Sine Function $y = A \sin(Bx + C)$:

i. $|A|$ corresponds to the amplitude of the graph. A negative value of A flipping the graph across the x axis.

ii. B corresponds to the number of complete cycles that occur in an interval of 360°.

iii. C corresponds to the horizontal phase shift. $C > 0$ means a phase shift to the left and $C < 0$ means a phase shift to the right.

To illustrate these discoveries, write down one of the sine functions, use the statements above to predict what the graph of the function will look like, and then graph the function to verify your prediction.

For example, suppose you use the function $y = 2 \times \sin(3x - 30)$. $A = 2$ tells you the graph will have an amplitude of 2; $B = 3$ indicates there will be three complete cycles between 0° and 360°, and $C = -30$ means the entire curve will be shifted 30° to the right. This is exactly what you find when you graph the function (Figure 11.3).

Your students are now ready for their visual discovery of the double angle formula for sine, $\sin(2x) = 2 \sin(x) \cos(x)$. Give each student a copy of **Activity Sheet 11.2** and let them work on it either individually or in small groups. When they are finished lead them in a discussion of their findings, using the Viewscreen for demonstration (or letting a student use it).

Step 3–Developing a Conjecture

Your students will discover from Activity Sheet 11.2 that the function $y = \sin(x) \cos(x)$ has an amplitude of 0.5, displays two complete cycles over the interval [0°, 360°], and has a phase shift of 0°. Using these three values for A, B, and C gives $y = 0.5 \sin(2x)$ as another form of the function they started with. This leads to the equation

$$0.5 \sin(2x) = \sin(x) \cos(x)$$

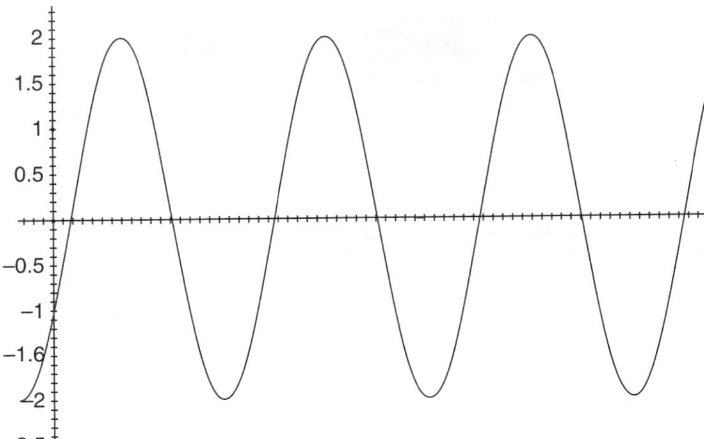

FIGURE 11.3

Multiplying both sides of this equation by 2 now gives

$$\sin(2x) = 2\sin(x)\cos(x)$$

the double angle formula for sine.

Step 4–Testing the Conjecture

Two different graphs can appear so close to each other that they look the same to the naked eye. One way of testing whether the expressions $\sin(2x)$ and $2\sin(x)\cos(x)$ are in fact identical is to compare actual numerical results for various values of x. The graphing calculator is the perfect tool for doing this. We can set up a table of values for both $y_1 = \sin(2x)$ and $y_2 = 2\sin(x)\cos(x)$ and compare the results. Your students will find that the tables are identical for all values of x, supporting the double angle formula found above.

Step 5–A Mathematical Proof

Several different proofs are available for the double angle formulas for sine and cosine as well as those for the sine and cosine of the sum and difference of two angles. You can find them in most trigonometry textbooks or by performing an Internet search. If these proofs are too difficult for your students, however, you can simply use the graphical and table of values comparisons shown above. These also provide a convincing mathematical argument of the equivalence of $\sin(2x)$ and $2\sin(x)\cos(x)$.

FOLLOW-UP DISCUSSION AND INVESTIGATIONS

Follow-up Investigation 1–You can help your students discover the double angle formula for cosine,

$$y = \cos(2x) = \cos^2(x) - \sin^2(x) = 2\cos^2(x) - 1$$

in a manner similar to that employed above, but you have to do a few things first. Start by showing that the coefficients A, B, and C have the same relationship to the graph of the general cosine function, $y = A\cos(Bx + C)$, that they had to the graph of the general sine function.

Then add a coefficient D to the end of the general cosine function to give $y = A\cos(Bx + C) + D$. Remind your students that changing this constant in first and second degree equations moved the graph up or down, and show that this is still the case here. Finally, ask them to graph $y_1 = \cos^2(x)$ on their calculators while you graph it on your Viewscreen.

Show that the graph of this trigonometric function has the general appearance of a cosine curve. Ask the students to find the values of A, B, C, and D to give a function of the form $y = A\cos(Bx + C) + D$ that fits this graph perfectly. They can then enter this new function as y_2 and verify that this is just another form of the function they began with by comparing the graphs and the tables of values.

The new function they find will be $y_2 = 0.5\cos(2x) + 0.5$. Setting the two forms of this function equal to each other and simplifying then gives $\cos(2x) = 2\cos^2(x) - 1$, the double angle formula for cosine.

Follow-up Investigation 2–Graphing $y = \sin(x) + \cos(x)$ or $y = \sin(x) - \cos(x)$ produces a graph that looks like either a sine or a cosine curve. Your students can try to express either or both of these functions in an appropriate sine or cosine form.

RELATED READINGS

DiDomenico, Angelo S. "A Trigonometric Exploration." *Mathematics Teacher* (NCTM, October 1992, Vol. 85, No. 7, pp. 582–583).

Dugdale, Sharon. "Beyond the Evident Content Goals Part III. An Undercurrent-Enhanced Approach to Trigonometric Identities." *Journal of Mathematical Behavior* (December 1990, Vol. 9, No. 3, pp. 233–287).

Ren, Guanshen. "Match Geometric Figures with Trigonometric Identities." *Mathematics Teacher* (NCTM, January 1995, Vol. 88, No. 1, pp. 24–25).

Usiskin, Zalman. "Products of Sines." *Two-Year College Mathematics Journal* (November 1979, Vol. 10, No. 5, pp. 334–340).

Vonder Embse, Charles. "Using a Graphing Utility as a Catalyst for Connections." *Mathematics Teacher* (NCTM, January 1997, Vol. 90, No. 1, pp. 50–56).

ACTIVITY SHEET

11.1 A Visual Discovery of Trigonometric Identities and Formulas

Press the MODE key and set your calculator to degree mode for trigonometric operations. Then press WINDOW and set your viewing window to the following values:

Xmin = −360	Xmax = 360	Xscl = 30
Ymin = −4	Ymax = 4	Yscl = 0.5

In this activity you will study the general sine function $y = A\sin(Bx + C)$. Try to discover what effect changing the values of A, B, and C has on the behavior of the corresponding graph. To do this, press Y= and enter the basic sine curve $y = \sin(x)$ in the following form as y_1:

$$y_1 = 1\sin(1x + 0)$$

Step 1. Enter $y_2 = 2\sin(1x + 0)$ into the Y= screen. Graph both y_1 and y_2 on the screen at the same time and note how they are different from each other. Change the number 2 in y_2 to 3 and compare y_1 to y_2 once again. Then try –1, –2, and –3.

Step 2. Change y_2 to $y_2 = 1\sin(2x + 0)$ and compare the graphs of y_1 and y_2. Now compare y_1 with $y_2 = 1\sin(3x + 0)$ and then with $y_2 = 1\sin(4x + 0)$.

Step 3. Change y_2 to $y_2 = 1\sin(1x + 30)$ and compare the graphs of y_1 and y_2. Now compare y_1 with $y_2 = 1\sin(1x + 60)$, then with $y_2 = 1\sin(1x - 30)$, and finally with $y_2 = 1\sin(1x - 60)$.

Based on what you found in the three steps above, what do you think the coefficients A, B, and C of the function $y = A\sin(Bx + C)$ represent in terms of the graph?

A Visual Discovery of Trigonometric Identities and Formulas

11.2 ACTIVITY SHEET

Make sure that your calculator is in degree mode. Set your viewing window to the following values:

Xmin = 0	Xmax = 360	Xscl = 30
Ymin = −2	Ymax = 2	Yscl = 0.5

Graph the function $y = \sin(x)\cos(x)$ as y_1. Notice that it looks like a sine curve. Use any feature of the calculator you need to study the following properties of this curve:

- the amplitude
- the number of complete cycles between 0° and 360°
- the size and direction of the phase shift

Using the values you found above, express this function in the form $y = A\sin(Bx + C)$ with appropriate values for A, B, and C. Then enter this new form of the function as y_2. Graph y_1 and y_2 at the same time to see if they overlap and are simply two different names for the same function.

INVESTIGATION 12

Exploring Derivatives Using Both Algebraic and Visual Representations

PLANNING: GRADES 9–12

RELATED NCTM STANDARDS: Algebra

- Understand and compare the properties of classes of functions, including exponential, polynomial, rational, logarithmic, and periodic functions.
- Use symbolic algebra to represent and explain mathematical relationships.

MATHEMATICAL SKILLS AND CONCEPTS

Verifying properties of the derivative of a polynomial function through visual inspection.

Discovering the derivatives of the sine, cosine, exponential, and logarithmic functions using graphs and tables of values.

CALCULATOR KEYS AND FEATURES

Y=	WINDOW	nDeriv(
GRAPH	TBLSET	TABLE
VARS		

MATERIALS

Copies of Activity and Solution Sheets 12.1, 12.2, and 12.3 for each student.

CLASSROOM IMPLEMENTATION

Background Information for the Teacher

Students usually first learn about derivatives, a basic concept of calculus, algebraically in terms of the limit of a difference quotient. If they ever encounter the derivative visually, it is only as the slope of the tangent line to the curve of the original function.

Students can use the graphing calculator to investigate the visual representation of the derivative and use it to a much greater extent. This gives students a better understanding of the derivative and how the algebraic and visual representations of it relate to each other. That is precisely what this investigation does.

Step 1–Introducing the Problem Solving Scenario

Using algebraic notation and illustrating with simple first and second degree functions, review the definition of the derivative: the limit of the difference quotient $\lim \frac{f(x + \Delta x) - f(x)}{\Delta x}$ as $\Delta x \to 0$, and the slope of the tangent line to the graph of the equation at a specified point.

Now, using your Viewscreen for whole class display and discussion, press the MATH key and select the derivative function nDeriv(. Then illustrate the use of this calculator feature to find the derivative of a function $f(x)$ at a specified value $x = x_0$. The function nDeriv(takes three inputs separated by commas. The first input is the function whose derivative is being calculated; the second input is the variable with respect to which the derivative is being taken; and the third input is the value of x at which the derivative is being calculated.

For example, to obtain the derivative of $f(x) = x^2$ with respect to x at the point $x = 3$ you would use the function nDeriv (x^2, x, 3) and obtain the result 6, which is simply the value of the derivative, $f'(x) = 2x$, calculated at $x = 3$.

You can now show your students a trick they can use with the derivative function to "fool" the calculator. Enter the function nDeriv(into the Y= screen, and insert the variable x as the third input instead of a numerical value. Then you can graph the derivative function or obtain a table of values for it just as if they had entered the derivative function directly. To illustrate, enter $y_1 =$ nDeriv(x^3, x, x) and $y_2 = 3x^2$, the derivative of $f(x) = x^3$. If you now graph x_1 and x_2 and then create a table of values, you will see that both are identical for the two functions.

Explain that it is fairly easy to algebraically manipulate the definition of the derivative as a limit of a difference quotient to find the derivative of a polynomial explicitly, but this procedure is not so easy with more complex functions such as $y = \sin(x)$, $y = \cos(x)$, $y = e^x$, or $y = \ln(x)$. For functions like these a good first step might be to make a reasonable conjecture about the derivative function graphically on the calculator using nDeriv(, and then verify it mathematically.

Problem. To discover the derivatives of the sine, cosine, e^x, and ln(x) functions visually using the function nDeriv(.

Step 2–Investigating the Problem

Activity Sheet 12.1 guides your students through a visual discovery of the derivatives, with respect to x, of $y = \sin(x)$ and $y = \cos(x)$ when x is measured in radians. This is a good activity to do in small groups in order to encourage discussion, but the students can do it individually if you prefer.

Step 3–Developing a Conjecture

The graphs of nDeriv(sin(x), x, x) and nDeriv(cos(x), x, x) in Activity Sheet 12.1 clearly show that the derivative of $y = \sin(x)$ is $y'(x) = \cos(x)$ and that the derivative of $y = \cos(x)$ is $y'(x) = -\sin(x)$ when x is measured in radians. Help your students to state these two observations as a conjecture.

> **Conjecture:** In radian mode, the derivative of $y = \sin(x)$ is $y = \cos(x)$ and the derivative of $y = \cos(x)$ is $y = -\sin(x)$.

Step 4–Testing the Conjecture

The conjecture above was developed using a visual comparison of graphs. One way of testing the result is to create and compare a table of values for nDeriv(sin(x), x, x) and cos(x); and then for nDeriv(cos(x), x, x) and $-\sin(x)$. Another test would be to extend the interval for the two graphs, perhaps from $[0, 2\pi]$ to $[-2\pi, 2\pi]$. Both of these tests will support the truth of the conjecture.

Step 5–A Mathematical Proof

The algebraic proof of the two results contained in the conjecture employs the definition of the derivative as the limit of a difference quotient. It then uses the formulas for the sine and the cosine of the sum of two angles, and the fact that $\lim_{x \to 0} \frac{\sin(\Delta x)}{\Delta x} = 1$ and $\lim_{x \to 0} \frac{1 - \cos(\Delta x)}{\Delta x} = 1$, to symbolically manipulate the difference quotients and prove the desired results. The *Related Readings* section provides references for these proofs for both you and your students, if they can follow them. Otherwise, simply let the graphical and numerical comparisons serve as convincing mathematical arguments for the conjecture.

FOLLOW-UP DISCUSSION AND INVESTIGATIONS

In **Activity Sheet 12.2** your students use a similar visual approach to discover the derivative for the exponential function $y = e^x$. Surprisingly, if $y(x) = e^x$ then $y'(x) = e^x$ as well. If you want to follow up the visual discovery of this result with a mathematical proof, the proof once again depends on a symbolic manipulation of the difference quotient for $y = e^x$ and the result that $\lim_{x \to 0} \frac{e^{\Delta x} - 1}{\Delta x} = 1$.

Activity Sheet 12.3 is a little bit different. It leads your students to the discovery that the derivative of the natural logarithm function $y(x) = \ln(x)$ is $y'(x) = 1/x$. It does this in a non-visual way, using the calculator feature in the VARS menu that allows you to define one function as the product of two other functions: $y^3 = y^1 \times y^2$.

RELATED READINGS

Bloom, Lynette M., et al. "A Microcomputer Approach to Exponential Functions and Their Derivatives." *Mathematics in School* (November 1986, Vol. 15, No. 5, pp. 30–32).

Goetz, Albert, and Kahan, Jeremy. "Surprising Results Using Calculators for Derivatives." *Mathematics Teacher* (NCTM, January 1995, Vol. 88, No. 1, pp. 30–33).

Lumb, Stephen, Monaghan, John, and Mulligan, Steve. "Issues Arising When Teachers Make Extensive Use of Computer Algebra." *International Journal of Computer Algebra in Mathematics Education* (2001, Vol. 7, No. 1, pp. 223–240).

Machin, Matias Camacho, and Rivero, Ramon Depool. "Students' Attitudes towards Mathematics and Computers When Using DERIVE in the Learning of Calculus Concepts." *International Journal of Computer Algebra in Mathematics Education* (2002, Vol. 9, No. 4, pp. 259–283).

Young, Anne Luddington. "A Calculus I Project: Discovering the Derivative of an Exponential." *PRIMUS* (March 1997, Vol. 7, No. 1).

Exploring Derivatives Using Both Algebraic and Visual Representations

12.1

ACTIVITY SHEET

Set your calculator to radian mode by pressing the MODE key and selecting the "Radian" option. Then, set your viewing window to:

Xmin = 0	Xmax = 2π	Xscl = $\pi/2$
Ymin = -2	Ymax = $+2$	Yscl = 0.5

Enter y_1 = nDeriv(sin(x), x, x) into the Y= screen and press the GRAPH key. The graph displayed is that of the derivative of the function $y = \sin(x)$ with respect to x. Does it look familiar? If you think you know what it is, enter your guess as y_2 and then graph both y_1 and y_2 at the same time to see if they are indeed the same. Verify your result by creating a table of values for the two functions and comparing the values to see if they are identical.

Now, repeat the procedure above to discover the derivative of $y = \cos(x)$. Enter y_1 = nDeriv(cos(x), x, x) and see if you recognize the graph that is drawn. Once again test your guess by entering it as y_2 and comparing the graphs and the tables of values for the two functions.

ACTIVITY SHEET

12.2 Exploring Derivatives Using Both Algebraic and Visual Representations

In Activity Sheet 12.1 you used the graphing calculator function nDeriv(to visually discover the derivatives for the functions $y = \sin(x)$ and $y = \cos(x)$ in radian mode. Here you use a similar approach to discover the derivative for the exponential function $y = e^x$ and then verify your discovery by creating and inspecting a corresponding table of values.

Step 1. Enter the functions $y_1 = \text{nDeriv}(e^x, x, x)$ and $y_2 = e^x$ into the [Y=] screen of your calculator and graph both functions on the screen at the same time using an appropriate viewing window. From a visual observation of these two graphs, complete the following conjecture.

Conjecture: If $y(x) = e^x$ then $y'(x) =$ __________.

Step 2. Verify your conjecture by creating a table of values for y_1 and for your guess of the derivative of $y = e^x$. Check to see if they are, in fact, numerically identical.

Exploring Derivatives Using Both Algebraic and Visual Representations

12.3 ACTIVITY SHEET

In this investigation you will discover the derivative for the natural logarithm function $y = \ln(x)$. Again you will enter the derivative function nDeriv(into the [Y=] screen as y_1. This time, however, we will use the [GRAPH] key, not the [TABLE] key, to make our discovery.

Step 1. Enter $y_1 = \text{nDeriv}(\ln(x), x, x)$ into the [Y=] screen of your calculator and then enter $y_2 = x$. Create a table of values for these two functions. Begin with the value 1 and using an increment size of 1.

Step 2. Compare the values in the y_1 list from the table of values you get with their corresponding values in the y_2 list. Can you write a relationship between y_1 and y_2? If not, continue to Step 3.

Step 3. Use the [VARS] key to define y_3 as $y_3 = y_1 \times y_2$. Then press [TABLE] and look at the values in the y_3 list. Now can you write a relationship between y_1 and y_2? Recall that y_1 represents the derivative of the function $y = \ln(x)$. Can you now state what the derivative of the natural logarithm function is?

INVESTIGATION 13

Converging and Diverging Infinite Series and Special Mathematical Constants

PLANNING: GRADES 9–12

RELATED NCTM STANDARDS: Algebra

- Use symbolic algebra to represent and explain mathematical relationships.
- Judge the meaning, utility, and reasonableness of the results of symbolic manipulations, including those carried out by technology.

MATHEMATICAL SKILLS AND CONCEPTS

Understanding the difference between convergent and divergent infinite series and the meaning of the limit value of a convergent infinite series.

Using the properties of a convergent alternating infinite series to obtain upper and lower bounds for the limit of such a series.

CALCULATOR KEYS AND FEATURES

LIST

Seq(

cumSum

MATERIALS

Copies of Activity and Solution Sheets 13.1 and 13.2 for each student.

CLASSROOM IMPLEMENTATION

Background Information for the Teacher

Infinite series can be great mathematical fun. These series obey some of the same rules as finite sums do, but differ in interesting and unexpected ways. In particular, infinite series can illustrate monotonic or alternating asymptotic behavior; certain types of convergent infinite series can change their sums when the order of the terms is changed; and the investigation of infinite series can lead to the discovery of important mathematical constants in unexpected ways.

The graphing calculator cannot, of course, compute the actual sum of an infinite series. But it can be used with the Seq(and cumSum features to find reasonable approximations of the actual sum. This can help students better understand these special mathematical objects and their interesting properties.

Step 1–Introducing the Problem Solving Scenario

In Investigation 5 we used the seq and cumSum options under the [LIST] key to closely estimate the sums of several infinite geometric series. These estimates then led to the creation and mathematical proof of a conjecture about the sum of an infinite geometric series in terms of the first term and the common ratio. If you have already done that investigation with your students, simply remind them of it and say that you are now going to use these same calculator functions to investigate other types of infinite series as well. If not, proceed more slowly with the introductory activity so that they can learn how to apply the *LIST* operations Seq(and cumSum to estimate the sums of certain infinite series.

Tell your students the story of Zeno's Paradox. Zeno, a Greek mathematician who lived around 400 BC, stated three famous paradoxes that seemed to contradict intuitively obvious real life experiences. One of these seeks to show that it would be impossible for a person making a journey to ever complete the journey. The reasoning is that the traveler must first complete half of the trip; then complete half of the remainder of the trip; then complete half of the new remainder of the trip; and so on forever. No matter how much of the trip the traveler covers, some part of the trip always remains, so it can never be completed.

Begin your investigation of this classical paradox by considering, first, the distances the traveler covers. Assume that the entire trip is 1 mile long. On the first day the traveler covers ½ mile; on the second day, half of the remainder, or ¼ mile; on the third day, one half of the new remainder, or ⅛ of a mile; and so on. Then the total distance traveled would be the sum of the infinite series

$$S = \tfrac{1}{2} + \tfrac{1}{4} + \tfrac{1}{8} + \ldots + (\tfrac{1}{2})^K + \ldots$$

To verify that all of these parts of the journey do in fact sum to 1 mile, we will use the *LIST* operations Seq(and cumSum to find the total distance traveled for each of the first 50 days. Enter the following expressions into your Viewscreen for whole class viewing:

$\text{Seq}(0.5^x, x, 1, 50) \rightarrow L_1$ [ENTER]

$\text{cumSum}(L_1) \rightarrow L_2$ [ENTER]

Explain that the values in list L_2 are called the "partial sums" of the infinite series because they represent adding up larger, but still finite "parts" of the entire infinite series. For the partial sums in list L_2 the total distance traveled gets closer and closer to 1, so close, in fact, that eventually the value displays as the number 1.

You can now verify this estimated result mathematically as follows. Start with the original infinite series

$$S = \tfrac{1}{2} + \tfrac{1}{4} + \tfrac{1}{8} + \tfrac{1}{16} + \tfrac{1}{32} + \ldots$$

Divide both sides of this equation by 2 to obtain an infinite series for $S/2$. Align the terms on the right side for both S and $S/2$ to place similar fractions below each other:

$$S = \tfrac{1}{2} + \tfrac{1}{4} + \tfrac{1}{8} + \tfrac{1}{16} + \tfrac{1}{32} + \ldots$$

$$\frac{S}{2} = \qquad \tfrac{1}{4} + \tfrac{1}{8} + \tfrac{1}{16} + \tfrac{1}{32} + \ldots$$

Subtracting now gives $S/2 = \tfrac{1}{2}$, or $S = 1$, as we found above from our calculator estimation.

Let's now return to this supposed paradox. If, in fact, each part of this trip required an entire day of travel, then it certainly would take an infinite number of days to complete the journey since there is an infinite number of terms in the series that sums to 1 mile. Each part of the trip, however, should only take half as much time to travel since it is only one half the length of the previous part of the trip.

In other words, if the first part of the trip (½ mile) takes ½ day to travel, then the second part of the trip (¼ mile) should only take ¼ day to travel, the third part of the trip (⅛ mile) ⅛ day, and so on. Therefore, the total travel time needed to reach the end of the journey would be given by

$$\text{Time} = \tfrac{1}{2} + \tfrac{1}{4} + \tfrac{1}{8} + \ldots = 1 \text{ day}$$

Problem. To develop a rule that will tell us when certain types of infinite series converge to a finite limit and how to estimate the value of that limit.

In other words, there is really no paradox at all: The shorter the part of the trip that needs to be traveled, the less time that part should take.

Our investigation of Zeno's Paradox has unearthed an important concept that underlies not only infinite series, but also most of the procedures of calculus. This concept is that the sum of an infinite number of terms can be finite if the individual terms are getting small enough fast enough.

Step 2–Investigating the Problem

Give your students **Activity Sheet 13.1** and ask them to use their graphing calculators to complete the activity. After this is done have a discussion of their findings. Use the Viewscreen calculator to demonstrate how to obtain the partial sums using the commands Seq(and cumSum, and display the lists of values that are obtained. The calculator commands used for the two series are shown below.

$$S = 1 + \tfrac{1}{2} + \tfrac{1}{3} + \tfrac{1}{4} + \tfrac{1}{5} + \ldots + \tfrac{1}{K} + \ldots$$

Seq(1/x, x, 1, 300) → L_1

cumSum (L_1) → L_2

$$S = 1 + \tfrac{1}{2} + \tfrac{1}{3} - \tfrac{1}{4} + \tfrac{1}{5} - \tfrac{1}{6} + \ldots + \frac{(-1)^{K-1}}{K} + \ldots$$

Seq((−1)^(x − 1)/x, x, 1, 300) → L_1

cumSum (L_1) → L_2

It's not immediately obvious, but the first series, the harmonic series, grows without bound even though the 300th partial sum in list L_2 is only slightly greater than 6. You can explain to your students, however, that this infinite series can be algebraically broken up into individual pieces, each of which adds up to ½ or greater. Consequently, by taking enough terms in the series you can obtain a partial sum greater than any finite number. We therefore say that the harmonic series "diverges to infinity." This breaking up of the harmonic series into pieces is illustrated below.

$$1 + \tfrac{1}{2} + \underbrace{(\tfrac{1}{3} + \tfrac{1}{4})}_{>\frac{1}{2}} + \underbrace{(\tfrac{1}{5} + \tfrac{1}{6} + \tfrac{1}{7} + \tfrac{1}{8})}_{>\frac{1}{2}} + \underbrace{(\tfrac{1}{9} + \tfrac{1}{10} + \tfrac{1}{11} + \tfrac{1}{12} + \tfrac{1}{13} + \tfrac{1}{14} + \tfrac{1}{15} + \tfrac{1}{16})}_{>\frac{1}{2}} + \ldots$$

Your students' investigation into the partial sums of the second infinite series will yield quite different results even though the only difference between the second series and the first is the alternating positive and negative signs for consecutive terms. Explain that a series with alternating signs is called an "alternating series." Ask them what they discovered about its convergence to a limit.

They should find that the partial sums for this series approach some number with decimal representation beginning 0.69. . ., and that the partial sums are alternately larger and smaller than this apparent limit value. You can now reveal to them that the sum of this alternating series is in fact ln(2). Display the value of ln(2) on the Viewscreen. Then show that since the partial sums are always alternately greater and less than this value, you can always bound the actual sum of the infinite series, *S*, between any two consecutive partial sums. This is illustrated below for the first several partial sums.

1st partial sum = 1

2nd partial sum = 0.5 so $0.5 \le S \le 1$

3rd partial sum = 0.83333 . . . so $0.5 \le S \le 0.83333\ldots$

4th partial sum = 0.58333. . . so $0.58333\ldots \leq S \leq 0.83333\ldots$

5th partial sum = 0.78333. . . so $0.58333\ldots \leq S \leq 0.78333\ldots$

. . . . . .

299th partial sum = 0.69481. . .

300th partial sum = 0.69148. . . so $0.69148 \leq S \leq 0.69481\ldots$

Notice that each successive approximating interval is shorter, so each approximation is more accurate than the previous one.

Step 3–Developing a Conjecture

Any infinite series with alternating positive and negative terms must have partial sums that are alternately larger and smaller; and if the individual terms of the alternating infinite series are increasingly smaller in absolute value, these partial sum oscillations should become increasingly smaller. So we can posit the following conjecture about the convergence of such series based on the results of Activity Sheet 13.1 and the discussion that followed.

Conjecture: Given an alternating infinite series in which the absolute value of the terms of the series decreases monotonically toward 0, the series has a finite sum (in other words, converges to a finite limit). This sum will lie between any two consecutive partial sums.

Step 4–Testing the Conjecture

We will test the conjecture by taking a few infinite series that satisfy the basic conditions of the conjecture (an alternating series with the absolute value of the terms decreasing monotonically toward 0) and seeing if the conclusion of the conjecture holds true (the series converges to a finite limit and this limit value lies between any two successive partial sums). **Activity Sheet 13.2** provides such a test. The results of this activity do support the conjecture.

Step 5–A Mathematical Proof

The proof of the conjecture is fairly simple; but it does involve the use of the theorem that a monotonically increasing sequence with an upper bound must also have a least upper bound and converge to this least upper bound. Several examples of the proof are available on a number of web sites. Simply use the phrase "alternating infinite series" in a web search to find them.

FOLLOW-UP DISCUSSION AND INVESTIGATIONS

Give your students the two infinite series shown below. Ask them first to estimate the sum using their calculators, then to discover what famous mathematical constant the sum is related to. You could also ask them to do an Internet search to find infinite series that converge to well-known mathematical constants. Two of these interesting infinite series and their sums are shown below.

$\frac{1}{1} + \frac{1}{4} + \frac{1}{9} + \frac{1}{16} + \frac{1}{25} + \ldots + \frac{1}{K^2} + \ldots$ Sum = $\pi^2/6$

$1 + \frac{1}{1!} + \frac{1}{2!} + \frac{1}{3!} + \frac{1}{4!} + \ldots + \frac{1}{K!} + \ldots$ Sum = *e*, the base of the natural logarithm

SPREADSHEET MODIFICATION

All the infinite series partial sum calculations of this investigation can be easily performed using a spreadsheet. Furthermore, a corresponding graph of the partial sums can then be created that provides a visual representation to support the algebraic results obtained. Just enter the individual terms of the partial sum in column A, then calculate the corresponding partial sums in column B.

For example, suppose you want to calculate the first 30 partial sums of the infinite series $S = \frac{1}{2} + \frac{1}{4} + \frac{1}{8} + \ldots + (\frac{1}{2})^K + \ldots$. Enter ½ or 0.5 in cell A1; highlight cells A2 through A30; enter the expression "=A1/2" into cell A2 (click on cell A1 to place the name of this cell in the expression; and then hold down the Ctrl key and press ENTER at the same time. This should place the first 30 terms of the infinite series into cells A1 through A30.

Now enter ½ or 0.5 into cell B1; highlight cells B2 through B30; enter the expression "=B1+A2" into cell B2; then hold down the Ctrl key and press ENTER at the same time. This will place the first 30 partial sums into cells B1 through B30, showing clearly that the limit of this infinite series is 1. This is illustrated below.

0.5000	0.5000
0.2500	0.7500
0.1250	0.8750
0.0625	0.9375
0.0313	0.9688
0.0156	0.9844
0.0078	0.9922
0.0039	0.9961
0.0020	0.9980
0.0010	0.9990
0.0005	0.9995
0.0002	0.9998
0.0001	0.9999
0.0001	0.9999
0.0000	1.0000
0.0000	1.0000
0.0000	1.0000
0.0000	1.0000
0.0000	1.0000
0.0000	1.0000
0.0000	1.0000
0.0000	1.0000
0.0000	1.0000
0.0000	1.0000

To obtain a corresponding graph, highlight cells B1 through B30, click on the graph icon near the top of the screen, and select an appropriate line graph. You will obtain a graph similar to the one shown in Figure 13.1.

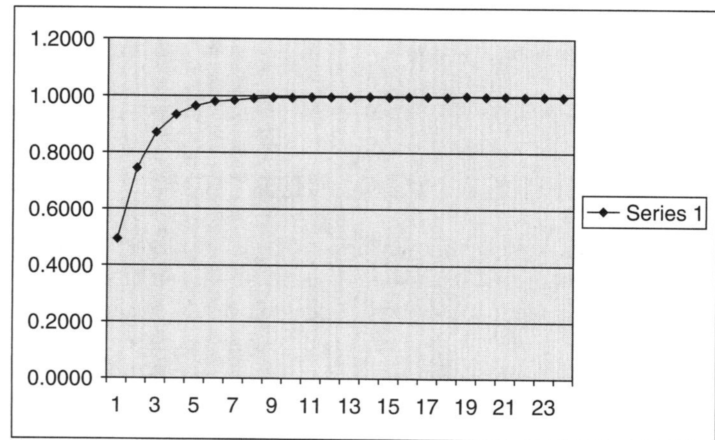

FIGURE 13.1

REFLECTIONS FOR THE TEACHER

1. At first glance infinite series seem to be a topic that's appropriate only for the top math students in your class, but that's not necessarily true. Treat the study of infinite series informally and use only procedures that are valid generalizations from finite series, and this topic can be a lot of fun for all students. It will also give them a feeling of real mathematical accomplishment.

2. Notice that the conjecture assumes not only that the terms of the series have a limit of 0 but that they converge *monotonically* toward 0. In other words, the terms can't get smaller for a while, then larger; then get even smaller for a while, then larger again. They must *always* get smaller in absolute value with a limit of 0. Surprisingly, in some alternating series, the absolute values of the terms approach 0, but not monotonically, so the series does *not* converge to a finite limit. The web site *Dr. Vogel's Gallery of Calculus Pathologies* (http://www.math.tamu.edu/˜tom.vogel/gallery/node9.html) provides an example of a divergent alternating series whose terms go to 0, but not monotonically.

RELATED READINGS

Basor, Estelle. "A Look at Infinite Series." *MATYC (Mathematics Association of Two Year Colleges) Journal* (1978, Vol. 12, No. 2, pp. 140–142).

Fay, Temple H. "Eulerization of an Alternating Series: A Calculus Laboratory Project." *Mathematics and Computer Education* (Spring 1998, Vol. 32, No. 2, pp. 120–126).

Harper, James D. "Estimating the Sum of Alternating Series." *College Mathematics Journal* (March 1988, Vol. 19, No. 2, pp. 149–153).

Schaumberger, N. "A Note on Testing the Convergence of an Alternating Series." *MATYC (Mathematics Association of Two Year Colleges) Journal* (1975, Vol. 9, No. 3, pp. 29–30).

ACTIVITY SHEET

13.1 Converging and Diverging Infinite Series and Special Mathematical Constants

Use the Seq(and cumSum operations on your graphing calculator to investigate the sums of the two infinite series below. (You can find these functions by pressing LIST and then arrowing over to the OPS menu.) The first series is called the "harmonic series," and the second differs from it only in that the signs of the terms alternate between positive and negative.

$$S = 1 + \tfrac{1}{2} + \tfrac{1}{3} + \tfrac{1}{4} + \tfrac{1}{5} + \ldots + \tfrac{1}{K} + \ldots$$

$$S = 1 - \tfrac{1}{2} + \tfrac{1}{3} - \tfrac{1}{4} + \tfrac{1}{5} - \tfrac{1}{6} + \ldots + \frac{(-1)^{K-1}}{K} + \ldots$$

Find the first 300 terms of each series and their corresponding sums. This is necessary because both series show their overall behavior only very slowly. Is there any difference in the partial sums for the two infinite series? If so, what is this difference?

Converging and Diverging Infinite Series and Special Mathematical Constants

13.2 ACTIVITY SHEET

Two alternating infinite series in which the absolute value of the terms decreases toward 0 are shown below. According to the conjecture developed in class both of these series should converge to a finite limit, and the value of the limit should lie between any two successive partial sums of the series.

$$\textbf{Series A: } S = 1 - \tfrac{1}{2} + \tfrac{1}{4} - \tfrac{1}{8} + \tfrac{1}{16} - \tfrac{1}{32} + \ldots + \frac{(-1)^{k-1}}{2^{k-1}} + \ldots$$

$$\textbf{Series B: } T = 1 - \tfrac{1}{3} + \tfrac{1}{5} - \tfrac{1}{7} + \tfrac{1}{9} - \tfrac{1}{11} + \ldots + \frac{(-1)^{k+1}}{2k - 1} + \ldots$$

Find the first 25 partial sums of each series. Look to see if, indeed, the partial sums are oscillating closer and closer to some finite limit value (S for the first series and T for the second series), and then bound the limits between the 10th and 11th partial sums.

Check the Solution Sheet to see if your estimates match the actual values S and T.

INVESTIGATION 14

The Use of Linear and Nonlinear Regression for Curve Fitting and Making Predictions

PLANNING: GRADES 9–12

RELATED NCTM STANDARDS: Data Analysis & Probability

- Understand histograms, parallel box plots, and scatterplots and use them to display data.
- For bivariate measurement data, be able to display a scatterplot, describe its shape, and determine regression coefficients, regression equations, and correlation coefficients using technological tools.

MATHEMATICAL SKILLS AND CONCEPTS

Plotting pairs of (x, y) points in the plane.

Finding the "best fitting line" for a set of (x, y) points.

Extrapolating a set of data to the future using a linear function model, an exponential function model, and a power function model and comparing the results.

CALCULATOR KEYS AND FEATURES

LIST	STAT PLOT	GRAPH
TBLSET	TABLE	STAT
LinReg (ax+b)	VARS	ExpReg
PwrReg		

MATERIALS

Copies of Activity and Solution Sheets 14.1 and 14.2 for each student.

CLASSROOM IMPLEMENTATION

Background Information for the Teacher

One purpose of mathematical modeling is to mathematically represent real world situations so as to better understand those situations and to make predictions about them. Many of these applications use statistical procedures, especially linear regression, which are now easily within the reach of a high school student through the statistical tools available on the graphing calculator.

Winning Women's and Men's Times in Seconds for the Olympic 100 Meter Swimming Event

	Year	Women's Winning Time	Men's Winning Time
	1912	82.2	63.4
	1920	73.6	61.4
	1924	72.4	59.0
FIGURE 14.1	1928	71.0	58.6

In this activity students take real life data, analyze the data using linear regression, make predictions, and discuss the appropriateness of extending a given set of data far into the future.

Step 1–Introducing the Problem Solving Scenario

Put the information from Figure 14.1 on the board or on the overhead. Tell your students that this data shows the women's and men's winning times in the Olympic 100-meter freestyle swimming event the first four years this event was held in the modern Olympics. (Of course, these are probably the first years the event was *ever* held since swimming was not a part of the original ancient Greek Olympics.)

Explain that although all the winning times improved steadily during these first four modern Olympics, the winning time in a particular Olympics still might not be as good as any one of the previous Olympics. Also point out that there was no Olympic competition in 1916 because of World War I.

When we calculate the difference between the women's and the men's winning times we see a clear trend toward equality: in 1912 the difference is 18.8 seconds in favor of the men, while in 1928 it is only 12.4 seconds. Tell your students that you will now use the graphing calculator's statistics tools to study this trend and try to predict when the women's and the men's winning times will be the same.

Problem. To use statistical curve fitting with past Olympic data for the winning women's and men's times in the 100-meter swimming event to predict when the women's and men's winning times will be the same.

Step 2–Investigating the Problem

To make sure that your students know how to use the linear regression feature of the graphing calculator and how to interpret the results, you and your students will do **Activity Sheet 14.1** together. You will use your Viewscreen calculator and the students their graphing calculators. Activity Sheet 14.1 focuses on the women's winning times from 1912 to 1996 by finding the best fitting line for this data, interpreting the meaning of the slope of this line, and finally using this line to make a prediction and interpret the reasonableness of that prediction.

After you have completed this activity and discussed the answers to the questions (you can hand out copies of the Solution Sheet when you begin to answer the questions) hand out copies of **Activity Sheet 14.2.** Let your students work on this activity sheet themselves, either individually or in small groups.

Step 3–Developing a Conjecture

Based on the results of Activity Sheet 14.2, if the trend toward improvement in the women's and men's winning times continues, the winning women's and men's times should be equal around the year 2030. So we can state this result as:

> **Conjecture:** If the current trend of improvement in the women's and men's winning Olympic times continues in the near future, women and men should have the same winning time in this event around the year 2030.

Step 4–Testing the Conjecture

We can't test this conjecture directly since we would have to wait until 2030 to verify the prediction. However, we can partially test the conjecture by using individual linear regression equations to predict the women's and men's winning times in this event as far beyond the last piece of data, 1996, as possible. If these predictions are fairly accurate then perhaps those for 2030 will be as well.

From a table of values for the linear regression functions y_1 and y_2 we predict that in 2004 the winning women's time in this Olympic event will be $y_1 = 49.51$ seconds; the winning men's time, $y_2 = 46.52$ seconds; and the difference, $y_1 - y_2 = 2.99$ seconds.

From the web site HickokSports.com (http://www.hickoksports.com/index.shtml) we actually find that in the 2004 Olympics in Athens the winning women's time in this event was $y_1 = 53.84$ seconds (Jodie Henry of Australia) and the winning men's time was $y_2 = 48.17$ seconds (Pieter van den Hoogenband of the Netherlands). Therefore, the actual difference for 2004 between the women's and the men's winning times was $y_1 - y_2 = 5.67$ seconds.

This difference for 2004 is almost twice as large as that predicted by the two linear regression equations. Apparently the difference between women's and men's winning times is not decreasing at a constant rate, even for the 8 years following our last data value. So perhaps we really should not try to use linear regression equations to make a prediction as far ahead as 2030.

FOLLOW-UP DISCUSSION AND INVESTIGATIONS

Using linear regression equations to predict the future showed that you cannot make a good prediction even 8 years ahead, let alone 34 years, so there is no point in trying to provide a convincing mathematical argument for the conjecture. Instead, you might want to discuss why using these two linear equations was unreasonable.

Records like the ones examined above cannot possibly be represented by a straight line over any but the shortest of intervals. Any such straight line with a negative slope would eventually have to intersect with, and then go below, the x axis; this means that at some point the winning time would be 0 seconds and then a negative number of seconds, both of which are impossible in the real world.

In fact, the scatterplots for the women's data and the men's data are not really linear after all. They appear instead to decrease at an increasingly slower pace and approach the x axis asymptotically rather than linearly. Even this is not realistic, however, because we know the time to swim 100 meters cannot really approach as close to 0 seconds as desired; but it is better than a linear model.

A good follow-up activity therefore is to repeat what we did previously with the data we entered into lists L_1, L_2, and L_3, but this time using either two exponential regression functions or two power regression functions, both of which are available on our calculator. Shown below are the regression equations that are found each way, the predictions of these equations for the year 2004, and a comparison of these predictions with the actual 2004 results.

Using Exponential Regression Equations

Rounding all constants to three decimal places, the regression equations are found to be:

$$\text{(Women)}\quad y_1 = 395930.042*0.996^x$$

$$\text{(Men)}\quad y_2 = 25608.204*0.997^x$$

Using these equations we find that for $x = 2004$ we obtain $y_1 = 50.75$ and $y_2 = 46.96$, yielding a difference of $y_1 - y_2 = 3.79$ seconds. This is somewhat closer to the actual value of 5.67 seconds than the 2.99 seconds we predicted with the linear regression equations.

Using Power Regression Equations

Rounding all constants to three decimal places, the regression equations are:

$$\text{(Women)}\quad y_1 = 3.865\text{E}30*\ x^{-8.747}$$

$$\text{(Men)}\quad y_2 = 9.136\text{E}21*\ x^{-6.144}$$

Using these equations we find that for $x = 2004$ we obtain $y_1 = 50.844$ and $y_2 = 47.026$, yielding a difference of $y_1 - y_2 = 3.82$ seconds. This is very similar to the result obtained using exponential regression.

As the final step of this investigation we will see, using either the exponential or the power regression equations, whether the women's and men's winning times will be the same. These predictors are both more accurate in the short run and more realistic in that they don't assume time will ever either actually reach or go below 0 seconds. To make our prediction, all we need to do is find where each pair of regression curves intersects.

The two exponential curves intersect approximately at the point (2062, 39.07); this indicates that the women and the men will have the same winning time of 39.07 seconds in the year 2062. The two power curves intersect approximately at the point (2065, 39.11), predicting that the women and the men will have the same winning time of 39.11 seconds in the year 2065. These two times are quite similar, so we might want to pay attention at the Olympics in 2064, the one closest to these two dates, to verify the predictions.

REFLECTIONS FOR THE TEACHER

1. You could simply end the investigation after using the linear regression equations to make your prediction since the predictions to 2004 are not bad. Just make sure to explain the pitfall of using these equations too far into the future: they must, eventually, take on negative values, which are impossible for describing the time needed to complete a race of any sort.

2. The Internet provides an amazing amount and variety of real world data to us at the press of a computer key. That means you can easily find any other sort of data (e.g., sports, movie receipts, or Guinness Book of World Records), you need to illustrate linear regression (or any other kind) by describing a set of data and making predictions, for the *near future* based on that data.

RELATED READINGS

Holliday, Berchie W., and Duf, Lauren R. "Activities: Using Graphing Calculators to Model Real-World Data." *Mathematics Teacher* (NCTM, May 2004, Vol. 97, No. 5, p. 328).

Powers, Robert A. "Big Box-Office Bucks." *Mathematics Teacher* (NCTM, February 2001, Vol. 94, No. 2, pp. 112–121).

The web site HickokSports.com (http://www.hickoksports.com/index.shtml) has information on a variety of sports including, but certainly not limited to, the Olympics.

The Entertainment Insiders web site (http://www.einsiders.com) provides a wide variety of entertainment information. Clicking on the "Box Office" tab displays information on the gross box office receipts for the top 10 movies of the week. By going back one week at a time, you can obtain data over several weeks. You can use this data to compare the number of weeks a film has been in theaters versus gross receipts each week, then see what kind of regression model fits the data. The web site The Numbers (http://www.the-numbers.com/index.php) provides similar information.

ACTIVITY SHEET

14.1 The Use of Linear and Nonlinear Regression for Curve Fitting and Making Predictions

At the end of this activity are the names, countries, and winning times in seconds for the women's Olympic 100-meter freestyle swimming event from 1912 to 1996. Follow the directions below and answer the questions that are included.

Step 1. Enter the years in list L_1 and the women's winning times in the corresponding positions in list L_2.

Step 2. Press STAT PLOT and use Plot 1 to set up a scatterplot of this data. Use L_1 for the x axis and L_2 for the y axis. The *ZoomStat* command in the ZOOM key menu will automatically set the viewing window for the specified data.

Step 3. Press STAT, arrow over to *CALC*, and select LinReg(ax+b). Then press ENTER to bring this command to the main screen. Finally, enter L_1, L_2 so that the command looks as shown below and then press ENTER to obtain the coefficients for the best fitting line for our data:

LinReg(ax+b) L_1, L_2

Step 4. Press Y= to open up the function window. Now press VARS; select the *Statistics* option and press ENTER; and arrow over to *EQ* and press ENTER. This will automatically place the linear regression equation from Step 3 into the Y= window as function y_1.

Step 5. Press GRAPH to display the scatterplot and the linear regression line on the screen at the same time.

Question 1. What is the slope of this linear regression line? What does this value represent in terms of the women's winning times from one Olympics to the next?

Question 2. Deactivate the scatterplot so only the line is showing. Then find where this line intersects the x axis either by tracing along the line or by using the CALC key. What does the x value for this point of intersection represent in terms of women's winning times in the Olympics?

Question 3. What does your answer to Question 2 tell you about using a linear regression equation to make predictions too far outside your set of data?

Winning Times in the Women's Olympic 100-meter Freestyle Swimming Event—1912 to 1996

Year	Name of Winner	Country	Time (sec.)
1912	Sarah Durack	Australia	82.2
1920	Ethelda Bleibtrey	United States	73.6
1924	Ethel Lackie	United States	72.4
1928	Albina Osipowich	United States	71.0
1932	Helene Madison	United States	66.8
1936	Hendrika Mastenbroek	Netherlands	65.9
1948	Greta Anderson	Denmark	66.3
1952	Katalin Szöke	Hungary	66.8
1956	Dawn Fraser	Australia	62.0
1960	Dawn Fraser	Australia	61.2
1964	Dawn Fraser	Australia	59.5
1968	Jan Henne	United States	60.0
1972	Sandra Neilson	United States	58.59
1976	Kornelia Ender	East Germany	55.65
1980	Barbara Krause	East Germany	54.79
1984	(Tie) Nancy Hogshead & Carrie Steinheifer	United States United States	55.92
1988	Kristin Otto	East Germany	54.93
1992	Zhuang Yong	China	54.64
1996	Le Jingyi	China	54.50

ACTIVITY SHEET

14.2 The Use of Linear and Nonlinear Regression for Curve Fitting and Making Predictions

In this activity you will use the calculator to compare the men's winning times for the Olympic 100-meter swimming event with the women's winning times. The men's winning times are provided on a sheet at the end of this activity.

Step 1. Deactivate both Plot 1 and function y_1 to retain, but not draw, the graphs for the women's data. Enter the men's winning times into list L_3, then use Plot 2 to create a scatterplot of the men's data. Use L_1 for the x axis and L_3 for the y axis.

Step 2. Find the linear regression equation for the men's data, as you did with the women's data. This time enter the equation into the [Y=] screen as y_2.

Step 3. Deactivate both scatterplots, Plot 1 and Plot 2, and activate both functions, y_1 and y_2. Then graph the two lines.

Question 1. Find the point of intersection of the two regression lines. What are the coordinates of this point?

Question 2. Explain what the x and y coordinates of the point of intersection represent in terms of winning times in the Olympics.

Question 3. Based on your response to Question 3 in Activity Sheet 14.1, what do you think about the accuracy of your findings in Question 2 above?

Winning Times in the Men's Olympic 100-meter Freestyle Swimming Event—1912 to 1996

Year	Name of Winner	Country	Time (sec.)
1912	Duke Kahanamoku	United States	63.4
1920	Duke Kahanamoku	United States	61.4
1924	Johnny Weissmuller	United States	59.0
1928	Johnny Weissmuller	United States	58.6
1932	Yasuji Miyazaki	Japan	58.2
1936	Ferenc Csik	Hungary	57.6
1948	Walter Ris	United States	57.3
1952	Clarke Scholes	United States	57.4
1956	Jon Henricks	Australia	55.4
1960	John Devitt	Australia	55.2
1964	Don Schollander	United States	53.4
1968	Mike Wenden	Australia	52.2
1972	Mark Spitz	United States	51.22
1976	Jim Montgomery	United States	49.99
1980	Jörg Woithe	East Germany	50.40
1984	Rowdy Gaines	United States	49.80
1988	Matt Biondi	United States	48.63
1992	Aleksandr Popov	Russia	49.02
1996	Aleksandr Popov	Russia	48.74

INVESTIGATION 15

Exponential Growth and Exponential Regression

PLANNING: GRADES 9–12

RELATED NCTM STANDARDS: Data Analysis & Probability

- Understand histograms, parallel box plots, and scatterplots and use them to display data.
- For bivariate measurement data, be able to display a scatterplot, describe its shape, and determine regression coefficients, regression equations, and correlation coefficients using technological tools.

MATHEMATICAL SKILLS AND CONCEPTS

Plotting pairs of (x, y) points in the plane.

Finding the best fitting exponential function and curve for a given set of (x, y) points.

Using the first term and common ratio of a sequence to develop an exponential function representing that sequence.

Extrapolating a set of data to the future using an exponential function model.

CALCULATOR KEYS AND FEATURES

LIST	STAT PLOT	GRAPH
TBLSET	TABLE	STAT
ExpReg	VARS	

MATERIALS

Copies of Activity and Solution Sheets 15.1, 15.2, and 15.3 for each student.

For each small group working on Activity Sheet 15.2: a paper or plastic cup, a paper or plastic plate, and approximately 100 plain M&M's with the letter *M* shown clearly on one side.

CLASSROOM IMPLEMENTATION

Background Information for the Teacher

In the previous investigation we used linear regression to represent a set of Olympic swimming data and to make a prediction based on this data. We then discovered that an exponential equation and a power equation provided a better mathematical model of the

Number of Folds X	Number of Rectangles Y
0	1
1	2
2	4
3	8
4	16

FIGURE 15.1

situation we were studying and made more accurate predictions. In this investigation we will again use exponential regression to model real life situations and to make predictions.

Step 1–Introducing the Problem Solving Scenario

Take a piece of paper and point out to the class that it's in the shape of one large rectangle. Fold the piece of paper once, then unfold it and show the class that the crease of the fold divides the paper into two smaller rectangles. Now fold the paper a second time and unfold it. Your students will now see that the creases of the two folds divide the paper into four smaller rectangles. Continue this process with two more folds.

On the board or on an overhead transparency write the table shown in Figure 15.1 comparing the number of folds, *x,* with the number of rectangles, *y*.

Using your Viewscreen, enter these five pairs of values into lists L_1 and L_2, respectively. Have your students do the same on their calculators. Then use [STAT PLOT] and [ZOOM] 9 to create the scatterplot of this data as illustrated in Figure 15.2. Of course, you could easily create a scatterplot by hand with only five pairs of values. But the calculator can find the best fitting exponential regression equation for this set of data, then examine the relationship between the coefficients of this equation and the data from which the equation comes.

Now press [STAT], highlight the word *CALC* at the top of the screen, and select ExpReg for exponential regression. Select lists L_1 and L_2 so that the command on the main screen appears as ExpReg L_1, L_2 and press [ENTER]. Your display should now appear as shown in Figure 15.3.

In other words, the best fitting exponential equation for this set of data is $y = 1*2^x$. Now go into the [Y=] screen and position the cursor to enter function y_1; then press the [VARS] key, select the *Statistics* option; arrow over to EQ, and press [ENTER]. This exponential equation will automatically be copied and pasted into the [Y=] screen as y_1. Now press [GRAPH] to show the graph of this function. It goes exactly through the five points of your scatterplot (Figure 15.4).

Tell your students that you will help them discover when an exponential function of the form $y = a*b^x$ is an appropriate mathematical model for a given situation, and how to determine what the values of *a* and *b* should be.

Problem. To determine when an exponential function of the form $y = a*b^x$ is an appropriate mathematical model for a given situation, and how to determine what the values of *a* and *b* should be for that situation.

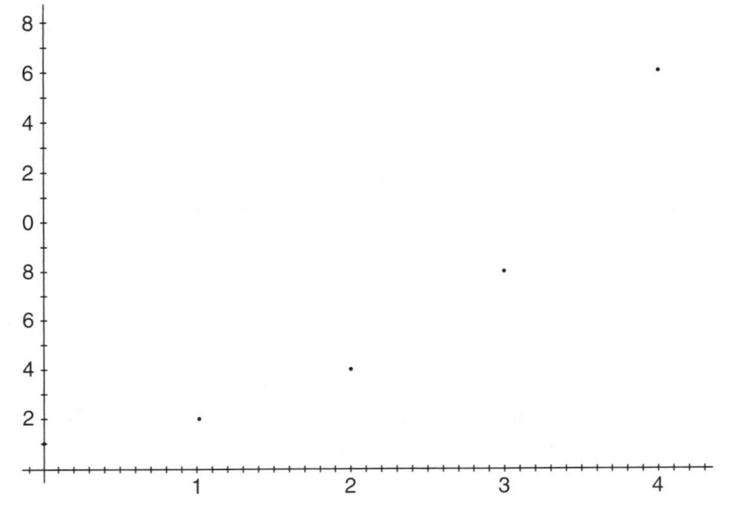

FIGURE 15.2

ExpReg
Y = a*b^X
a=1
b=2

FIGURE 15.3

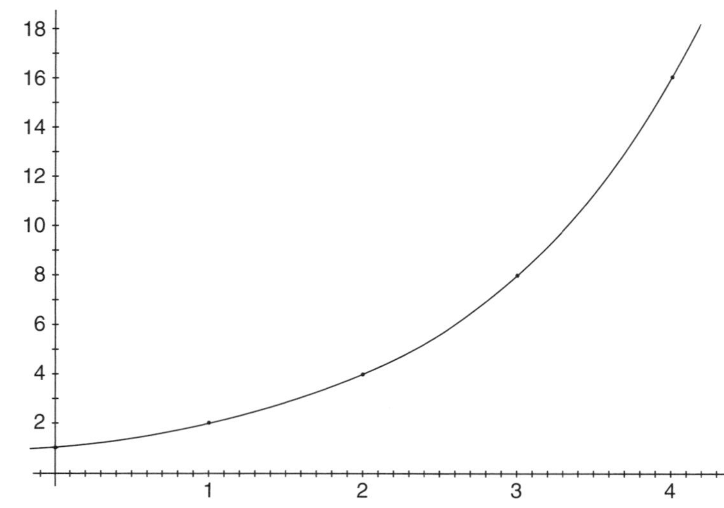

FIGURE 15.4

Step 2–Investigating the Problem

Compare the exponential equation $y = 1*2^x$ to the data in Figure 15.1 that this equation represents. Point out that the first coefficient, $a = 1$, is just the value in the chart corresponding to $x = 0$ (in other words, the value you began with, 1 rectangle); and that the second coefficient, $b = 2$, is just the common ratio for sequential values of y (in other words, the common multiplier to go from one y value to the next).

Tell your students that, in general, a set of data satisfies an exponential function if each value in the sequence is some constant multiple of the preceding value, and for such a set of data this is always what the coefficients a and b represent. Now illustrate this using an imaginary chain letter.

Explain to your students what a chain letter is and tell them to imagine that they themselves will start a chain letter. (Of course, this part has to be imaginary since sending chain letters through the United States mail is illegal.) Then give each student a copy of **Activity Sheet 15.1** and let them work on it using their calculators. When they are finished, discuss their work. Make sure they really understand when it is appropriate to represent a set of data by an exponential equation and how to find the values of a and b for the equation using the data values themselves.

Now hand out copies of **Activity Sheet 15.2.** It's a good idea to have your students work on this activity sheet in small groups. That way they can discuss the activity as they are doing it and you don't have to give each student a large number of M&M's.

Step 3–Developing a Conjecture

You can stop your students after they've completed Steps 1 and 2 on this activity sheet. You can also do the work up to this point together with them, using the Viewscreen for whole class display while the students follow along on their own calculators. State the results of Steps 1 and 2 as a conjecture:

> **Conjecture:** The M&M population increase can be theoretically represented by the exponential function $y = 8*1.5^x$, where x represents the number of years that have passed and y represents the corresponding population size.

Step 4–Testing the Conjecture

Use the theoretical representative function to predict the population size for some value of x. Then actually carry out the experiment and see how accurate the prediction was. This is just what the students are instructed to do in this activity beginning with Step 3.

Step 5–A Convincing Mathematical Argument

The appropriateness of the exponential function $x = 8*1.5^x$ to represent the M&M population growth situation depends on two criteria: first, the accuracy of its predictions; second, its accuracy in the values of the constants a and b. Step 3 and Question 3 of the activity sheet address the first criterion. You cannot guarantee that the results of all the groups will be within 5% of the predicted value, but some of them should be, with many of the others within 10%.

For the second criterion each group will enter the x and y data from their experiment into the L_1 and L_2 lists of their calculators. Then they will use the ExpReg option of *CALC* after pressing the [STAT] key to find the best fitting exponential regression equation for their experimental data. Put a chart on the board to list each group's equation and values of a and b. Then compare these values to those of a and b in the theoretical model ($a = 8$ and $b = 1.5$). These values should be relatively close, and the averages of all the values of a and b for the different groups should be reasonably close to the theoretical values.

FOLLOW-UP DISCUSSION AND INVESTIGATIONS

The M&M population decay investigation provided in **Activity Sheet 15.3** is a good follow-up activity to the M&M population growth investigation just completed. In this investigation your students remove M&M's from a large population of M&M's instead of adding them if the letter *M* appears on the top. Similar to Activity Sheet 15.2, it gives the students an idea of what to do, but it also requires some real understanding and thinking, not simply repeating what they did before.

RELATED READINGS

Appelbaum, Elizabeth Berman. "A Simulation to Model Exponential Growth." *Mathematics Teacher* (NCTM, October 2000, Vol. 93, No. 7, pp. 614–615).

Blume, Glendon W. "A Calculator-Based Unit on Exponential Functions and Logarithms." *Computing Teacher* (May 1979, Vol. 6, No. 4, pp. 47–48).

Forster, Pat. "Exponential Functions: Teaching for Insight with a Constructivist Approach." *Australian Senior Mathematics Journal* (1998, Vol. 12, No. 2, pp. 13–19).

Kunkle, Dan, and Burch, Charles I., Jr. "Modeling Growth—A Discrete Approach." *Mathematics Teacher* (NCTM, April 1984, Vol. 77, No. 4, pp. 266–268).

ACTIVITY SHEET

15.1 Exponential Growth and Exponential Regression

In a chain letter one person sends a letter to several other people; they each make copies of the letter and send the copies to additional people; these new people send copies of the letter to more people; and the process continues as long as letter recipients keep sending copies to other people.

Imagine you are starting a chain letter by sending a letter to five friends that instructs them each to send a copy of the letter to five other people, and so on. Assume that a letter takes one day to be delivered and the recipients send copies out that same day. Make a chart comparing *x*, the number of days that have passed, with *y*, the number of recipients of a copy of the letter on that day. This is shown below.

Days Passed (*x*)	0	1	2	3	4	...
Letters Received (y)	1	5	25	125	625	...

At the beginning ($x = 0$) only you have a copy of the letter so $y = 1$. After one day ($x = 1$) the five people you sent the letter to have a copy, so $y = 1 \times 5 = 5$. After the second day ($x = 2$) each of the five people you sent letters to have sent five new people copies of this letter, for a total of $5 \times 5 = 25$, and so on. Answer the following questions related to this situation.

Question 1. Using what you learned in the paper folding activity about how the coefficients a and b in $y = a*b^k$ relate to the values the function represents, create an exponential function that represents the x, y data in the chart above.

Question 2. Enter the function you found in Question 1 into the [Y=] screen of your calculator as y_1. Then use either the graph of this function or a table of its values to find out on what day 1 million (1,000,000) people will receive a copy of this letter.

Question 3. Enter the number 1 into your calculator's display. Then see how many times you must press the sequence of keystrokes [*] [5] [ENTER] to obtain a value greater than or equal to 1 million in your display. Does this result agree with your result in Question 2?

Exponential Growth and Exponential Regression 15.2

In this activity you will study the growth of a population of M&M's, using an exponential function of the form $y = a*b^x$ to model the situation and to make predictions. Simply follow the steps below and answer the questions. Use what you discovered about exponential functions and the sets of data they represent in the paper folding and chain letter investigations.

Step 1. Place 8 M&M's on the plate to represent your starting population so that when $x = 0$ you have $y = 8$. Use the following procedure to obtain the population size for each succeeding year: Place the population of M&M's in the cup, shake it for randomness, pour the M&M's out onto the plate, and then add an extra M&M to the population for each M&M that has the letter *M* on the top. Repeat this procedure several times to obtain a set of (x, y) data representing successive years and population sizes.

Step 2. Assuming the M&M's are randomly mixed each time you pour them out of the cup, this situation theoretically could be represented by an exponential function of the form $y = a*b^x$. Theoretically, what should be the values of the constants *a* and *b*?

Step 3. Use the exponential function found in the answer to Question 1 to predict the population size *y* in 6 years ($x = 6$).

Step 4. Now perform the experiment and collect your data for $x = 1, 2, 3, 4, 5$, and 6. Then list all your data in a chart like the one shown below.

Year (x)	0	1	2	3	4	5	6
Population (y)	8						

Step 5. Using the prediction made in Step 3 and the actual result found in Step 4 for $x = 6$, calculate the following measure of "Error of Prediction":

$$\text{Error of Prediction} = \frac{|\textit{Actual Result} - \textit{Prediction}|}{\textit{Actual Result}}$$

Step 6. Consider an error of 5% or less (Error of Prediction ≤ 0.05) to be fairly accurate. Did your result in Step 3 support the conjecture or not?

ACTIVITY SHEET

15.3 Exponential Growth and Exponential Regression

This activity is similar to the one in Activity Sheet 15.2 except that here your population will decrease in size, simulating population decay rather than population growth.

Step 1. Put 80 M&M's in the cup to represent the beginning population size ($y = 80$ when $x = 0$). To find the population size after one year (when $x = 1$), shake the M&M's in the cup, pour them out onto the plate, and *remove* all the M&M's that have the letter *M* on the top.

Step 2. Write down an exponential function of the form $y = a*b^x$ that theoretically can be used to model this situation. Explain how you decided on the values of a and b to use.

Step 3. Use your answer to Question 1 to predict the population size y when $x = 6$.

Step 4. Repeat the procedure described in Step 1 to obtain population sizes for $x = 1, 2, 3, 4, 5$, and 6 and put your x and y data into a chart. Calculate the "Error of Prediction" when comparing this result with your prediction.

INVESTIGATION 16

Generalized Fibonacci Sequences Using Matrices

PLANNING: GRADES 9–12

RELATED NCTM STANDARDS: Number & Operations

- Understand vectors and matrices as systems that have some of the properties of the real-number system.
- Develop an understanding of properties of, and representations for, the addition and multiplication of vectors and matrices.
- Develop fluency in operations with real numbers, vectors, and matrices, using mental computation or paper-and-pencil calculations for simple cases and technology for more-complicated cases.

RELATED NCTM STANDARDS: Algebra

- Generalize patterns using explicitly defined and recursively defined functions.
- Use symbolic algebra to represent and explain mathematical relationships.

MATHEMATICAL SKILLS AND CONCEPTS

Use matrix representations and operations to analyze numerical relationships.

Use symbolic representation and manipulation to find the limits of certain types of infinite series.

CALCULATOR KEYS AND FEATURES

MATRX PRGM

MATERIALS

Copies of Activity Sheets 16.1 and 16.2 for each student.

CLASSROOM IMPLEMENTATION

Background Information for the Teacher

Information about the history of mathematics can make the learning of mathematics more interesting and real to many students. One of the most fascinating mathematicians of medieval times was Leonardo Pisano Bonacci, better known as Fibonacci. One of his most famous discoveries involved the properties of a seemingly simple infinite sequence, the Fibonacci sequence. The Fibonacci sequence starts with the values 0 and 1, then obtains successive terms by adding together the previous two. So, $0 + 1$ gives 1 as the third term (0, 1, 1); $1 + 1$ gives 2 as the fourth term (0, 1, 1, 2); $1 + 2$ gives 3 as the fifth term (0, 1, 1, 2, 3); and so on.

This very simple but intriguing sequence of positive integers quickly and easily leads you to one of the most famous numbers in mathematics, the "Golden Mean," $\frac{1+\sqrt{5}}{2} =$ 1.618033989. . . . But the Fibonacci sequence has other surprises for the mathematics student as well. This investigation is about discovering some of these surprises.

Step 1–Introducing the Problem Solving Scenario

Tell your students a little bit about Fibonacci (see the *Related Readings* section for web sites providing information about him). Then write down the first several terms of his famous sequence, explaining that new terms are obtained by adding the two terms that came before:

$$0, \quad 1, \quad 0+1=1, \quad 1+1=2, \quad 1+2=3, \quad 2+3=5, \quad 3+5=8, \ldots$$

giving the sequence:

$$0, 1, 1, 2, 3, 5, 8, \ldots$$

Now make a chart showing the first 10 or so terms of this sequence and the corresponding ratio of successive terms as shown below:

U_N:	0	1	1	2	3	5	8	. . .
$\dfrac{U_N}{U_{N-1}}$:			1	2	1.5	1.66. . .	1.6	. . .

Extend this chart a bit further, or let your students extend it themselves. Now you can show them that this sequence of ratios approaches a very famous infinite decimal as a limit, called the "Golden Mean." This number in closed form is $\frac{1+\sqrt{5}}{2}$, while in decimal form it is 1.618033989. . . . Provide your students with examples of the occurrence of this number in art and in nature from the Related Readings provided later in this investigation.

Problem. To investigate the Fibonacci sequence and discover some of its interesting properties.

Now tell your students that this relationship with the Golden Mean is only one of many interesting things about the Fibonacci sequence, and this investigation will enable them to discover what some of these other things are.

Step 2–Investigating the Problem

Give your students copies of **Activity Sheet 16.1** and let them work on it using their calculators. When they are finished discuss the activity together, letting them tell you what they did. Allow them to show their computations on the overhead projector or the chalkboard and explain how they developed their conjecture.

Step 3–Developing a Conjecture

Your students should have discovered that the sequence of ratios of successive terms in the Fibonacci sequence always seems to approach the same value, the Golden Mean, whatever two positive values they used to begin the sequence. This can be stated as:

> **Conjecture:** The limit of the ratios of successive terms of the Fibonacci sequence does not depend on the choice of the first two values. It is always equal to the Golden Mean.

Step 4–Testing the Conjecture

The results your students obtained in Activity Sheet 16.1 could themselves be considered a test of this conjecture. But you may want to do additional tests with various choices of a and b using the Viewscreen calculator for whole class display. As we've seen, however, listing the terms of such a sequence and calculating the ratios one at a time can be time consuming and prone to computational error. So we need some way to use the special features of the graphing calculator to simplify and speed up this process.

In fact, there are three different ways in which the graphing calculator can simplify all the computations we've been doing. These three methods all involve the use of the matrix capabilities of the calculator and are presented below for you to choose from. The first two procedures use only basic matrix operations while the third uses a simple program involving matrices.

Procedure 1–Define a 1×2 matrix [A] and a 2×2 matrix [B] as:

$$[\mathrm{A}] = [a\ b] \qquad \text{and} \qquad [\mathrm{B}] = \begin{pmatrix} 0 & 1 \\ 1 & 1 \end{pmatrix}.$$

Matrix [A] contains the first and second terms of the Fibonacci sequence that begins with the values a and b. Multiplying matrix [A] by matrix [B] results in the product [A] * [B] = $[b \;\; a + b]$, which gives the second and third terms of this Fibonacci sequence. Multiplying by matrix [B] once again on the right gives the third and fourth terms of the sequence, [A] * [B] * [B] = $[a + b \;\; a + 2b]$, and so on.

With matrices [A] and [B] defined in this way, the keystroke sequence below will display, one at a time, the successive pairs of terms in the Fibonacci sequence, beginning with the values a and b, each time you press ENTER. You can then easily list the terms of this se quence and calculate the successive ratios.

A * B ENTER * B ENTER ENTER ENTER ...

Procedure 2–Define matrices [A] and [B] as in Procedure 1. But this time, instead of finding every pair of successive terms in the sequence, find just one pair reasonably far out in the sequence and calculate its ratio to see if it is close to the Golden Mean. To do this you simply need to use the appropriate power of matrix [B]. For example, the following expression gives a 1×2 matrix containing the $K+1^{\text{st}}$ and $K+2^{\text{nd}}$ terms of the sequence:

A * B ^ K ENTER

Procedure 3–Once again, define matrices [A] and [B] as above. Then enter the following program, called FIB, into your calculator. This program will calculate and display the ratios of successive terms of the sequence, waiting until you press the ENTER key each time before calculating and displaying the next ratio. To break out of the program, simply press the ON key and select "Quit".

```
PROGRAM:FIB
:ClrHome
:0 → X
:ClrList L1, L2
:Lbl 1
:X+1 → X
:[A] * [B] → [A]
:Disp [A] (1,2) / [A] (1,1)
:Pause
:Goto 1
:End
```

Step 5–A Mathematical Proof

Let U_N, U_{N+1}, and U_{N+2} be three consecutive terms in the Fibonacci sequence that begins with the terms a and b. Then, with a little algebraic manipulation we can show that

$$\frac{U_{N+2}}{U_{N+1}} = \frac{U_{N+1} + U_N}{U_{N+1}} = 1 + \frac{U_N}{U_{N+1}} = 1 + \cfrac{1}{\cfrac{U_{N+1}}{U_N}}$$

If N is very large, and this sequence of ratios actually has a finite limit L, then both of the ratios $\frac{U_{N+2}}{U_{N+1}}$ and $\frac{U_{N+1}}{U_N}$ will be very close to L. We then can replace each of these ratios of successive terms by L to obtain the equation

$$L = 1 + \frac{1}{L} \text{ equivalently, } L^2 - L - 1 = 0$$

Solving for L gives $L = \frac{1+/-\sqrt{5}}{2}$. Using the negative sign would lead to a negative value for L, so we use the positive sign instead and obtain $L = \frac{1+\sqrt{5}}{2}$, the Golden Mean. Notice that this algebraic representation, manipulation, and solution never involved the actual first two terms of the sequence. This shows that you get the same limit value for the ratios no matter what two values you use to generate your sequence.

FOLLOW-UP DISCUSSION AND INVESTIGATIONS

Your students can gain a feeling of involvement in the story of the Fibonacci sequence and its relationship with the Golden Mean by creating their own rules for developing a sequence and naming the limit of the resulting ratios after themselves. This is done in **Activity Sheet 16.2.**

SPREADSHEET MODIFICATION

You can carry out the nonmatrix parts of this Fibonacci sequence investigation quite nicely and easily using a spreadsheet. Just calculate and display the values of the Fibonacci sequence, or any modification of it, in the cells of column A, and the corresponding ratios of successive terms in the cells of column B. This would be accomplished as follows.

Enter the first two numbers of the Fibonacci sequence, 0 and 1, into cells A1 and A2, respectively. Then highlight cells A3 through A20, enter the formula "=A1+A2" into cell A3, and press the [Ctrl] and [ENTER] keys at the same time. You will now have the first 20 terms of the Fibonacci sequence in cells A1 through A20.

Now highlight cells B3 through B20, enter the formula "=A3/A2" into cell B3, and press [Ctrl] and [ENTER] at the same time. The first 18 ratios of successive terms of the Fibonacci sequence will now display in cells B3 through B20. Note that the last several ratios of this sequence are the same for several decimal places. This hints that the sequence of ratios is approaching a finite limit L, which can then be shown algebraically to be equal to the Golden Mean.

Now change either or both of the original two terms of the Fibonacci sequence in cells A1 and A2. You can see quite clearly that while the Fibonacci sequence changes, the ratios still seem to approach the same limit as before. You can also change the formula in cell A3 to any other linear combination. You will immediately see the effect of this change on both the terms of the sequence and the limit of the ratios.

REFLECTIONS FOR THE TEACHER

The proof given above assumes that the sequence of ratios does have a limit. The proof also shows that, if this limit exists, it must be equal to the Golden Mean. You can either leave the proof with this implicit assumption, or give a more formal proof showing that the sequence of ratios must have a limit in the first place. Such a proof is easily found by doing an Internet search using the phrase "Fibonacci sequence."

RELATED READINGS

Bradley, Sean. "Generalized Fibonacci Sequences." *Mathematics Teacher* (NCTM, October 2000, Vol. 93, No. 7, pp. 604–606).

Engstrom, Philip G. "Sections, Golden and Not So Golden." *Fibonacci Quarterly* (May 1987, 25.2, pp. 118–124).

Rulf, Benjamin. "A Geometric Puzzle That Leads to Fibonacci Sequences." *Mathematics Teacher* (NCTM, January 1998, Vol. 91, pp. 21–23).

Shaw, Kenneth L., and Aspenwall, Leslie. "The Recurring Fibonacci Sequence: Using a Pose-and-Probe Rubric." *Mathematics Teacher* (NCTM, March 1999, Vol. 92, pp. 192–196).

The home page for Ron Knott's web site, is a wonderful resource for the Fibonacci sequence, the Golden Mean, Fibonacci Numbers and the Golden Section, and many other related mathematical topics (http://www.mcs.surrey.ac.uk/Personal/R.Knott/Fibonacci/fib.html).

ACTIVITY SHEET

16.1 Generalized Fibonacci Sequences Using Matrices

The Fibonacci sequence 0, 1, 1, 2, 3, 5, 8, . . . is obtained by starting with 0, 1 and finding subsequent terms by adding the previous two terms. In class we discovered that the corresponding sequence of ratios of successive terms in this sequence $1/1 = 1$, $2/1 = 2$, $3/2 = 1.5$, and so on appears to approach an infinite decimal value known as the "Golden Mean."

In this activity you will investigate what happens when you change the first two terms of the Fibonacci sequence but keep everything else the same; then create a conjecture based on your findings.

Step 1. Select any two non-negative integers a and b, with $0 \leq a < b$, to serve as the first two terms of your new Fibonacci sequence. Then construct the rest of the sequence the same way you did with the original sequence in class.

Step 2. Calculate the sequence of ratios of successive terms for this new Fibonacci sequence. Compare the limit of this new sequence of ratios with the limit of the original sequence, the Golden Mean. What do you find?

Step 3. Redo Steps 1 and 2 with a different choice of non-negative integer values a and b. What is the limit of the sequence of ratios of successive terms this time?

Step 4. Redo Steps 1 and 2, but this time select noninteger values for a and b. Did your result change?

Step 5. Create a conjecture, based on your results above, about how the two starting values a and b for the Fibonacci sequence are related to the resulting limit of the ratio of successive terms.

Generalized Fibonacci Sequences Using Matrices

16.2 ACTIVITY SHEET

The Fibonacci sequence begins with the numbers 0 and 1 and uses a simple addition rule to obtain additional terms of the sequence: $U_{N+2} = U_N + U_{N+1}$. Create your own sequence by changing this rule to some other linear combination rule such as

$$U_{N+2} = SU_N + TU_{N+1}$$

where S and T are any positive integers. For example, you could use $U_{N+2} = 1*U_N + 2U_{N+1}$, $U_{N+2} = 2*U_N + 1U_{N+1}$, or any other linear combination you want. For example, you could develop a Fibonacci-type sequence by using the month and day of your birth as the coefficients S and T. If you were born on December 9, your coefficients would be $S = 12$ and $T = 9$, giving the generating formula

$$U_{N+2} = 12U_N + 9U_{N+1}$$

for the terms of this new, very personalized sequence.

Step 1. Use any of the methods you've seen in this investigation to obtain the first 15 or so terms of your new sequence. Begin with 0 and 1 and see if the ratios of successive terms appear to approach some finite limit value.

Step 2. Change the first two terms of the sequence. See if this has any effect on the limit of the sequence of ratios.

Step 3. Use an algebraic procedure, as we did in class, to find a closed form representation for the limit of your sequence of ratios. Verify your numerical guess from Steps 1 and 2. Check to see if this limit value depends in any way on the first two terms you used to generate your sequence.

PART THREE

Dynamic Geometry Software

Research Results and Effective Classroom Practice

17 Relating the Properties of Quadrilaterals
18 Inscribed Quadrilaterals
19 The Sum of the Perpendicular Distances
20 Perimeter and Area Relationships on a Line Segment
21 Area Relationships between Inscribed and Circumscribed Circles
22 The Product of the Segments of Intersecting Chords in a Circle
23 The Geometric Solution of a Minimization Problem

BACKGROUND AND OVERVIEW

The precursor of today's dynamic geometry software was a piece of educational software called *The Geometric Supposer.* It was developed in the mid- to late 1980's for Apple Computers at the Educational Development Center (EDC) and won *Classroom Computer Learning's* Software of the Year Award in 1986 and 1987.

The original versions of *The Geometric Supposer* were menu driven rather than windows based. By selecting from a series of menu options the user could construct various geometric figures and measure properties of these figures, such as angles and side lengths. The user could then perform the same operations on other, randomly selected geometric figures of the same type to verify conjectures based on the first drawings and measurements.

Dynamic geometry software extended this early merging of technology with classical Euclidean geometry by creating a geometry environment that was windows based. This allowed the user not only to create geometric objects but also to link them together through geometric construction procedures. The user could then drag these geometric objects around the screen; all constructions and measurements would change automatically and virtually seamlessly to match the changes in the corresponding figure.

There are two commonly used dynamic geometry programs today. *Cabri Geometry* originally developed in 1988–89 in France, was brought to the United States by Texas Instruments as the geometry component of their handheld calculators. *Geometer's Sketchpad* developed around the same time, is commercially sold and supported in the United States by Key Curriculum Press.

Without a doubt, the effective use of dynamic geometry software for enhancing the teaching and understanding of geometry is of major interest to mathematics teachers and researchers. For example, Drexel University's web site *The Math Forum* (mathforum.org) now has a section on this topic called the "Corner for Interactive Geometry Software (CIGS)." This special area offers discussion groups, classroom resources, and an archive of additional information, all related to dynamic geometry software and its instructional implementation.

Recent conferences and projects further illustrate this interest in the educational use of dynamic geometry software. These include "Dynamic Mathematics Visualization for Young Learners: Sketchpad in Grades 3–8," a conference held at the University of Illinois at Chicago on February 7–9, 2003; "CabriWorld: the Third Cabri/Geometry International Conference," held September 9–12, 2004, in Rome, Italy; and a two-year research project on dynamic geometry run by the Educational Development Center under a grant from the National Science Foundation.

Given all this international interest and discussion, similar to that concerning graphing calculators when they first appeared, some questions need to be answered. Does the use of this geometry software have positive benefits for students? If so, what are those benefits? And what issues should teachers consider when using such software as a component of geometry in the curriculum?

THE RESEARCH

The development of dynamic geometry software is much more recent than that of calculators, and requires more sophisticated equipment (or the use of a computer lab) rather than a Viewscreen and an overhead projector. And so, naturally, there is both less use of dynamic geometry software in schools and less research on its instructional use than there is for either scientific or graphing calculators. Some research on dynamic geometry software does exist, however, although much of it is anecdotal. It is worth looking at this research since this software has so much to offer to both teachers and students.

We begin with the impact of dynamic geometry software on mathematics education. Professor John Olive of the University of Georgia delivered a presentation on this topic at the December 2000 International Conference on Technology in Mathematics Education (TIME) held in Auckland, New Zealand. The title of this presentation was *"Implications of Using Dynamic Geometry Technology for Teaching and Learning."*

Olive first discusses anecdotal reports from other educators who used dynamic geometry software with students at many different grade levels. Then Olive notes the potential benefits:

> At the secondary level dynamic geometry can (and should) completely transform the teaching and learning of mathematics. Dynamic geometry turns mathematics into a laboratory science rather than the game of mental gymnastics, dominated by computation and symbolic manipulation, that it has become in many of our secondary schools.

In his conclusion, however, he also warns about the pitfalls of this approach:

> While there have been many personal accounts of the powerful learning that can take place when students of all ages work with dynamic geometry technology (my own included), there have been very few well designed research projects to study the effects on learning in such environments.

Luckily for us, much additional research on dynamic geometry software has taken place since Professor Olive's presentation at *TIME 2000.* A review of this research can help us to better understand the potential and realized benefits of dynamic geometry in mathematics education.

Keith Jones presents summary of this research in "Research on the Use of Dynamic Geometry Software: Implications for the Classroom," an article published in 2002 in *MicroMath* (volume 18, issue 3, pages 18–20). Jones says the following about research relating to dynamic geometry software:

> Over the last two decades, dynamic geometry software has become one of the most widely used pieces of software in schools and colleges all over the world. . . . In terms of research, Straber thinks that dynamic geometry software may be one of the best, if not the best, researched type of software within mathematics education research.

Jones concludes by presenting an overview of what research on dynamic geometry software has revealed.

> A variety of research shows that interacting with dynamic geometry software can help students to explore, conjecture, construct and explain geometric relationships. It can even provide them with the basis from which to build deductive proofs. Overall, this research has found that discussions and group work in the classroom are important components.

Three final statements sum up Jones' conclusions from studying this research on dynamic geometry software.

- Dynamic geometry software used inappropriately makes no significant difference (and might make things worse).
- Dynamic geometry software integrated intelligently with curriculum and pedagogy produces measurable learning gains.
- What matters is *how* dynamic geometry software is used.

In other words, dynamic geometry software is a tool that can improve mathematical understanding. But the teacher must know how to use it as an appropriate part of instruction. Interestingly, and not unexpectedly, the same could be said of the instructional use of scientific and graphing calculators. We saw this in the Research sections of the first two parts of this text.

Relating the Properties of Quadrilaterals to the Properties of Their Diagonals and Creating a Book of Shapes

PLANNING: GRADES 9–12

RELATED NCTM STANDARDS: Geometry

- Analyze properties and determine attributes of two- and three-dimensional objects.
- Explore relationships (including congruence and similarity) among classes of two- and three-dimensional geometric objects, make and test conjectures about them, and solve problems involving them.
- Establish the validity of geometric conjectures using deduction, prove theorems, and critique arguments made by others.
- Draw and construct representations of two- and three-dimensional geometric objects using a variety of tools.

MATHEMATICAL SKILLS AND CONCEPTS

Identify the properties of the diagonals of a square, a rectangle, a rhombus, and a parallelogram.

Show that the properties of the diagonals of a quadrilateral uniquely determine the type of quadrilateral: square, rectangle, rhombus, or parallelogram.

SKETCHPAD FEATURES

Constructions	Construct menu	Measure menu
Multipage documents	Custom tools	

MATERIALS

Copies of Activity and Solution Sheet 17.1 for each student.

CLASSROOM IMPLEMENTATION

Background Information for the Teacher

This investigation really serves two purposes. First, it allows your students to determine the properties of the diagonals of a quadrilateral based on the type of quadrilateral they are working with (square, rectangle, rhombus, or parallelogram); then *reverse* the process to show that by knowing the properties of the diagonals you can identify the type of quadrilateral they come from.

Second, this investigation prepares students for the remaining activities in this text. In future investigations your students will begin with a certain type of figure such as a square, or a parallelogram, or an equilateral triangle. If, each time this happened, they actually had to construct the desired base figure before starting the investigation, they would get bogged down, and lose sight of the investigation's purpose. Therefore, as part of this investigation, your students will construct a file (or *document* as *Sketchpad* calls them) that contains six different pages, each of which contains one of the six types of figures that will be needed in future investigations (square, rectangle, rhombus, parallelogram, isosceles triangle, and equilateral triangle). Furthermore, students will create a *custom tool* for each figure that allows them to automatically draw these figures whenever needed, provided they have first opened this *Book of Shapes* document in the background.

Step 1–Introducing the Problem Solving Scenario

Ask your students to define a square. They will probably give the standard definition: a four-sided polygon with all sides equal and all four angles equal to each other and to 90°. Use *Sketchpad* to either construct such a square or display a ready-made square to the entire class. Then have the students verify that it has these properties.

Now construct the two diagonals of this square and the point of intersection of the diagonals. Then, measure the diagonals, the lengths of the four segments into which the diagonals are cut, and the four angles formed by the diagonals and their point of intersection. The results are illustrated in Figure 17.1 (the measurements you obtain may be different from those shown).

Problem. To investigate the properties of the diagonals of a square, a rectangle, a parallelogram, and a rhombus; and to determine if these properties uniquely define which of these quadrilaterals the diagonals come from.

Point out that the diagonals appear to be equal in length, to be perpendicular, and to bisect each other. Then drag the figure by all of its vertices and segments to show that these three characteristics are intrinsic to the figure of a square. Two natural questions now arise. First, do the diagonals of other quadrilaterals such as the rectangle, rhombus, and parallelogram also have certain unique properties; and, second, if you know the properties of the diagonals of a quadrilateral can you reverse the process of deduction and determine what type of quadrilateral they come from? These questions will be studied in this investigation.

Step 2–Investigating the Problem

Hand out **Activity Sheet 17.1.** Your students can work on it individually or in pairs at computers next to each other sharing what they find. After the students have finished, hand out the solution sheet and discuss the results. Show how these results make sense. The parallelogram is the most basic quadrilateral since its diagonals have only one property: They bisect each other. If the diagonals also are perpendicular (an additional property) you get a rhombus. If, instead, you add the property that the diagonals are of equal length, you get a rectangle. If you add both of these diagonal properties, you get a square. This hierarchy of quadrilaterals (from simple, parallelogram, to complex, square) is readily deduced from the information contained in the completed Activity Sheet 17.1 chart.

Step 3–Developing a Conjecture

It's clear from the chart that no two of our four special quadrilaterals has exactly the same diagonal properties. We now may wonder whether in fact these diagonal properties are defining characteristics of the four shapes. This can now be stated as a conjecture as follows.

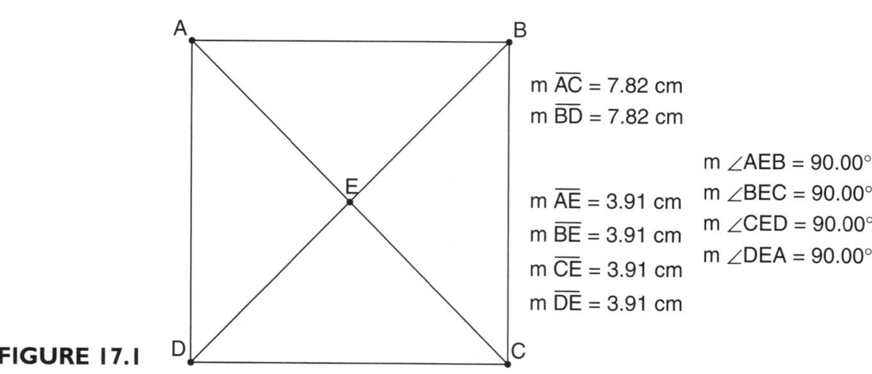

FIGURE 17.1

Conjecture: If the diagonals of a quadrilateral have exactly the properties listed in one of the rows of the chart from Activity Sheet 17.1, then that quadrilateral must be the type of figure identified for that row.

In other words, if the diagonals of a quadrilateral are of equal length and perpendicularly bisect each other, then the quadrilateral must be a square; if the diagonals of a quadrilateral are of equal length and bisect each other but are not perpendicular, then the quadrilateral must be a rectangle; and so on.

Step 4–Testing the Conjecture

We will test this conjecture as follows. For each row of the Activity Sheet 17.1 chart, we will construct a pair of line segments having the properties specified in that row; connect the endpoints of those segments consecutively to form a quadrilateral having those segments as its diagonals; and then take appropriate measurements to verify that the figure so obtained is of the specified type.

For the first row of the chart, for example, we would first construct two line segments of equal length that perpendicularly bisect each other, as shown in Figure 17.2a. We would then connect the endpoints of these segments to form a quadrilateral, as shown in Figure 17.2b. Finally, we would hide all the segments and points except those that form the quadrilateral and measure its sides and angles, as in Figure 17.2c.

We discover that this figure appears to be a square, even when we drag it by any of its vertices or sides. Now let your students perform the same test for the other three rows of the completed chart from Activity Sheet 17.1.

Step 5–A Mathematical Proof

The proof for all four rows of the chart is very straightforward. It uses the properties of congruent triangles and parallel lines cut by a transversal. Shown below is the proof for the row of the chart corresponding to a parallelogram.

Given: A quadrilateral $ABCD$ with diagonals that bisect each other at point E (Figure 17.3).

Prove: Quadrilateral $ABCD$ is a parallelogram.

Proof: Triangles ABE and CDE are congruent because $AE = EC$ and $BE = ED$ (diagonals AC and BD bisect each other); and angle AEB = angle CED (vertical angles are equal).

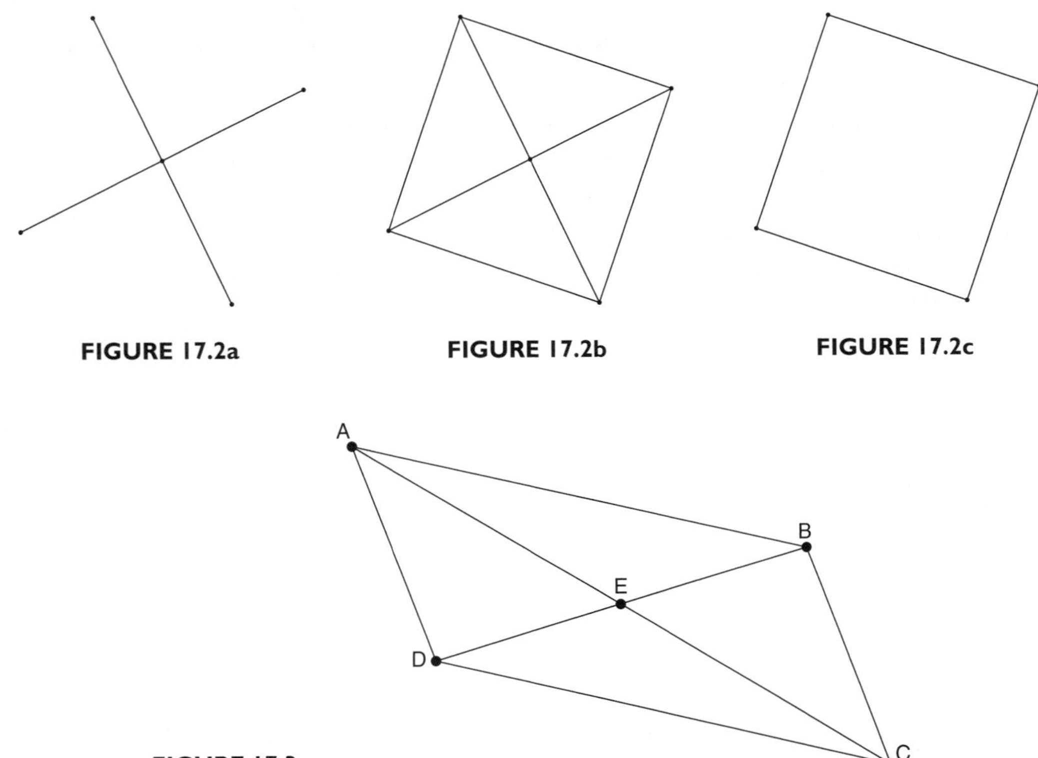

FIGURE 17.2a **FIGURE 17.2b** **FIGURE 17.2c**

FIGURE 17.3

Therefore side AB is the same length as side CD. Furthermore, AD is parallel to CD because, from the congruence of the two triangles, the opposite interior angles of transversal AC, angle BAE and angle DCE are equal. Therefore, sides AB and CD are equal and parallel. A similar argument shows that sides BC and DA are equal and parallel. However, there is no way to prove any additional properties or relationships among the sides or angles of this figure. Therefore quadrilateral $ABCD$ is a parallelogram and only a parallelogram.

FOLLOW-UP DISCUSSION AND INVESTIGATIONS

Have your students create two additional pages in this document, one containing an equilateral triangle and the other containing an isosceles triangle, and name them *Equilateral* and *Isosceles,* respectively. Then have them create a custom tool for each of the six pages of this document. The documentation that comes with the *Sketchpad* software explains how to do this; or they can use the built-in *Help* command at the top of the *Sketchpad* screen. When the students are done they should save the entire *Book of Shapes* document with the six pages, the six shapes, and the six corresponding custom tools for creating these shapes. Now, whenever they need one of these shapes they can simply open this file and use one of the six custom tools to create it.

RELATED READINGS

Britton, Barbara J., and Stump, Sheryl L. "Unexpected Riches from a Geoboard Quadrilateral Activity." *Mathematics Teaching in the Middle School* (NCTM, April 2001, Vol. 6, No. 8, p. 490).

Burger, William F., and Shaughnessy, Michael J. "Characterizing the van Hiele Levels of Development in Geometry." *Journal for Research in Mathematics Education* (NCTM, January 1986, Vol. 17, No. 1, pp. 31–48).

Craine, Timothy V., and Rubenstein, Rheta N. "A Quadrilateral Hierarchy to Facilitate Learning in Geometry." *Mathematics Teacher* (NCTM, January 1993, Vol. 86, No. 1, pp. 30–36).

Hershkowitz, Rina, et al. "Geometrical Adventures in Functionland." *Mathematics Teacher* (NCTM, May 1987, Vol. 80, No. 5, pp. 346–352).

Thornton, Steve. "Constructing Geometric Reasoning." *Australian Mathematics Teacher* (August 1998, Vol. 54, No. 3, pp. 6–11).

Toumasis, Charalampos. "When Is a Quadrilateral a Parallelogram?" *Mathematics Teacher* (NCTM, March 1994, Vol. 87, No. 3, pp. 208–211).

Relating the Properties of Quadrilaterals to the Properties of Their Diagonals and Creating a Book of Shapes

17.1 ACTIVITY SHEET

Open a new sketch in *Sketchpad* and save this document with the name *Book of Shapes*. Under the *File* menu select *Document Options* and create four pages in this document. Name the pages *Square, Rectangle, Rhombus,* and *Parallelogram,* in that order. On each page construct a shape that matches the name for the page, so that on the *Square* page you have a square, and so on for the other three pages.

Now construct the diagonals and the intersection point of the diagonals for the figure that's displayed on each page of this document. Then measure the diagonals, the four segments created by the intersection of the diagonals, and the angles formed by the diagonals. Finally, use your measurements to fill in the chart below. Put an "X" into each box that describes a property of the diagonals of that figure. As an example, we have already marked each property in the row of the chart that represents a square, since the diagonals of a square have all three of the properties listed.

Properties of Diagonals

	Bisect Each Other	Equal Length	Perpendicular to Each Other
Square	×	×	×
Rectangle			
Rhombus			
Parallelogram			

INVESTIGATION 18

Inscribed Quadrilaterals

PLANNING: GRADES 9–12

RELATED NCTM STANDARDS: Geometry

- Analyze properties and determine attributes of two- and three-dimensional objects.
- Explore relationships (including congruence and similarity) among classes of two- and three-dimensional geometric objects, make and test conjectures about them, and solve problems involving them.
- Establish the validity of geometric conjectures using deduction, prove theorems, and critique arguments made by others.
- Draw and construct representations of two- and three-dimensional geometric objects using a variety of tools.

MATHEMATICAL SKILLS AND CONCEPTS

Identify the defining properties of different types of quadrilaterals and triangles.

Relate the algebraic representation of a limiting process to the geometric representation of the same process.

SKETCHPAD FEATURES

Construct menu   Measure menu   Calculate
Custom tools

MATERIALS

Custom tools for constructing various types of quadrilaterals and triangles (from the *Book of Shapes*).

Copies of Activity and Solution Sheet 18.1 for each student.

CLASSROOM IMPLEMENTATION

Background Information for the Teacher

Students often memorize the properties of various geometric shapes without having any idea why they might ever be useful in a problem solving situation. In this investigation they use properties to identify the figure they obtain by connecting the midpoints of different types of quadrilaterals with line segments.

Using the results of this initial investigation as a springboard, students then investigate the relationships between the perimeters and areas of the original and new figures; and how these relationships change when the vertices of the new figures are moved from the midpoints to new positions on the sides of the original figures.

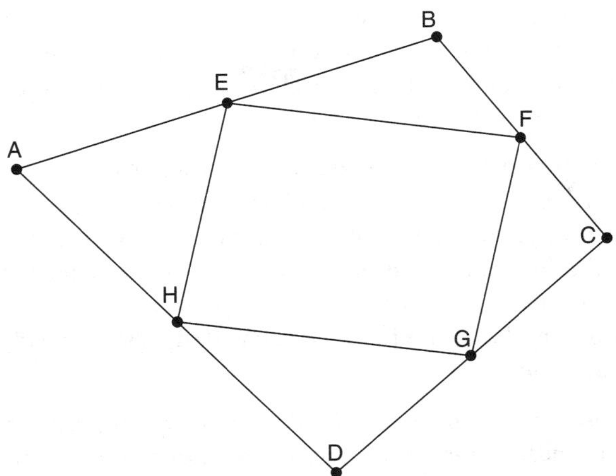

FIGURE 18.1

Step 1–Introducing the Problem Solving Scenario

Using a large screen monitor or other method of display, draw an arbitrary convex quadrilateral; construct the midpoints of its four sides; and connect these midpoints to form a new quadrilateral. The results are illustrated in Figure 18.1.

Measure the side lengths and angles of inscribed quadrilateral *EFGH*. Show your class that this figure is a parallelogram and remains a parallelogram after dragging any of the vertices or sides of the original figure. Finally, construct the interior of both the original and the inscribed quadrilaterals, measure the area and the perimeter of both quadrilaterals, and use the *Calculate* feature of the *Measure* menu to calculate the ratios of the larger to the smaller area, and of the larger to the smaller perimeter.

You can now show your students that as you drag vertex *A* to various positions, the ratio of the areas remains fixed at 2 while the ratio of the perimeters changes value. In other words, the area of the parallelogram formed by joining the midpoints of the sides of an arbitrary quadrilateral is always one-half the area of the original figure.

Remind your students that in Investigation 17 they discovered a hierarchy of quadrilaterals in terms of the properties of their diagonals. The parallelogram has the fewest special properties (its diagonals bisect each other); the rhombus and rectangle have one additional property each (the diagonals of a rhombus are perpendicular but not of equal length, while the diagonals of a rectangle are of equal length but not perpendicular; and the square has both of these extra properties (its diagonals are of equal length, are perpendicular), and bisect each other).

Now ask the following: If you begin with a special quadrilateral such as a parallelogram, a rhombus, a rectangle, or a square, is the inscribed quadrilateral you obtain also one of these special quadrilaterals? And, if so, which one is it? This is the problem that they will use *Sketchpad* to investigate.

Problem. To determine, when you begin with a parallelogram, a rhombus, a rectangle, or a square and connect the midpoints of its sides, what type of quadrilateral you obtain.

Step 2–Investigating the Problem

Tell your students to open the *Book of Shapes* document they created in Investigation 17 and use the built-in custom tools to create the four types of quadrilaterals they need for this investigation. They should be able to find the following relationships between the original figure and the inscribed figure fairly easily.

- A **parallelogram** gives another **parallelogram.**
- A **rhombus** gives a **rectangle.**
- A **rectangle** gives a **rhombus.**
- A **square** gives another **square.**

Explain that you're now going to change things a bit and see if any of the results obtained so far change as well. Then give them **Activity Sheet 18.1** to work on and allow them to share their findings with each other. When they have completed the activity, discuss what they found, using your large screen display for illustration if necessary.

Tell them that you're especially interested in their answers to Question 2, which focuses on how the ratio of the area of the original quadrilateral to that of the inscribed figure changes as the points on the sides of the original quadrilateral are moved. Clearly, the inscribed figure is completely contained *within* the original figure, so its area has to be less than the area of the original figure. Thus the ratio must be greater than 1. From the answer to Question 3, however, it appears that the value of this ratio decreased from 2, when the midpoints were connected, to 1.60, when the points one-fourth of the way from each vertex to the next were connected. You are now ready to make a conjecture about these values.

Step 3–Developing a Mathematical Conjecture

Mention to your students that a monotonically decreasing sequence of numbers that is bounded below must converge to a limit that is greater than or equal to this lower bound. In this case it seems that as the points to be connected are moved closer to the vertices of the original figure, the ratio of areas decreases and that all of these ratios have a lower bound of 1. Therefore this sequence of ratios must have a limit, which you will suggest is actually equal to 1. This can be stated as the following conjecture:

> **Conjecture:** As the points on the sides of the quadrilateral that are connected to form an inscribed quadrilateral move closer and closer to the vertices of the original figure, the ratio of the area of the original figure to that of the inscribed figure approaches 1 as a limit.

Step 4–Testing the Conjecture

In class you connected the points that were one-half of the way from each vertex to the next and found an area ratio of 2. In Activity Sheet 18.1 your students connected the points that were one-fourth of the way from each vertex to the next and found an area ratio of 1.60. Let your students now repeat the procedure, this time connecting the points that are one-eighth of the way from each vertex to the next. They will find that the ratio of areas is equal to 1.28. As predicted, this value is less than the previous ratio and is approaching 1 as a possible limit.

Step 5–A Convincing Mathematical Argument

If the *Sketchpad* constructions used to find the area ratios of 2, 1.60, and 1.28 are placed next to each other (Figures 18.2a, 18.2b, and 18.2c), we see that as the vertices of the inscribed figure approach those of the original figure, the two figures overlap more and more until they are virtually the same. Consequently, the ratio of their areas must approach 1.

Alternatively, if the area ratio does not depend on the particular type of quadrilateral used, we can simplify the calculation of the area ratio by starting with the simplest of all quadrilaterals, a square, and see where it takes us. In Figure 18.3, we begin with a square of side length 1 and connect the points that are a distance S from each vertex to the next.

Using the Pythagorean theorem it's easy to find that $X^2 = S^2 + (1 - S)^2 = 1 - 2S + 2S^2$. Consequently, the ratio of areas is $ratio = \frac{1}{1 - 2S + 2S^2}$, and as S approaches 0 this approaches $\frac{1}{1 - 0 + 0} = \frac{1}{1} = 1$.

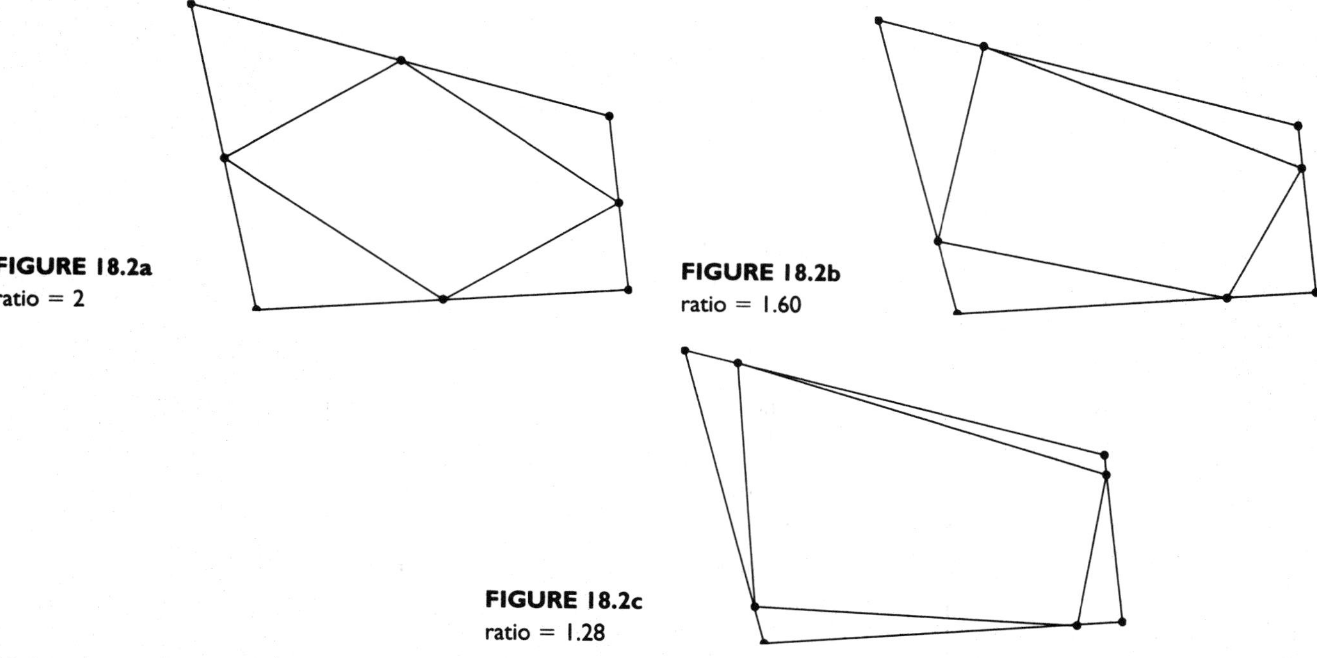

FIGURE 18.2a
ratio = 2

FIGURE 18.2b
ratio = 1.60

FIGURE 18.2c
ratio = 1.28

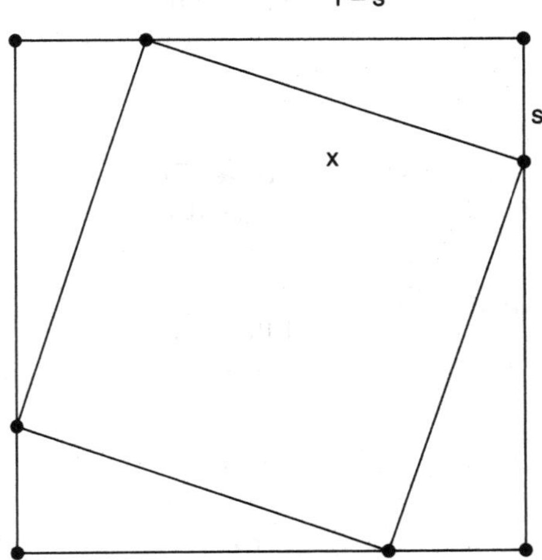

FIGURE 18.3

FOLLOW-UP DISCUSSION AND INVESTIGATIONS

This entire investigation was based on inscribing a quadrilateral inside another quadrilateral. You could have your students use the same procedure, but this time start with an arbitrary triangle. They will discover that connecting the midpoints of the three sides leads to a constant ratio of areas of 4, but also to a constant ratio of perimeters of 2; that an isosceles triangle leads to another isosceles triangle; and that an equilateral triangle leads to another equilateral triangle.

They can now go on to investigate how all of these results change when the points on the sides of the triangle that are connected are positioned one-fourth of the way from each vertex to the next, one-eighth of the way from each vertex to the next, and so on. The results, of course, will be similar to what they found with quadrilaterals.

REFLECTIONS FOR THE TEACHER

You could use this investigation as a lead-in to the questions of how to find the area of a quadrilateral, whether there is a general formula for such an area, and how much information is needed to find a quadrilateral's area.

If you do an Internet search for "quadrilateral area," you will find numerous web sites looking into these questions. Some use trigonometry, some use coordinate geometry, and some use other approaches entirely.

RELATED READINGS

Gau, Y. David, and Tartre, Lindsay A. "The Sidesplitting Story of the Midpoint Polygon." *Mathematics Teacher* (NCTM, April 1994, Vol. 87, No. 4, pp. 249–256).

Greenberg, Benjamin. "That Area Problem." *Mathematics Teacher* (NCTM, January 1971, Vol. 64, No. 1, pp. 79–80).

Oliver, Peter N. "Pierre Varignon and the Parallelogram Theorem." *Mathematics Teacher* (NCTM, April 2001, Vol. 94, No. 4, pp. 316–319).

Oliver, Peter N. "Consequences of the Varignon Parallelogram Theorem." Mathematics Teacher (NCTM, May 2001, Vol. 94, No. 5, pp. 406–408).

Scher, Daniel. "A Triangle Divided: Investigating Equal Areas." Mathematics Teacher (NCTM, October 2000, Vol. 93, No. 7, p. 608).

ACTIVITY SHEET

18.1 Inscribed Quadrilaterals

In class you discovered several interesting things about the quadrilateral you obtain by connecting the midpoints of certain types of quadrilaterals. You found that a parallelogram leads to a parallelogram, a rhombus leads to a rectangle, a rectangle leads to a rhombus, and a square leads to a square.

You also discovered that the area of the inscribed figure is always half the area of the original figure. In this activity you will change the positions of the points that are connected and see how this affects those results.

Question 1. Draw an arbitrary quadrilateral *ABCD* and construct the points one-fourth of the way from each vertex to the next. (Hint: Construct the midpoint *E* of *AB*. Then construct segment *AE* and find its midpoint *F*. *F* will be one-fourth of the way from *A* to *B*. Repeat this procedure for the other three sides of *ABCD* and connect the four points. This procedure is illustrated in the figure below.) Is the new quadrilateral still a parallelogram?

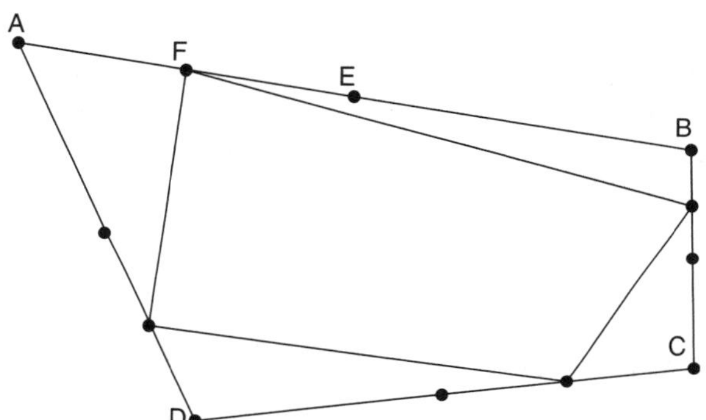

Question 2. Calculate the ratio of the areas of the original and inscribed quadrilaterals from Question 1. Is this ratio still equal to 2? Is this ratio invariant when dragging vertices and sides? What does this result tell you about the ratio of areas if you start with a special quadrilateral like a parallelogram, a rhombus, a rectangle, or a square?

Question 3. Starting with a parallelogram, a rhombus, a rectangle, and then a square, connect the points that are one-fourth of the way from each vertex to the next. Are any of the inscribed quadrilaterals you obtain special types of quadrilaterals?

The Sum of the Perpendicular Distances from an Interior Point of a Regular Polygon to Its Sides

PLANNING: GRADES 9–12

RELATED NCTM STANDARDS: Geometry

- Analyze properties and determine attributes of two- and three-dimensional objects.
- Explore relationships (including congruence and similarity) among classes of two- and three-dimensional geometric objects, make and test conjectures about them, and solve problems involving them.
- Establish the validity of geometric conjectures using deduction, prove theorems, and critique arguments made by others.
- Draw and construct representations of two- and three-dimensional geometric objects using a variety of tools.

MATHEMATICAL SKILLS AND CONCEPTS

Understand the definition and properties of regular polygons.

Decompose a regular polygon into triangles.

Represent a sum of triangular areas algebraically and use symbolic manipulation to simplify this expression.

SKETCHPAD FEATURES

Construct menu Measure menu Custom tools

MATERIALS

Custom tools from the *Book of Shapes.* Copies of Activity and Solution Sheet 19.1 for each student.

CLASSROOM IMPLEMENTATION

Background Information for the Teacher

The concept of invariants—properties that remain unchanged when other characteristics of the situation are changed—plays an important role in many different areas of mathematics. For example, algebraic solutions of equations take advantage of the fact that the set of solutions remains unchanged even though the original equation or equations are changed in various ways.

Similarly, trigonometry uses the fact that the ratios of the side lengths of a triangle remain the same when we increase or decrease the size of the triangle provided that the three angles remain the same. And when we work with matrices in advanced high school or college mathematics, the determinant of the matrix remains the same when we perform certain row and column transformations on the matrix.

In this investigation your students will discover another invariant, a geometric one. They will make this discovery using the special construction, measurement, and dragging features of *Sketchpad.*

Step 1–Introducing the Problem Solving Scenario

Use your custom tools to construct an equilateral triangle and place a point somewhere near the center. Construct perpendicular lines from this point that extend through each side of the triangle. Then use the points of intersection of the lines and the sides of the triangle to construct perpendicular line segments from the point to each side of the triangle. This is illustrated in Figures 19.1a, 19.1b, and 19.1c, respectively.

Measure the lengths of the three line segments and use the *Calculate* feature in the *Measure* menu to find the sum of these three lengths. Now drag this point to various positions inside the triangle. You can see that while the individual lengths of the three segments may change, the sum remains constant. (Of course, this sum changes if you move the point outside the triangle and you might want to demonstrate this.)

Problem. To determine what types of polygons have the property that the sum of the perpendicular distances from an interior point to all the sides of the polygon is the same for all positions of the point inside the figure.

Tell your students that you want them to help you discover just which polygons possess this geometric invariance characteristic. Do only equilateral triangles have it? Or do triangles of any shape have it? What about polygons with any number of sides as long as they are *regular polygons* (equal side lengths and equal interior angles) like the equilateral triangle? That's for them to investigate and to discover.

Step 2–Investigating the Problem

Give your students **Activity Sheet 19.1** to work on using *Sketchpad.* This is a good activity for them to work on in small groups since different members of the group can work on different questions. Then they can discuss their findings and verify each other's work and conclusions. The final question on the activity sheet asks them to complete a conjecture that generalizes their results and what the students think they mean.

Step 3–Developing a Mathematical Conjecture

Have one of the groups tell the class how they completed the conjecture in Question 4 of the activity sheet and why they completed it the way they did. Let them use *Sketchpad* with a large screen display if that helps them explain what they found and how it led them to the conjecture. Then write the conjecture on the board for everyone to see and discuss.

> **Conjecture:** Given an *N*-sided ***regular** polygon* and a point *P* inside this polygon, the **sum of the perpendicular line segments from *P* to the sides of the polygon** will remain invariant as point *P* moves to any other position in the interior of the polygon.

Step 4–Testing the Conjecture

As a test, ask each group to use the equilateral triangle custom tool to construct six such triangles around a common center to form a regular six-sided polygon (Figure 19.2a). They can then hide

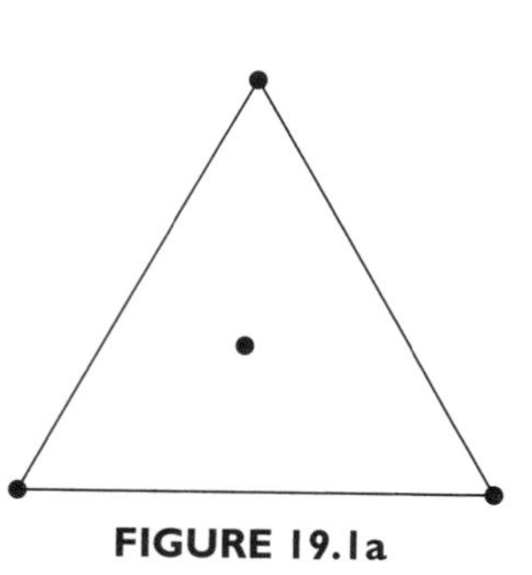

FIGURE 19.1a

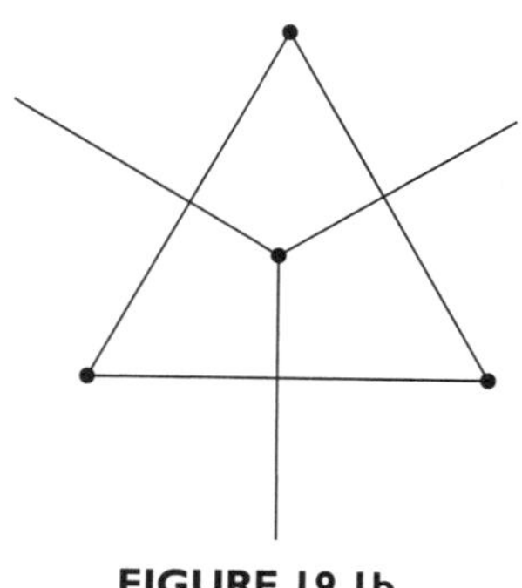

FIGURE 19.1b

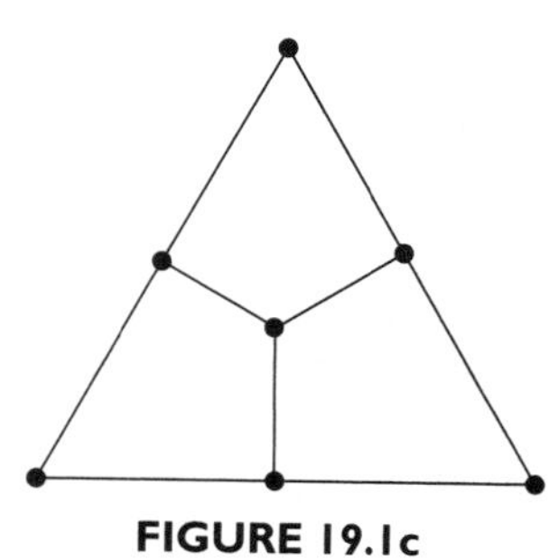

FIGURE 19.1c

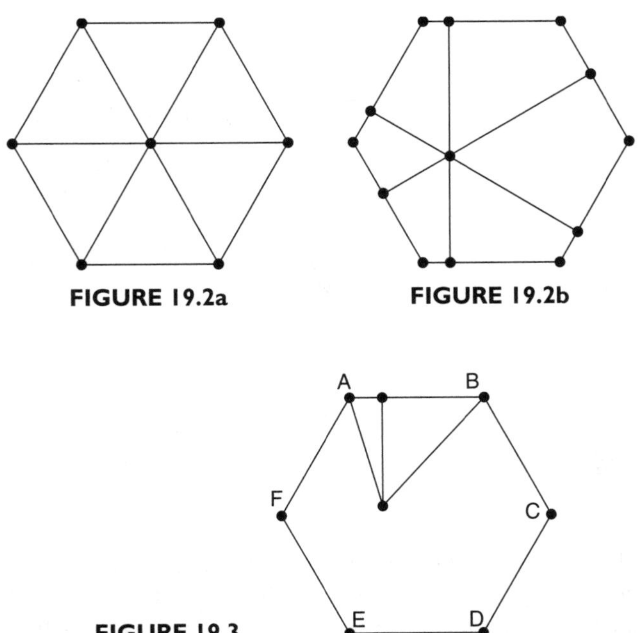

FIGURE 19.2a

FIGURE 19.2b

FIGURE 19.3

the internal line segments and proceed to test the conjecture on this new regular polygon as shown in Figure 19.2b.

Once your students have this construction, they should discover that the conjecture again holds true for this six-sided regular polygon. With all of these specific examples supporting the conjecture we now need a more complete mathematical justification.

Step 5–A Mathematical Proof

Let S be a regular N-sided polygon with side length L and let P be a point in the interior of S. If you connect P to each vertex of S with line segments, you decompose S into N triangles. Each triangle has a base of length L and an altitude equal to the perpendicular distance from P to that side of the triangle. This is illustrated in Figure 19.3 for $N = 6$ (where we show only the first of the six triangles into which S will be decomposed).

The area of each triangle is the product of its base, L, and its altitude, and the altitude is the perpendicular distance from the interior point to that side of the polygon. So we find that

$$\text{Sum of Triangle Areas} = L \times (\text{Sum of Perpendicular Segments})$$

But the sum of the areas of the triangles is just the area of the entire polygon S. So we can rewrite this expression as

$$\text{Sum of Perpendicular Segments} = (\text{Area of } S)/L$$

Since both the area of polygon S and its side length L are fixed, the sum of the perpendicular segments must be a fixed number as well, and that number does not depend on the position of interior point P. This completes the proof.

FOLLOW-UP DISCUSSION AND INVESTIGATIONS

The result we've just discovered and proved is true only for *regular* polygons, but many similar results hold true for *arbitrary* polygons of certain types. One very interesting relationship that your students can now investigate is the *Erdos-Mordell theorem.*

The *Erdos-Mordell theorem* can be stated as follows. (Your students will have a lot of fun using *Sketchpad* to investigate the truth of this theorem.)

> Let P be a point inside an arbitrary triangle. If D is the sum of the distances from P to the three vertices and E is the sum of the perpendicular distances from P to the three sides, then $D \geq 2E$ or, equivalently, $\frac{D}{E} \geq 2$.

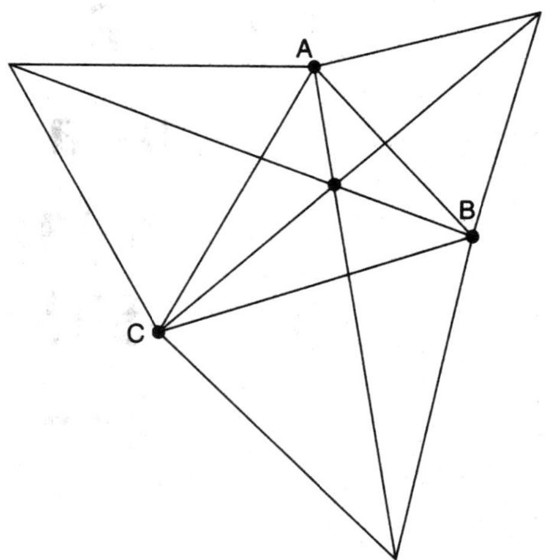

FIGURE 19.4

Another related topic is *Fermat points in a triangle*. Given an arbitrary acute triangle ABC, the *first Fermat point* is the point P that minimizes the sum of the distances from P to the three vertices. You can find the first Fermat point in the following way (Figure 19.4).

- Construct an equilateral triangle on the *outside* of each side of triangle ABC.
- Connect the vertex of each equilateral triangle that is *not on* ABC to the vertex of ABC that is farthest from it.
- These three line segments will meet at the first Fermat point P.

REFLECTIONS FOR THE TEACHER

You will notice that as the number of sides of the regular polygon increases in our original investigation there are positions for P in the interior of the polygon where some of the perpendicular segments to the sides of the polygon disappear. In other words, the set of points for P so that all the perpendicular segments appear decreases as the number of sides of the regular polygon increases.

Of course, we see that as the number of sides of the regular polygon increases to infinity, the polygon gets closer to a perfect circle. But as this happens, the set of points for P so that all the perpendicular segments appear approaches only one point: the center of the limit circle.

RELATED READINGS

Glass, Brad, and Deckert, Walter. "Making Better Use of Computer Tools in Geometry." *Mathematics Teacher* (NCTM, March 2001, Vol. 94, No. 3, p. 224).

Leikin, Roza. "Dividable Triangles—What Are They?" *Mathematics Teacher* (NCTM, May 2001, Vol. 94, No. 5, p. 392).

Mathews, John H., and Leonard, William A. "A Discovery Activity in Geometry." *Mathematics Teacher* (NCTM, February 1977, Vol. 70, No. 2, p. 126).

Shilgalis, Thomas W., and Benson, Carol T. "Centroid of a Polygon—Three Views." *Mathematics Teacher* (NCTM, April 2001, Vol. 94, No. 4, p. 302).

Waters, William M. "Notes on the Partial Converses of a Familiar Theorem." *Mathematics Teacher* (NCTM, May 1977, Vol. 70, No. 5, pp. 458–460).

The Sum of the Perpendicular Distances from an Interior Point of a Regular Polygon to Its Sides

19.1 ACTIVITY SHEET

Question 1. Repeat what you did in class with an equilateral triangle, but this time use an arbitrary triangle. Do you get the same invariance result?

Question 2. Repeat what you did in class, but with a square, which is a regular quadrilateral. Do you get the same invariance result as with the equilateral triangle?

Question 3. Repeat Question 2 but this time use an arbitrary quadrilateral. Do you get the same invariance result as with the equilateral triangle?

Question 4. Based on what you found in class and in Questions 1, 2, and 3 above complete the following conjecture.

Conjecture: Given an *N*-sided __________ *polygon* and a point inside this polygon, the __________ will remain invariant as the point moves to any other position in the interior of the polygon.

INVESTIGATION

20

Perimeter and Area Relationships on a Line Segment

PLANNING: GRADES 9–12

RELATED NCTM STANDARDS: Geometry

- Analyze properties and determine attributes of two- and three-dimensional objects.
- Explore relationships (including congruence and similarity) among classes of two- and three-dimensional geometric objects, make and test conjectures about them, and solve problems involving them.
- Establish the validity of geometric conjectures using deduction, prove theorems, and critique arguments made by others.
- Draw and construct representations of two- and three-dimensional geometric objects using a variety of tools.

MATHEMATICAL SKILLS AND CONCEPTS

Use perimeter and area formulas for various geometric shapes.

Use symbolic manipulation to simplify perimeter and area formulas.

Recognize invariants in the measurement of perimeters and areas of a set of geometric shapes.

SKETCHPAD FEATURES

Construct menu Measure menu Custom tools

Motion Controller for animation

MATERIALS

Custom tools from the *Book of Shapes*.

Copies of Activity Sheet 20.1 for each student.

CLASSROOM IMPLEMENTATION

Background Information for the Teacher

Teachers know that students can often be intrigued and motivated to use mathematics when presented with problems that appear, at first glance, to be similar, yet lead to very different consequences.

For example, students asked to find the largest-area rectangle with a perimeter of 40 can easily discover that the answer is a square of side length 10 with an area of

$10 \times 10 = 100$. When they are asked, however, to find the largest-perimeter rectangle with an area of 100 they are amazed to discover that there is no such rectangle. In fact, a rectangle with an area of 100 can have a perimeter greater than any desired value.

In this investigation students will examine two similar shapes constructed on a fixed line segment such that when one increases in size the other decreases correspondingly. They will obtain different results when they study the perimeters of the two figures and when they study their areas.

Step 1–Introducing the Problem Solving Scenario

Using a large screen display construct a line segment *AB*. Place a point *C* at an arbitrary position on this segment. Then construct an equilateral triangle on both segments *AC* and *CB* as shown in Figure 20.1. For efficiency use your custom equilateral tool from your *Book of Shapes* for the equilateral triangles.

Now measure segments *AC* and *CB*, the side lengths of the two equilateral triangles, respectively. Use *Calculate* in the *Measure* menu to find the perimeter of each triangle and then the sum of the two perimeters. Finally, construct the interior of each triangle, measure the area of each triangle, and calculate the sum of these two areas.

Now drag point *C* along segment *AB*. Your students will see that all the individual segment, perimeter, and area measurements change, including the sum of the two areas, but the sum of the two perimeters remains constant. Finally, construct the midpoint of segment *AB*, point *F*, and drag point *C* toward and eventually onto point *F*. You will discover that the sum of the two areas is minimized at the midpoint of the original segment, point *F*. This is illustrated in Figure 20.2.

This initial demonstration easily leads to the following problem based on this example.

Problem. To determine whether, for shapes constructed on a fixed line segment as in the demonstration in class, the sum of the perimeters remains fixed as point *C* is moved, and the sum of the areas is minimized when point *C* is placed at the midpoint of the segment.

Step 2–Investigating the Problem

Hand out copies of **Activity Sheet 20.1.** Your students are asked to repeat your demonstration with two equilateral triangles constructed on a common line segment. But this time they first use squares instead of equilateral triangles, and then use circles. In both cases they will find that the conjecture is supported in both respects: The sum of the two perimeters is invariant, and the sum of the two areas is minimized when point *C* is placed at the midpoint of the segment. This is illustrated in Figures 20.3 and 20.4, respectively.

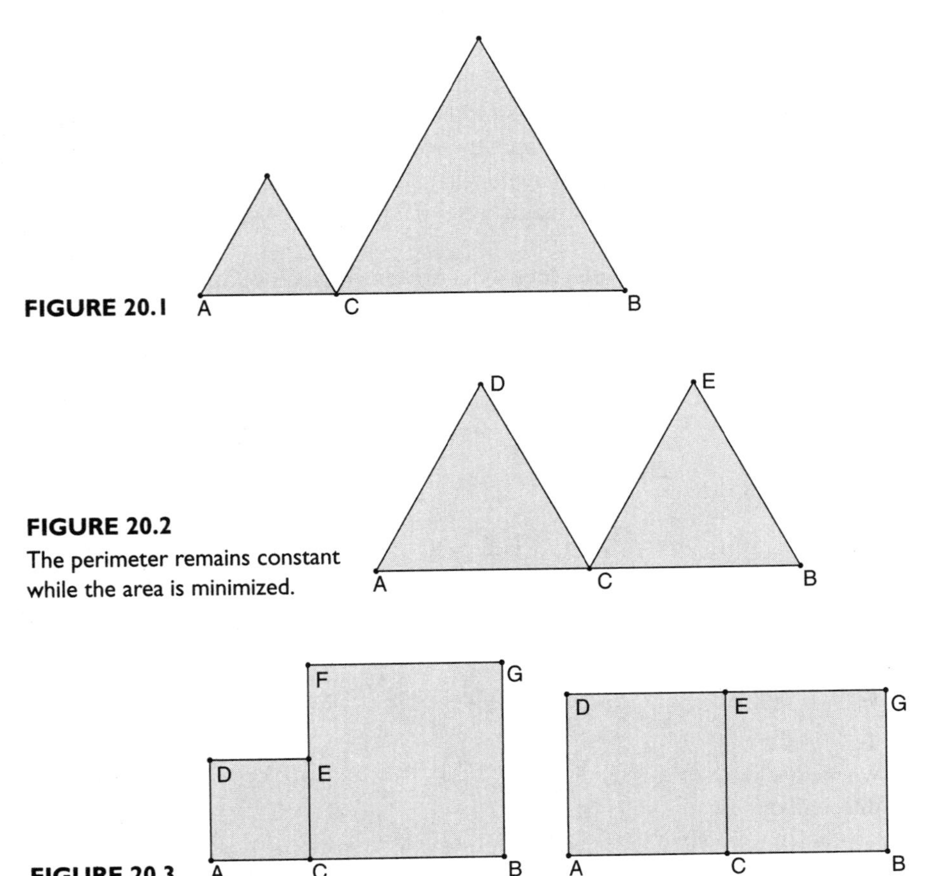

FIGURE 20.1

FIGURE 20.2
The perimeter remains constant while the area is minimized.

FIGURE 20.3

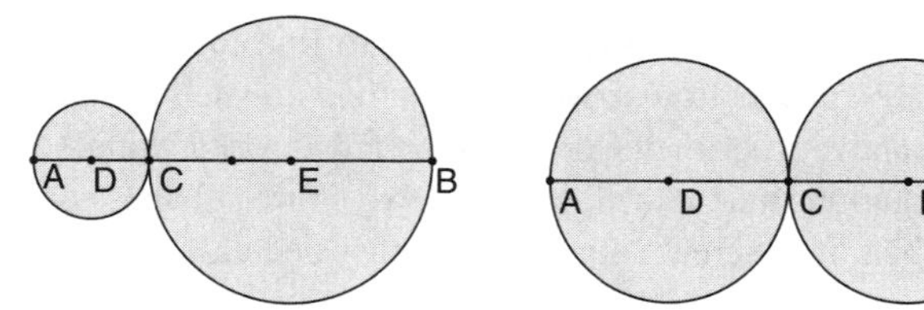

FIGURE 20.4

Step 3–Developing a Mathematical Conjecture

Now help the class develop a conjecture that generalizes what they have seen and then found with their own constructions and measurements. The following is one way of stating such a conjecture.

> **Conjecture:** Given a line segment *AB* and a point *C* on the segment. If an *N*-sided regular polygon has segment *AC* as one of its sides, and a similar *N*-sided regular polygon has segment *CB* as one of its sides, then the sum of the perimeters of the two polygons will remain constant as point *C* is moved along segment *AB*; and the sum of the areas of the two polygons will be minimized when *C* is positioned at the midpoint of segment *AB*.

Step 4–Testing the Conjecture

As a test, ask each group to construct six equilateral triangles using the custom tool to form a regular six-sided figure with one side on segment *AC*, and then repeat the procedure to place another regular six-sided figure with one side on segment *CB*. Students can measure the perimeters and areas of these two figures, calculate the sums of the perimeters and the areas, and then drag point *C* along the segment to verify the conjecture for this additional regular polygon even though the two figures overlap. This is illustrated in Figure 20.5.

Step 5–A Mathematical Proof/Convincing Mathematical Argument

Suppose you have two *N*-sided regular polygons. One has segment *AC* as one of its sides, and the other segment *CB* as one of its sides. All *N* sides of the first polygon are the same, so the perimeter of this polygon must be $N \times AC$. Similarly, the perimeter of the second polygon must be $N \times CB$. Adding the two perimeters shows that

$$\text{Sum of Perimeters} = N \times AC + N \times CB = N{*}AB$$

This result is independent of the position of point *C* on the line segment.

You can easily find the general formula for the area of a regular *N*-sided figure online, but it is somewhat complicated. So you might want to prove the area conjecture for the particular case of a square and, if you wish, of an equilateral triangle as well. The proof for the square is given below. (The proof for the equilateral triangle is similar.)

Proof of the Area Part of the Conjecture for a Square–Given two squares on segment *AB* as shown in Figure 20.6.

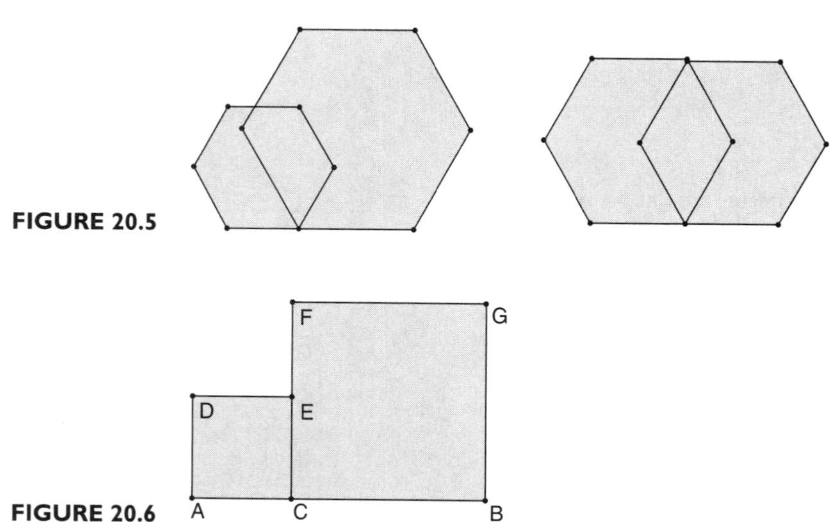

FIGURE 20.5

FIGURE 20.6

Let the length of segment AB be represented by L, and the length of segment AC by x. Then the length of segment CB can be represented by $L-x$, and the sum of the two areas can be given by $x^2 + (L - x)^2$. Using algebraic manipulation:

$$\begin{aligned}\text{Sum of Areas} &= x^2 + (L - x)^2 = 2x^2 - 2Lx + L^2 \\ &= 2[x^2 - Lx] + L^2 \\ &= 2\left[x^2 - Lx + \frac{L^2}{4}\right] + L^2 - \frac{L^2}{2} \\ &= 2\left[x - \frac{L}{2}\right]^2 + \frac{L^2}{2}\end{aligned}$$

The expression inside the brackets is non-negative, so the smallest value it can have is 0. That occurs when $x = L/2$ which is exactly when point C is at the midpoint of segment AB. This completes the proof.

FOLLOW-UP DISCUSSION AND INVESTIGATIONS

In this investigation your students will look at the value of the expression that represents either the sum of the two perimeters or the sum of the two areas. Then they will determine whether, and how, these values change as they drag the point C along segment AB. Suggest to your students that they use the animation feature of *Sketchpad* to drag point C along the segment rather than do it manually. That way they can really focus on the values of the two expressions.

Have the students simply move the cursor to point C and right click their mouse button. Tell them to select the *Animate Point* option. The *Motion Controller* then will appear on their screen, and point C will be put in motion back and forth along segment AB.

The students can now use the *Motion Controller* to reduce the speed of point C to see clearly the changes in the values of the two expressions. They should also notice that the expression for the sum of the two areas reaches its minimum when point C is at the midpoint of segment AB.

RELATED READINGS

Chappell, Michaele F., and Thompson, Denisse R. "Perimeter or Area? Which Measure Is It?" *Mathematics Teaching in the Middle School* (NCTM, September 1999, Vol. 5, No. 1, p. 20).

Davis, Elwyn H. "Area of Spherical Triangles." *Mathematics Teacher* (NCTM, February 1999, Vol. 92, No. 2, p. 150).

Malloy, Carol E. "Perimeter and Area through the van Hiele Model." *Mathematics Teaching in the Middle School* (NCTM, October 1999, Vol. 5, No. 2, p. 87).

ACTIVITY SHEET

20.1 Perimeter and Area Relationships on a Line Segment

Construct a line segment. Place a point on the segment that divides the segment into two pieces. Construct a square on each part of the segment, as shown below, and measure the perimeter and area of each square.

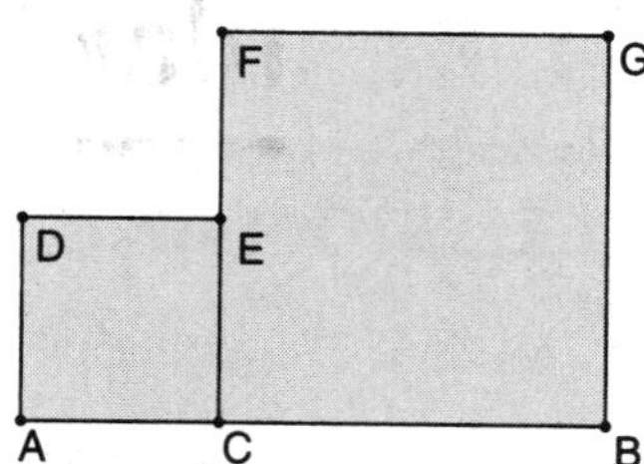

Drag the point along the interval. Show that the sum of the perimeters remains constant while the sum of the areas is minimized when this point is midway through the interval and the squares are of the same size.

Now repeat this construction and measurement, but use circles instead of squares as shown below. Show that the circumference sum remains constant while the area sum is minimized when both circles are the same size.

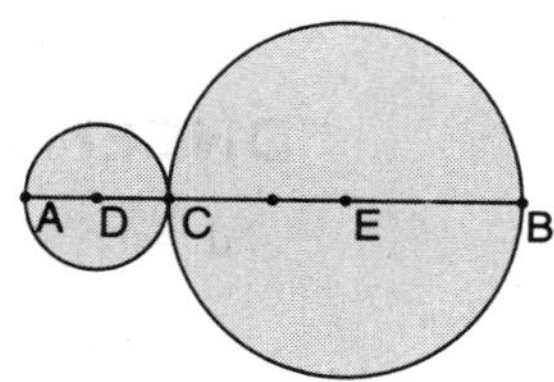

INVESTIGATION 21

Area Relationships between Inscribed and Circumscribed Circles of Regular Polygons

PLANNING: GRADES 9–12

RELATED NCTM STANDARDS: Geometry

- Analyze properties and determine attributes of two- and three-dimensional objects.
- Explore relationships (including congruence and similarity) among classes of two- and three-dimensional geometric objects, make and test conjectures about them, and solve problems involving them.
- Establish the validity of geometric conjectures using deduction, prove theorems, and critique arguments made by others.
- Draw and construct representations of two- and three-dimensional geometric objects using a variety of tools.

MATHEMATICAL SKILLS AND CONCEPTS

Construct, for a given circle, circumscribed and inscribed polygons with various numbers of sides.

Use algebraic representation to represent and analyze the ratio of the areas of the circumscribed and inscribed polygons of a circle.

SKETCHPAD FEATURES

Construct menu Measure menu Custom tools

MATERIALS

Custom tools from the *Book of Shapes*. Copies of Activity and Solution Sheets 21.1 and 21.2 for each student.

CLASSROOM IMPLEMENTATION

Background Information for the Teacher

In this investigation students try to generalize a result found for equilateral triangles and squares, first to regular polygons with a larger number of sides; then to a limiting situation as the number of sides of the regular polygons approaches infinity.

Step 1–Introducing the Problem Solving Scenario

Problem. To discover what happens to the ratio of areas of the circumscribed circle to the inscribed circle of a regular polygon as the number of sides of the regular polygon increases without bound.

Give your students **Activity Sheet 21.1** to work on. Allow them to work together or to simply discuss what they are doing with each other. After sufficient time has passed ask a volunteer to tell you what he or she found. Then use a large screen display to demonstrate the student's work for the entire class.

Question 3 on the activity sheet asks them whether the ratio of areas will be smaller or larger than 2 if they repeat the procedure of Questions 1 and 2 using a regular polygon with more than four sides. This question can lead to more general questions: Do the ratios of areas change for regular polygons with greater and greater numbers of sides? Is there some limiting value for this sequence of ratios as the number of sides gets increasingly larger without bound? These questions can now be stated as follows:

Step 2–Investigating the Problem

Ask your students now to complete **Activity Sheet 21.2.** They will use the custom equilateral tool from their *Book of Shapes* to construct a regular six-sided polygon. Then they will calculate the ratio of areas of the circumscribed and inscribed circles for this figure. This will give them three ratios to compare in order to see any emerging pattern.

After they have completed Activity Sheet 21.2 they will discover that area ratios decrease as the number of sides of the regular polygon increases: a ratio of 4 for the three-sided figure, a ratio of 2 for the four-sided figure, and a ratio of approximately 1.33 (actually $\frac{4}{3}$) for a six-sided figure.

Step 3–Developing a Mathematical Conjecture

Based on these results it's natural to conjecture that this area ratio will continue to decrease as the number of sides of the regular polygon increases. Furthermore, since the circumscribed circle contains the inscribed circle, this ratio cannot be less than 1. A reasonable conjecture, therefore, is:

> **Conjecture:** Given an *N*-sided regular polygon, the ratio of the area of its circumscribed circle to that of its inscribed circle will get smaller and smaller as *N* increases, and has a limit of 1, as *N* approaches infinity.

Step 4–Testing the Conjecture

Your students could test the conjecture by constructing a regular polygon with more than six sides and calculating the ratio of areas for this figure. Alternatively, you could simply point out to them that as the number of sides of the regular polygon increases, this figure gets closer and closer to a circle, and its circumscribed and inscribed circles increasingly resemble the shape of the polygon itself; so the ratio of the areas clearly decreases.

In the limit case the regular polygon would itself turn into a circle. Consequently, the figure and its circumscribed and inscribed circles would all be identical to each other, so the ratio of the two areas would be 1.

Step 5–A Mathematical Proof

Figure 21.1 shows a small part of a regular polygon with N sides. Point A is the center of the polygon, segment BC is a side of the polygon, and point D is the midpoint of side BC.

Our constructions of the circumscribed and inscribed circles for the three figures in Activity Sheets 21.1 and 21.2 show that segment AB is a radius of the circumscribed circle, and segment AD a radius of the inscribed circle for this regular polygon. Furthermore, ABD is a right triangle, so $AB^2 = AD^2 + BD^2$.

But then the ratio of the areas of these two circles will be the same as the ratio of the squared values of the radii AB and AD. In other words

$$\text{Area Ratio} = \frac{AB^2}{AD^2} = \frac{AD^2 + BD^2}{AD^2} = 1 + \left(\frac{BD}{AD}\right)^2$$

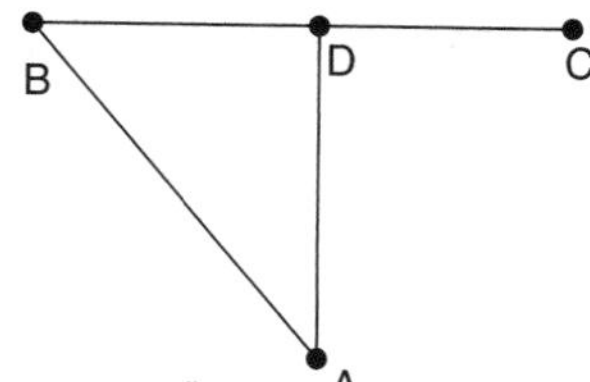

FIGURE 21.1

As the number of sides N increases, BD approaches 0 while AD increases. Consequently, $(\frac{BD}{AD})^2$ decreases to 0 and $1 + (\frac{BD}{AD})^2$ approaches $1 + 0 = 1$ as a limit. This completes the proof.

RELATED READINGS

Hansen, David W. "On Inscribed and Escribed Circles of Right Triangles, Circumscribed Triangles, and the Four-Square, Three-Square Problem." *Mathematics Teacher* (NCTM, May 2003, Vol. 96, No. 5, p. 358).

Rokach, Arie. "Finding the Maximal Area of Bounded Polygons in a Circle." *Mathematics Teacher* (NCTM, March 2005, Vol. 98, No. 7, p. 491).

Worrall, Charles. "Circumscribable Quadrilaterals: A Journey in Honors Geometry." *Mathematics Teacher* (NCTM, October 2004, Vol. 98, No. 3, p. 192).

ACTIVITY SHEET

21.1 Area Relationships between Inscribed and Circumscribed Circles of Regular Polygons

Use the custom tools from your *Book of Shapes* document to construct an equilateral triangle. Then construct two circles, one inscribed within the triangle and the other circumscribed around the triangle. Your construction should look as shown in the illustration below. Notice that the center of the circle is at the intersection of the altitudes of the triangle; that the inscribed circle passes through the midpoints of the sides; and that the circumscribed circle passes through all three vertices.

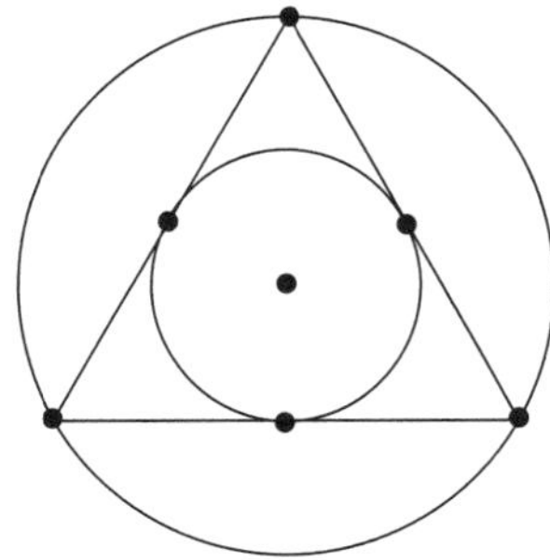

Question 1. Find the areas of the two circles. Then calculate the ratio of the larger circle's area to the smaller circle's area. What is the value of this ratio?

Question 2. Repeat the procedure outlined above, but this time start with a square. Then find the ratio of the larger circle's area to the smaller circle's area just as you did in Question 1. The center of the circles will be at the intersection of the diagonals of the square, the inner circle will pass through the midpoints of the sides, and the outer circle will pass through the vertices, as shown in the illustration below.

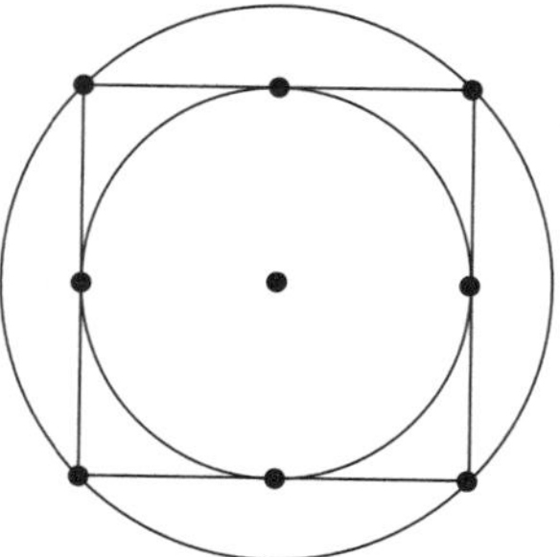

Question 3. Suppose you repeat this procedure with a regular polygon having more than four sides. Would the ratio of the areas of the circumscribed and inscribed circles be smaller or larger than your answer to Question 2?

Area Relationships between Inscribed and Circumscribed Circles of Regular Polygons

21.2

ACTIVITY SHEET

Use the custom equilateral tool from your *Book of Shapes* document to construct six equilateral triangles. Then arrange them as shown below to form a regular six-sided polygon.

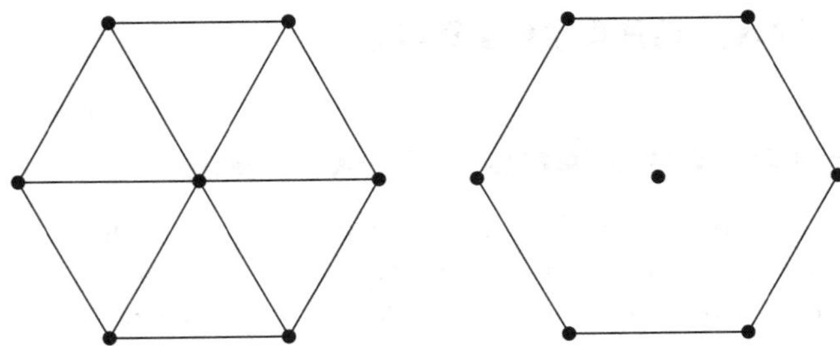

Construct the midpoint of any side of this figure. Then use the midpoints of the figure and the side to construct the inscribed circle; and the midpoint and any vertex of the figure to construct the circumscribed circle. This is illustrated below.

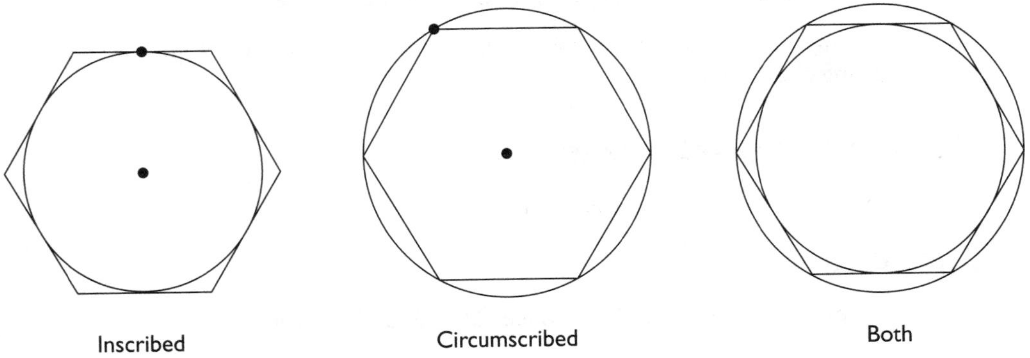

Inscribed | Circumscribed | Both

Now calculate the ratio of the areas of these two circles. Is the ratio less than 2, as predicted?

INVESTIGATION

22

The Product of the Segments of Intersecting Chords in a Circle

PLANNING: GRADES 9–12

RELATED NCTM STANDARDS: Geometry

- Analyze properties and determine attributes of two- and three-dimensional objects.
- Explore relationships (including congruence and similarity) among classes of two- and three-dimensional geometric objects, make and test conjectures about them, and solve problems involving them.
- Establish the validity of geometric conjectures using deduction, prove theorems, and critique arguments made by others.
- Draw and construct representations of two- and three-dimensional geometric objects using a variety of tools.

MATHEMATICAL SKILLS AND CONCEPTS

Discover and state the relationship between the products of the segments of intersecting chords of a circle.

SKETCHPAD FEATURES

Construct menu   Measure menu

MATERIALS

Copies of Activity and Solution Sheet 22.1 for each student.

CLASSROOM IMPLEMENTATION

Background Information for the Teacher

Properties of geometric shapes presented in a static and traditional format are often boring to students. These same properties, however, can be quite surprising and interesting when students discover them as part of a dynamic, participatory investigation.

In this investigation your students will discover, rather than be told, a basic property of intersecting chords in a circle: The product of the segments of one chord is equal to the product of the segments of the other chord.

Step 1–Introducing the Problem Solving Scenario

Give your students **Activity Sheet 22.1** to work on. In this activity sheet they are asked where they can place a vertex of a quadrilateral to make a certain expression equal to 0. This can be stated as:

Problem. To discover the geometric significance of the position of a vertex of a quadrilateral that makes a certain expression equal to 0.

Step 2–Investigating the Problem

Explain the following to your students: When the expression they have been looking at, $AE \times EC - BE \times ED$, is equal to 0, it can be rewritten as $AE \times EC = BE \times ED$. Furthermore, this happens when, and only when, the fourth vertex of the quadrilateral is on the same circle as the other three vertices of the quadrilateral. And, finally, when this happens, the four segments *AE*, *EC*, *BE*, and *ED* are those formed by the intersection of the two chords *AC* and *BD*.

Step 3–Developing a Mathematical Conjecture

Based on the results found in Activity Sheet 22.1 and the classroom discussion that follows, we can now state a conjecture. It presents a familiar statement regarding the product of the segments of intersecting chords of a circle.

> **Conjecture:** Given a circle with intersecting chords *AC* and *BD* and intersection *E*, the product of the lengths of segments *AE* and *EC* of chord *AC* will be equal to the product of the lengths of segments *BE* and *ED* of chord *BD*.

Step 4–Testing the Conjecture

To test this conjecture have your students draw an arbitrary circle. Have them place points *A*, *B*, *C*, and *D* on the circumference of the circle. Then they will connect points *A* and *C* and points *B* and *D* to form chords and move the chords until they intersect in a point labeled *E*. Finally, have them construct the four segments *AE*, *EC*, *BE*, and *ED* and calculate the values of the products $AE \times EC$ and $BE \times ED$. As the students drag the points *A*, *B*, *C*, and *D* around the circle they will see that the values of $AE \times EC$ and $BE \times ED$ do change, but always remain equal to each other.

Step 5–A Mathematical Proof

The proof of this geometric relationship is available in any high school geometry text and on many web sites. Simply do an Internet search for "intersecting chords theorem" and you will find many sites that offer a proof of this theorem.

RELATED READINGS

Eccles, Frank M. "The Euler Line and Nine-Point-Circle Theorems." *Mathematics Teacher* (NCTM, January 1999, Vol. 92, No. 1, p. 50).

Jiang, Zhonghong, and Pagnucco, Lyle. "Discuss with Your Colleagues: Exploring the Four-Points-on-a-Circle Theorems with Interactive Geometry Software." *Mathematics Teacher* (NCTM, December 2002, Vol. 95, No. 9, p. 668).

ACTIVITY SHEET

22.1 The Product of the Segments of Intersecting Chords in a Circle

Construct an arbitrary quadrilateral with vertices *A*, *B*, *C*, and *D*. Construct the two diagonals of this quadrilateral as segments *AC* and *BD*. Then, construct the intersection of these two segments and denote the point of intersection as point *E*, as shown in the figure below.

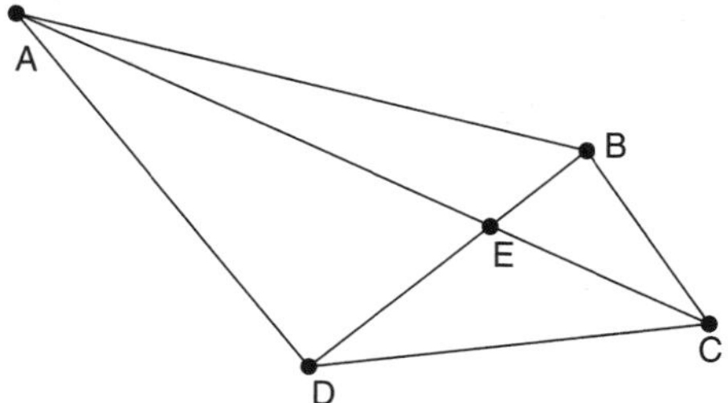

Now create segments *AE*, *EC*, *BE*, and *ED*. Measure all four of these segments, and calculate the value of the expression

$$AE \times EC - BE \times ED$$

Finally, construct an arc through points *B*, *C*, and *D* in that order; and then an arc through points *D*, *B*, and *C* in that order. This should give you a circle passing through points *B*, *C*, and *D* as illustrated below.

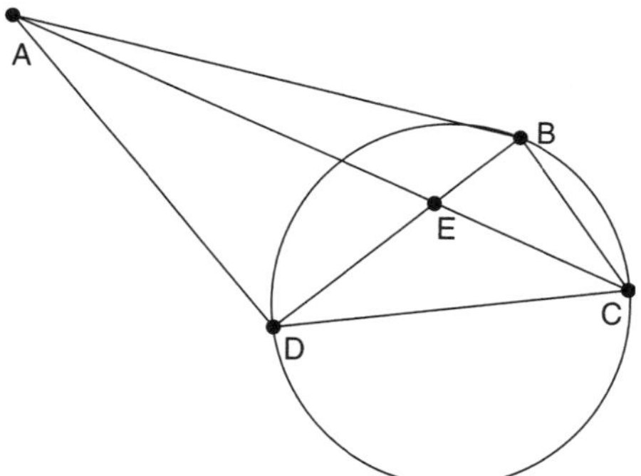

Drag point *A* around and watch what happens to the value of the expression $AE \times EC - BE \times ED$. Is there any place you can drag point *A* so that this expression takes on the value 0? Where does this happen?

The Geometric Solution of a Minimization Problem Using Reflection of a Point Across a Line Segment

PLANNING: GRADES 9–12

RELATED NCTM STANDARDS: Geometry

- Analyze properties and determine attributes of two- and three-dimensional objects.
- Explore relationships (including congruence and similarity) among classes of two- and three-dimensional geometric objects, make and test conjectures about them, and solve problems involving them.
- Establish the validity of geometric conjectures using deduction, prove theorems, and critique arguments made by others.
- Draw and construct representations of two- and three-dimensional geometric objects using a variety of tools.

MATHEMATICAL SKILLS AND CONCEPTS

Understand and use the geometric property that the shortest distance between two points is a straight line.

Understand and use the geometric relationship between a point and its reflection across a line segment.

SKETCHPAD FEATURES

Built-in tools Animation

The *Reflect* option under the *Transform* menu

MATERIALS

Copies of Activity Sheets 23.1 and 23.2 for each student.

CLASSROOM IMPLEMENTATION

Background Information for the Teacher

Your students will use a visual approach to investigate a minimization problem that is usually approached algebraically. They will discover that the solution depends on the simplest of all geometric properties: The shortest distance between two points is the straight line connecting those points.

Problem. To discover the geometric relationship between the location of points D and E and the location of point C that minimizes the sum $DC + CE$.

Step 1–Introducing the Problem Solving Scenario

Give your students **Activity Sheet 23.1** to work on. They will discover, and you can then demonstrate on a large screen display, that there is a unique position C along segment AB that minimizes the sum of the two segment lengths $DC + CE$; but this position changes when you change the locations of D and E. In other words, the minimizing position depends on where D and E are. We would now like to determine whether there is some geometric relationship between the locations of points D and E and the location of point C that minimizes the sum $DC + CE$.

Step 2–Investigating the Problem

Give your students **Activity Sheet 23.2** to work on. This activity is a continuation of what they did in Activity Sheet 23.1. Use a large screen display to review their work in this second activity sheet, or let one of the students do it. You are now ready to state the findings as a conjecture.

Step 3–Developing a Mathematical Conjecture

Your students will discover from **Activity Sheet 23.2** that the ray starting at point D and passing through point C goes right through reflected point E'. Actually, a small interval of positions on segment AB will all give the same minimum value for $DC + CE$. So, if the ray does not go exactly through E' when you construct it you can move point C slightly so that the ray does go through E' and point out that the value of $DC + CE$ is still minimized. The conjecture that this discovery leads to can be stated as:

> **Conjecture:** Given the situation we have been investigating in Activity Sheets 23.1 and 23.2, the point where the ray from point D and passing through point E' intersects segment AB will always minimize the value of $DC + CE$.

Step 4–Testing the Conjecture

To test this conjecture have your students move point E to a new position on the sketch they already have. (Alternatively, you can perform this procedure on the large screen display for the entire class to see.) This will automatically move point E' as well since E' is the reflection of E across segment AB. They can now move point C along AB until the ray once again passes through E'. Notice that this is exactly the position of point C that minimizes the value of $DC + CE$.

Step 5–A Mathematical Proof

The figures below show our geometric situation. Figure 23.1 has point C not in the minimizing position and Figure 23.2, in the minimizing position.

Point E' is the reflection of point E across segment AB, so the length of segment CE' is the same as the length of segment CE. So minimizing $DC + CE$ is equivalent to minimizing $DC + CE'$. From the property that the sum of any two sides of a triangle is greater than the third side, it is clear that $DC + CE' \geq DE$ as shown in Figure 23.3.

However, when point C is at the intersection of ray DE' and segment AB, length DE' is equal to length DC plus length CE'. So C at this position must give the minimal value for $DC + CE'$. This completes the proof.

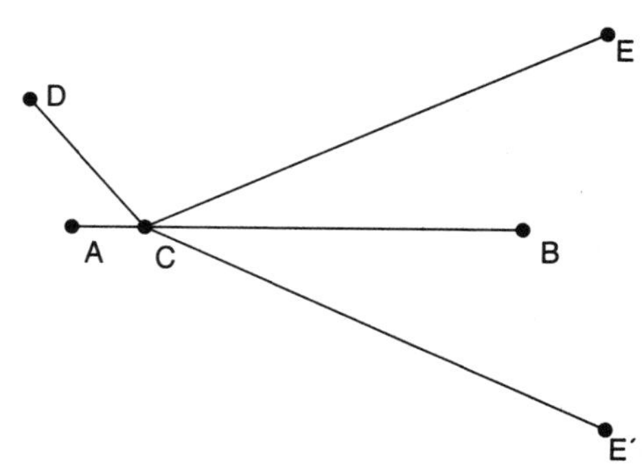

FIGURE 23.1

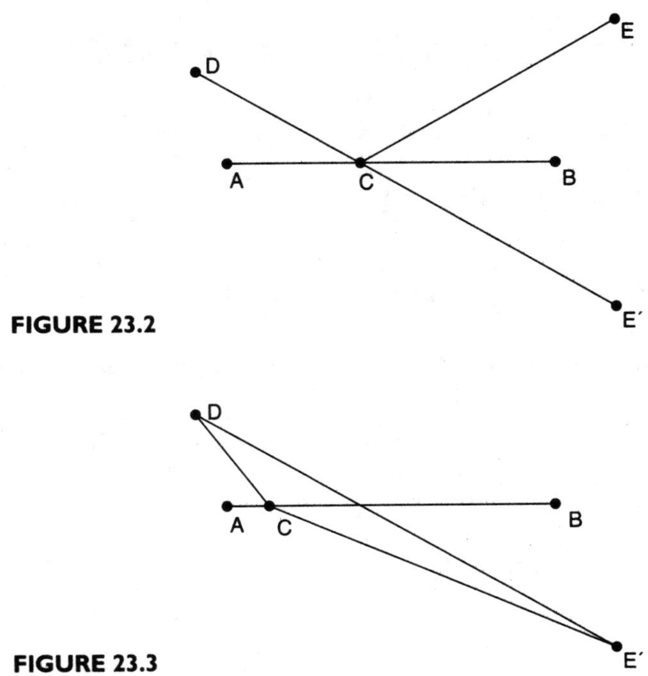

FIGURE 23.2

FIGURE 23.3

RELATED READINGS

Purdy, David C. "Using The Geometer's Sketchpad to Visualize Maximum-Volume Problems." *Mathematics Teacher* (NCTM, March 2000, Vol. 93, No. 3, p. 224).

Sherfinski, John. "Sharing Teaching Ideas: Multilayered Maximum-Minimum Problem." *Mathematics Teacher* (NCTM, March 2002, Vol. 95, No. 3, p. 218).

ACTIVITY SHEET

23.1 The Geometric Solution of a Minimization Problem Using Reflection of a Point Across a Line Segment

Construct a line segment AB and an arbitrary point C on the segment. Then construct points D and E above and near opposite ends of the segment. Connect D to C and C to E with line segments. The final sketch should look as shown below.

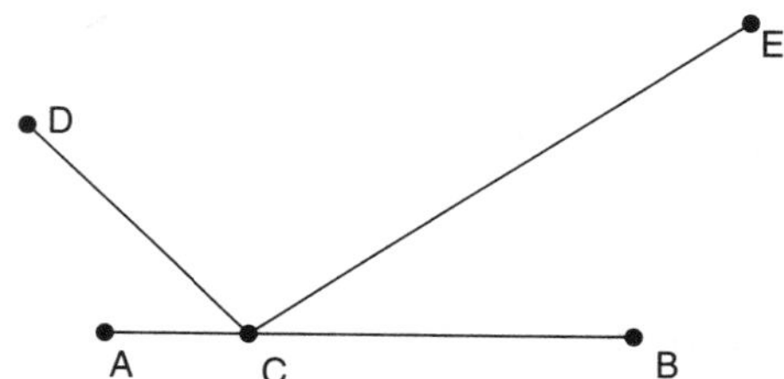

Now measure segments DC and CE and calculate their sum $DC + CE$. Drag point C along segment AB. Notice what happens to the sum $DC + CE$. Now answer the following questions.

Question 1. How does the sum of the lengths of segments DC and CE change as you move point C to different positions on segment AB? Is there a position that minimizes this sum? If so, place point C at that spot.

Question 2. Now move points D and E. Look at the value of the sum $DC + CE$ where you left point C. Drag C away from the position that minimized this sum in Question 1. Does this same position give the minimum for the new placements of D and E, or has the minimum position changed?

The Geometric Solution of a Minimization Problem Using Reflection of a Point Across a Line Segment

23.2 ACTIVITY SHEET

Construct the same type of sketch as you did in Activity Sheet 23.1. Then construct point E', the reflection of point E across segment AB. To do this, select both point E and segment AB; then go to the *Transform* menu and select the *Reflect* option. Your sketch should now look as shown below.

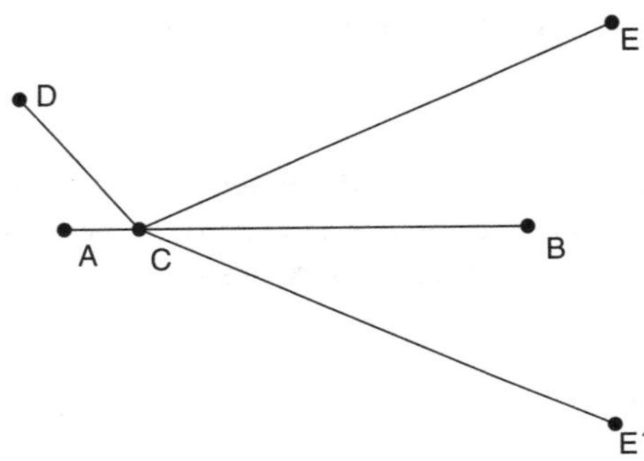

Move point C along segment AB until it is at the position that minimizes the sum $DC + CE$. Then construct a ray starting at point D and passing through point C. Do you notice anything interesting about this ray and the reflected point E'?

Solutions

ACTIVITY SHEET 1.1

Question 1. Beginning with $\frac{1}{3} + \frac{1}{6}$, every third pair gives a unit fraction sum.

Question 2. The larger denominator (and in fact the smaller denominator as well) is always divisible by 3 whenever the sum is itself a unit fraction. This is the only time the sum is a unit fraction.

Question 3.

Conjecture: Given two unit fractions with the second denominator equal to twice the first denominator, the sum of these two unit fractions itself can be written as a unit fraction if and only if the larger denominator is divisible by 3.

Question 4.

Conjecture: If the sum of two unit fractions with the second denominator equal to twice the first denominator can be written as a unit fraction, the denominator of the sum will be equal to the denominator of the second fraction divided by 3.

ACTIVITY SHEET 2.1

Question 1. $0.15 \times L = 120$

Question 2. $L = 800$

Note. Since 15% of the trees are cut down at the end of each year, 85% are left. Therefore the basic keystroke sequence for calculating the number of trees each successive year is

[×] [.85] [+] [120] [=]

Question 3.

Year	1	2	3	4	5	6	7	8	...
Trees	1000	970	945	923	904	889	875	864	...

The number of trees eventually reaches and remains at 800.

Question 4.

Year	1	2	3	4	5	6	7	8	...
Trees	500	545	583	616	643	667	687	704	...

The number of trees eventually reaches and remains at 800.

Question 5.

Year	1	2	3	4	5	6	7	8	...
Trees	800	800	800	800	800	800	800	800	...

ACTIVITY SHEET 2.2

Question 1. Any values of $A\%$ and B for which

$$A\% \times 250 = B$$

will give a limit of $L = 250$. For example, the following pairs would work, but so would infinitely many others.

$A\% = 10\%$	and	$B = 25$	since	$10\% \times 250 = 25$
$A\% = 20\%$	and	$B = 50$	since	$20\% \times 250 = 50$
$A\% = 30\%$	and	$B = 75$	since	$30\% \times 250 = 75$

Question 2. Use $A\% = 10\%$ and $B = 25$ for purposes of illustration, keeping in mind that if 10% of the trees are cut down each year then 90% of them are left. We find using the keystroke sequence [×] [.90] [+] [25] [=]:

Year	1	2	3	4	5	6	7	8	9	...
Trees	500	475	453	432	414	396	381	368	356	...

If you continue this chart you will see that the limit value for the number of trees is $L = 250$.

Question 3. Once again use the values $A\% = 10\%$ and $B = 25$. We find using the same keystroke sequence [×] [.90] [+] [25] [=]:

Year	1	2	3	4	5	6	7	8	9	...
Trees	100	115	129	141	152	161	170	178	185	...

If you continue this chart you will see that the limit value is $L = 250$.

ACTIVITY SHEET 2.3

Question 1. (i) The initial dose of 200 cc of the drug is equivalent to the starting size of the forest; (ii) the 75% of the drug that leaves the patient's body each hour is equivalent to the percent of trees that are cut down; and (iii) the 30 cc of the drug that is injected each hour is equivalent to the number of new trees planted each year.

Question 2.

i. $0.75 \times L = 30$

ii. $L = 40$ cc is the limit value over time.

iii. [×] [.25] [+] [30] [=] since, if 75% of the drug leaves the patient's body every hour, then 25% or 0.25 of the drug remains.

iv. To two decimal places we find

Hours	1	2	3	4	5	6	7	...
Drug	200	80	50	42.5	40.63	40.16	40.04	...

It appears fairly clear that this sequence of values is approaching 40 as a limit.

ACTIVITY SHEET 3.1

Example 1. The original price of the item is $100 and the two discounts are 10% and 15%.

	Store 1	**Store 2**
Original Price	$100	$100
1st Discount	10% × $100 = $10	15% × $100 = $15
Reduced Price	$100 − $10 = $90	$100 − $15 = $85
2nd Discount	15% × $90 = $13.50	10% × $85 = $8.50
Final Price	$90 − $13.50 = $76.50	$85 − $8.50 = $76.50

The final price is the same both ways. The order doesn't matter.

Example 2. The discounts are now 15% and 25%.

	Store 1	**Store 2**
Original Price	$100	$100
1st Discount	15% × $100 = $15	25% × $100 = $25
Reduced Price	$100 − $15 = $85	$100 − $25 = $75
2nd Discount	25% × $85 = $21.25	15% × $75 = $11.25
Final Price	$85 − $21.25 = $63.75	$75 − $11.25 = $63.75

The final price is the same both ways. The order doesn't matter.

Example 3. The original price of the item is $150 and the two discounts are 5% and 20%.

	Store 1	**Store 2**
Original Price	$150	$150
1st Discount	5% × $150 = $7.50	20% × $150 = $30
Reduced Price	$150 − $7.50 = $142.50	$150 − $30 = $120
2nd Discount	20% × $142.50 = $28.50	5% × $120 = $6
Final Price	$142.50 − $28.50 = $114	$120 − $6 = $114

The final price is the same both ways. The order doesn't matter.

Conclusion. As long as you use the same two percentage discounts, the final price is the same no matter what order the discounts are applied.

ACTIVITY SHEET 3.2

The calculations for the first two orderings are provided below. The calculations for the other four orderings are similar. All six give the same final price for the sneakers, \$75.60.

1 – 10%, then 20%, then 30%	
Original Price	\$150
10% Discount	10% × \$150 = \$15
Price After Discount	\$150 – \$15 = \$135
20% Discount	20% × \$135 = \$27
Price After Discount	\$135 – \$27 = \$108
30% Discount	30% × \$108 = \$32.40
Final Price	\$108 – \$32.40 = \$75.60

2 – 10%, then 30%, then 20%	
Original Price	\$150
10% Discount	10% × \$150 = \$15
Price After Discount	\$150 – \$15 = \$135
30% Discount	30% × \$135 = \$40.50
Price After Discount	\$135 – \$40.50 = \$94.50
20% Discount	20% × \$94.50 = \$18.90
Final Price	\$94.50 – \$18.90 = \$75.60

ACTIVITY SHEET 4.1

Two interesting things should happen. First, whatever positive number you begin with, if you repeatedly press the square root key the sequence of numbers you obtain will always approach 1. On a calculator, once the numbers are close enough to 1, they are displayed as exactly 1 even though they are only approximately equal to this value.

Second, if you begin with a positive number greater than 1, all the numbers you obtain by pressing the square root key will be greater than 1 and decrease toward 1 as a limit. Similarly, if you begin with a positive number less than 1, all the numbers you obtain by pressing the square root key will be less than 1 and increase toward 1 as a limit.

ACTIVITY SHEET 4.2

Yes, all three properties of the square root function also hold for the operation of averaging with 1: If you begin with a positive number greater than 1 and continually average it with 1, all the numbers you obtain are greater than 1 and decrease toward 1 as a limit; if you begin with a positive number less than 1 and continually average it with 1, all the numbers you obtain are positive numbers less than 1 and increase toward 1 as a limit; and if you begin with the number 1 and continually average it with 1, you repeatedly get 1 as a result.

ACTIVITY SHEET 4.3

No matter what starting value you begin with, applying the formula $x_{N+1} = Ax_N + B$ repeatedly with $0 < A < 1$ will give values that approach $\frac{B}{1 - A}$ as a limit. The reason for this result is that if the sequence does have a limit, and the value of this limit is L, then from some point on both x_{N+1} and x_N will be so close to L that we will almost have $L = AL + B$ or, solving for L, $L = \frac{B}{1 - A}$.

If, however, either $A = 1$ or $A > 1$, we find that the sequence of values obtained from the formula $x_{N+1} = Ax_N + B$ has no finite limit. We can state this result as follows:

> **Conjecture:** If we use the linear function $x_{N+1} = Ax_N + B$ to generate a sequence of numbers, then this sequence will have the finite limit $\frac{B}{1 - A}$ if $0 < A < 1$, and will diverge if $A = 1$ or if $A > 1$.

ACTIVITY SHEET 5.1

Question 1. In the first investigation the sum of the infinite series, 32, was twice the first term of the series, 16. Therefore it is reasonable to predict that the sum of any infinite geometric series with a constant ratio of ½ will be twice the first term. Therefore the sum of the first series, which begins with 40, should be 2 × 40 or 80; and the sum of the second series, which begins with 100, should be 2 × 100 or 200.

Question 2. Using the same set of steps as with the original infinite series in class, we find the following values for the first several partial sums of each series. In both cases the partial sums do appear to approach the sums predicted in Question 1.

Partial Sums for the First Series, Approaching 80

L_2:	40	60	70	75	77.5	78.75	79.375	79.688	...

Partial Sums for the Second Series, Approaching 200

L_2:	100	150	175	187.5	193.75	196.88	198.44	...

ACTIVITY SHEET 5.2

Question 1. The first several partial sums are:

L_2:	30	40	43.333	44.444	44.815	44.938

After several more of these values it seems clear that they are approaching a limit of $S = 45$.

Question 2. Since $45 = \frac{3}{2} \times 30$ we have:

> **Conjecture:** Given an infinite geometric series with constant ratio $r = \frac{1}{3}$ and first term A, the sum of the series can be written as "Sum $= \frac{3}{2} \times A$."

Question 3. If the series has first A and constant ratio of $\frac{1}{3}$, it can be written as

$$S = A + A/3 + A/9 + A/27 + A/81 + \dots$$

Multiply both sides of this equation by $\frac{1}{3}$, line up the common terms underneath each other, and subtract. We find:

$$\begin{aligned} S &= A + A/3 + A/9 + A/27 + A/27 + \dots \\ -\tfrac{1}{3}S &= \phantom{A +{}} A/3 + A/9 + A/27 + A/81 + \dots \\ \hline \tfrac{2}{3}S &= A \end{aligned}$$

so $S = \frac{3}{2} \times A$ and the proof is complete.

Question 4. The first several partial sums are:

L_2:	36	45	47.25	47.813	47.953	47.988

After several more of these values it seems clear that they are approaching a limit of $S = 48$.

Since $48 = \frac{4}{3} \times 36$, we can state the following conjecture:

Conjecture: Given an infinite geometric series with constant ratio $r = \frac{1}{4}$ and first term A, the sum of the series can be written as "Sum $= \frac{4}{3} \times A$."

Proof of Conjecture: If the series has first term A and constant ratio of $\frac{1}{4}$, it can be written as

$$S = A + A/4 + A/16 + A/64 + A/256 + \ldots$$

Multiply both sides of this equation by $\frac{1}{4}$, line up the common terms underneath each other, and subtract. We find

$$\begin{aligned} S &= A + A/4 + A/16 + A/64 + A/256 + \ldots \\ \tfrac{1}{4}S &= \phantom{A + {}} A/4 + A/16 + A/64 + A/256 + \ldots \\ \hline \tfrac{3}{4}S &= A \end{aligned}$$

so $S = \frac{4}{3} \times A$ and the proof is complete.

ACTIVITY SHEET 6.1

Possible Units Digits	% of Time 1 to 10	% of Time 1 to 20	% of Time 1 to 30
0	10%	10%	10%
1	20%	20%	20%
2	0%	0%	0%
3	0%	0%	0%
4	20%	20%	20%
5	10%	10%	10%
6	20%	20%	20%
7	0%	0%	0%
8	0%	0%	0%
9	20%	20%	20%

Whether you look at the squares from 1^2 to 10^2, or 1^2 to 20^2, or 1^2 to 30^2, the same digits occur with the same relative frequency. Perhaps we would have the same result if we looked at the set of *all* perfect squares and their units digits.

ACTIVITY SHEET 6.2

Step 1. For 1 to 10, 1 to 20, and 1 to 30 every digit from 0 to 9 occurs as the units digit of the cubes and they all occur the same percent of the time, 10% each.

Step 2.

Conjecture: For the set of all positive integers, the digits 0 through 9 all occur as the units digit of the corresponding set of cubes and they each occur 10% of the time.

Step 3. Using the modified program with $N = 100, 200$, and 300 gives exactly the same results as before. This provides further evidence of the truth of the conjecture.

Note. The proof of this conjecture uses the same steps and logic as that of the conjecture in the original investigation. In this case, however, you must use the fact that if $N = a_0 + 10a_1 + 100a_3 + 1000a_4 + \ldots$ then

$$N^3 = a_0^3 + 30a_0^2a_1 + \ldots$$

and only the term a_0^3 contributes to the units digit of the sum.

ACTIVITY SHEET 6.3

Step 1. The following chart shows the units digits of perfect squares, A^2, with their relative frequencies, and the units digits of numbers of the form A^4 that these digits lead to when they are squared.

A^2 Units Digit	Relative Frequency	A^4 Units Digits
0	.1	$0^2 \to 0$
1	.2	$1^2 \to 1$
4	.2	$4^2 \to 6$
5	.1	$5^2 \to 5$
6	.2	$6^2 \to 6$
9	.2	$9^2 \to 1$

As you can see, the only digits that can appear as the units digit of a number of the form A^4 are 0, 1, 5, and 6. 0 and 5 each occur .1 of the time, and 1 and 6 each occur .2 + .2 = .4 of the time. The conjecture would be that these same results hold for the set of *all* numbers of the form A^4.

Step 2. Yes, the conjecture holds true for $N = 100$ and 200.

ACTIVITY SHEET 7.2

		Die 2					
		1	**2**	**3**	**4**	**5**	**6**
	1	A	A	A	B	B	B
	2	A	A	A	A	B	B
Die 1	3	A	A	A	A	A	B
	4	B	A	A	A	A	A
	5	B	B	A	A	A	A
	6	B	B	B	A	A	A

Player A wins in 24 out of the 36 results, or 67% of the time.

Player B wins in 12 out of the 36 results, or 33% of the time.

Based on these results, we would expect Player A to win approximately twice as often as Player B.

ACTIVITY SHEET 7.3

```
PROGRAM: GAME2
:ClrHome
:0 → A: 0 → B
:For(X, 1, 50, 1)
:randInt(1, 6) → C
:randInt(1, 6) → D
:max(C, D) → E
:If E ≤ 3 or E = 5
:A + 1 → A
:If E = 4 or E = 6
:B + 1 → B
:End
:Disp A, B
```

		Die 2					
		1	**2**	**3**	**4**	**5**	**6**
	1	A	A	A	B	A	B
	2	A	A	A	B	A	B
Die 1	3	A	A	A	B	A	B
	4	B	B	B	B	A	B
	5	A	A	A	A	A	B
	6	B	B	B	B	B	B

Player A wins in 18 out of the 36 results, or 50% of the time.

Player B wins in 18 out of the 36 results, or 50% of the time.

Is the game fair? If not, whom does it favor? Yes, it is fair.

ACTIVITY SHEET 7.4

```
PROGRAM: GAME3
:ClrHome
:0 → A: 0 → B
:For(X, 1, 50, 1)
:randInt(1, 6) → C
:randInt(1, 6) → D
:min(C, D) → E
:If E ≤ 3
:A + 1 → A
:If E > 3
:B + 1 → B
:End
:Disp A, B
```

		Die 2					
		1	**2**	**3**	**4**	**5**	**6**
	1	A	A	A	A	A	A
	2	A	A	A	A	A	A
Die 1	3	A	A	A	A	A	A
	4	A	A	A	B	B	B
	5	A	A	A	B	B	B
	6	A	A	A	B	B	B

Player A wins in 27 out of the 36 results, or 75% of the time.

Player B wins in 9 out of the 36 results, or 25% of the time.

Is the game fair? If not, whom does it favor? It is not fair. It favors Player A three to one.

ACTIVITY SHEET 8.1

Step 1. If you double the initial velocity, the time to go up and come down will be doubled as well ($2 \times 1 = 2$ seconds to go up and $2 \times 1 = 2$ seconds to come down for a total of 4 seconds for the entire trip), but the maximum height reached will be multiplied by 2^2 ($4 \times 16 = 64$ feet).

Step 2. Based on the results of Step 1 we predict that if the initial velocity of the object is multiplied by 3, then the time to go up and come down will also be multiplied by 3 (3 second to go up and 3 seconds to come down for a total of 6 seconds); and that the maximum height will be multiplied by 3^2 or 9 to give a maximum height of $9 \times 16 = 144$ feet. When we develop a graph and table of values for the modified equation we find that these predictions are correct.

Step 3.

Conjecture: If the initial velocity of the object is multiplied by K, then the time it takes to go up will be $K \times 1 = K$ seconds; the time to come down will be $K \times 1 = K$ seconds; and the maximum height will be $K^2 \times 16 = 16\,K^2$ feet.

ACTIVITY SHEET 8.2

Step 1. It takes 2 seconds to go up and 2 seconds to come down, and the maximum height is 32 feet. It therefore appears that multiplying the force of gravity by ½ multiplies the time to go up, the time to come down, and the maximum height each by 2.

Step 2. Based on the result in Step 1 we predict that if we multiply the force of gravity by $\frac{1}{4}$, all three measurements will be multiplied by 4 to give a time to go up of $4 \times 1 = 4$ seconds; a time to come down of $4 \times 1 = 4$ seconds; and a maximum height of $4 \times 16 = 64$ feet. Using the calculator we find that these predictions are exactly correct.

Step 3.

Conjecture: If the force of gravity is multiplied by $\frac{1}{K}$, giving a corresponding equation $y = 32x - \frac{16}{K}x^2$, the time to go up, the time to come down, and the maximum height will all be multiplied by K.

ACTIVITY SHEET 9.1

Degree of Polynomial Function	Maximum Number of Turns	Maximum Number of Real Roots
1	0	1
2	1	2
3	2	3
4	3	4

ACTIVITY SHEET 9.2

Step 1.

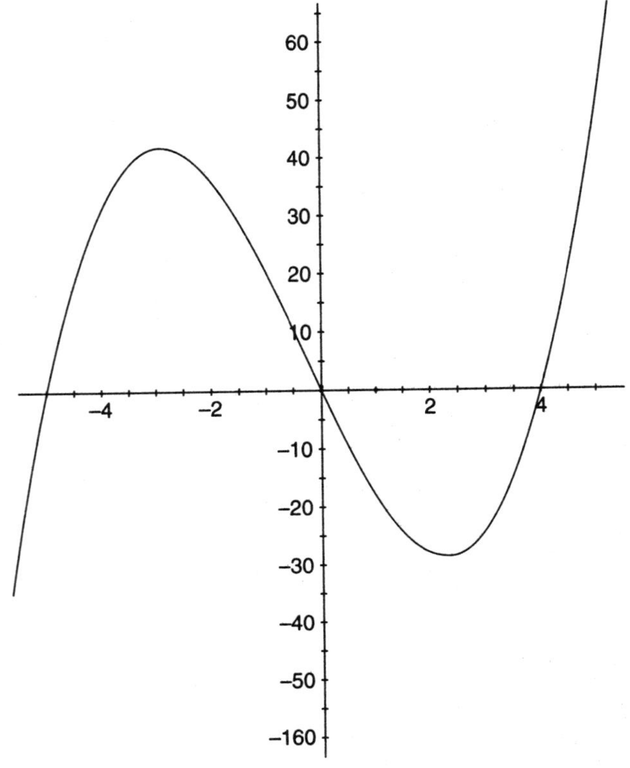

y = (x)(x – 4)(x + 5). Three real roots.

Step 2. There are an infinite number of possible answers to this question. Shown below is one solution with the corresponding graphs.

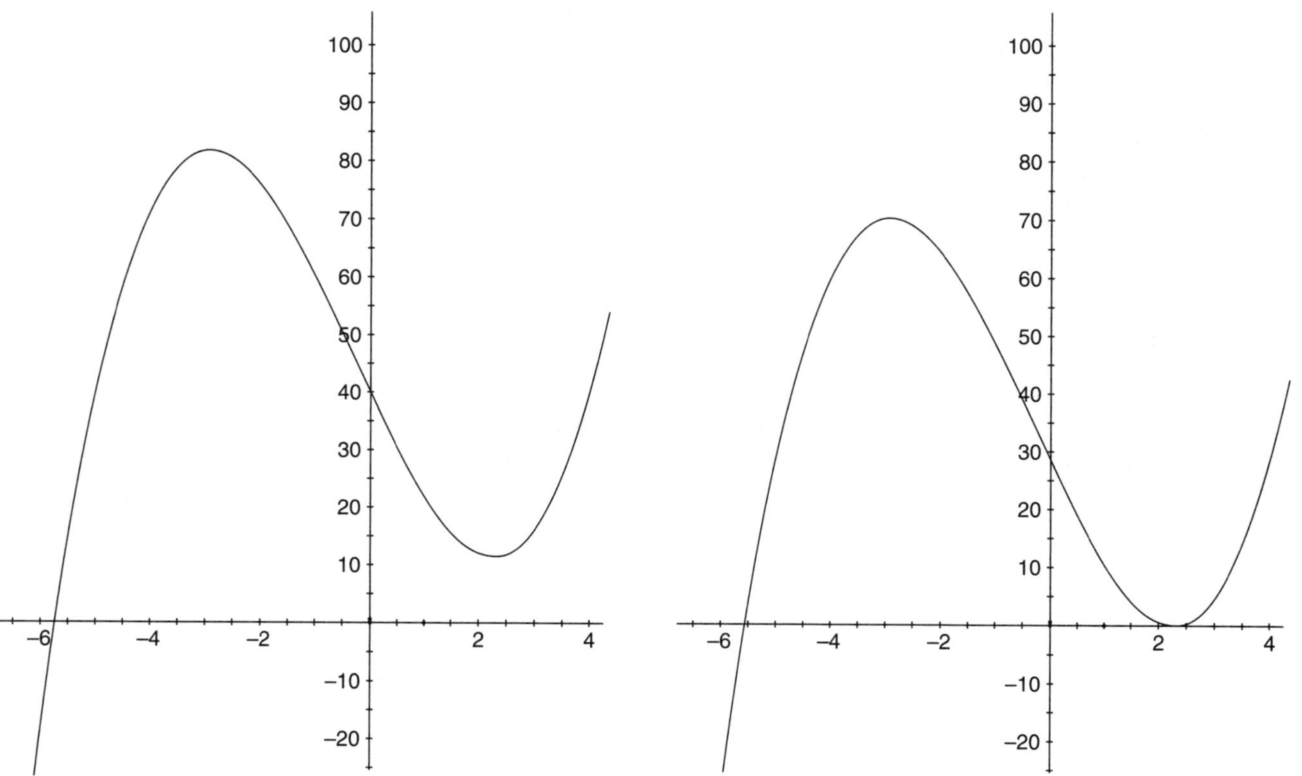

y = x(x − 4)(x + 5) + 40. One real root.

y = x(x − 4)(x + 5) + 28.55 (approximately). Two real roots.

Step 3.

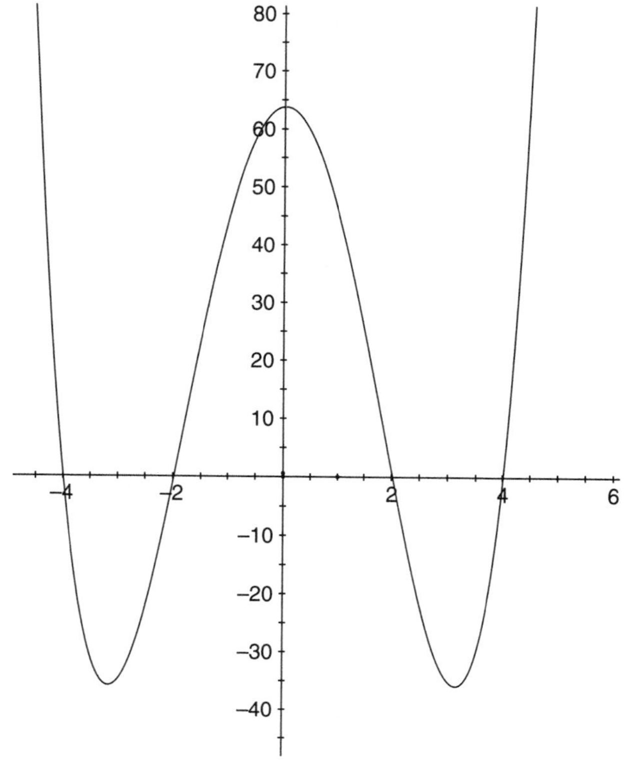

y = (x + 4)(x + 2)(x − 4)(x − 2). Four real roots.

Step 4. There are an infinite number of possible answers to this question. One solution is shown below with the corresponding graphs.

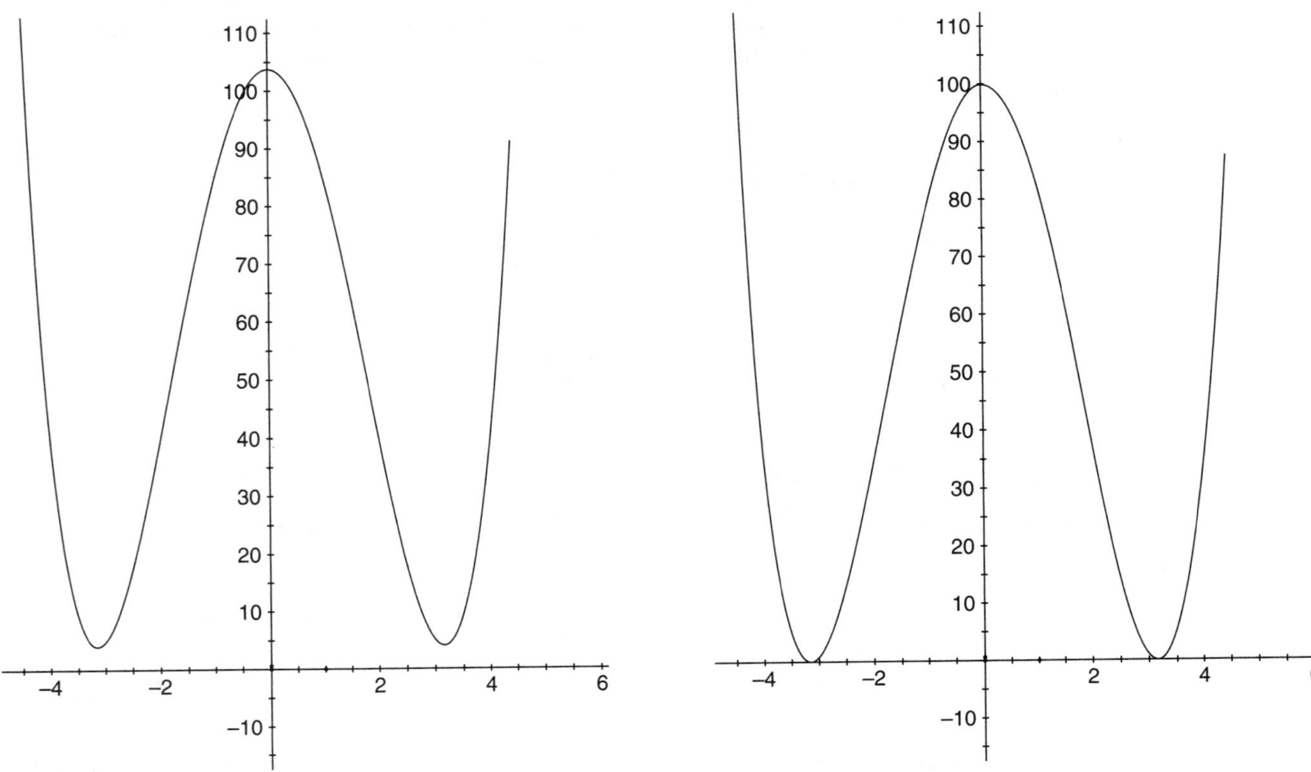

y = (x + 4)(x + 2)(x – 4)(x – 2) + 40. No real roots.

y = (x + 4)(x + 2)(x – 4)(x – 2) + 36. Two real roots.

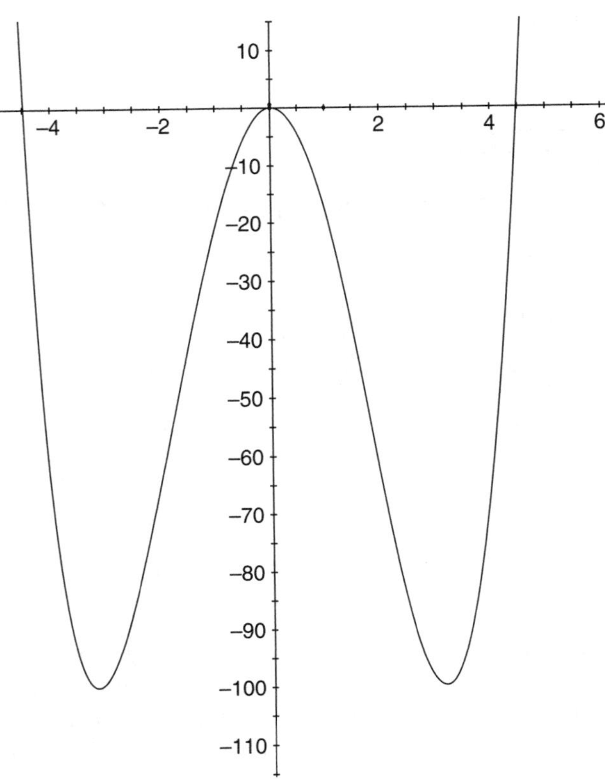

y = (x + 4)(x + 2)(x – 4)(x – 2) – 64. Three real roots.

The function in Step 3 has an even degree, so its graph begins and ends at the same end of the y axis. Consequently, by adding a large enough constant to the original function we can raise it so that it doesn't intersect the x axis at all. The function in Step 1 has an odd degree, so its graph begins and ends at opposite ends of the y axis. Therefore, no matter how much we either raise or lower the graph, it will still intersect the x axis in at least one point.

ACTIVITY SHEET 12.3

Step 1. The table will look as shown below.

x	y_1	y_2
1	1	1
2	.5	2
3	.33333	3
4	.25	4
5	.2	5
6	.16667	6
7	.14286	7

Step 2. The values in the y_2 list are just the inverses of the corresponding values in the y_1 list. Based on this observation, you can write $y_1 = 1/y_2$.

Step 3. The values in the y_3 list are all 1. This means the product of y_1 and y_2 is 1 so $y_1 = 1/y_2$, or, equivalently, the derivative of $y = \ln(x)$ is $1/x$.

ACTIVITY SHEET 13.1

A few of the partial sums for the two infinite series are shown below. The symbol S_K stands for the Kth partial sum.

	$S = 1 + \frac{1}{2} + \frac{1}{3} + \frac{1}{4} + \frac{1}{5} + \ldots + \frac{1}{K} + \ldots$	$S = 1 - \frac{1}{2} + \frac{1}{3} - \frac{1}{4} + \frac{1}{5} - \frac{1}{6} + \ldots + \frac{(-1)^{K-1}}{K} + \ldots$
S_1	1	1
S_2	1.5	0.5
S_3	1.8333 . . .	0.8333 . . .
S_4	2.0833 . . .	0.5833 . . .
S_{100}	5.1873 . . .	0.6881 . . .
S_{200}	5.8780 . . .	0.6906 . . .
S_{300}	6.2826 . . .	0.6914 . . .

The terms in the first infinite series are all positive, so we expect that the sequence of partial sums will steadily increase, and that is just what we observe from the list above. However, we cannot tell just from this short list whether the partial sums will grow without bound, indicating divergence of the infinite series; or they will approach some finite value, indicating convergence.

The terms in the second infinite series are alternately positive and negative, so we expect the sequence of partial sums to alternately increase and decrease, which is precisely what we observe from the list above. Here the partial sums seem to oscillate closer and closer to some finite value from above and from below. If this is the case, then the infinite series is convergent, and the limit of the series is the value that the partial sums are approaching.

ACTIVITY SHEET 13.2

For Series A

$$\text{seq}(((-1)\hat{}(x-1))/(2\hat{}(x-1)), x, 1, 25) \rightarrow L_1$$

$$\text{cumSum}(L_1) \rightarrow L_2$$

This series converges to the limit $S = 2/3 = 0.666\ldots$, and this value does lie between the 10th partial sum, S_{10}, and the 11th partial sum, S_{11}, of the series, as shown below.

$$S_{10} = 0.66602\ldots \leq 0.6666\ldots \leq 0.66699\ldots = S_{11}$$

For Series B

$$\text{seq}((-1)\hat{}(x+1)/(2x-1), x, 1, 25) \rightarrow L_1$$

$$\text{cumSum}(L_1) \rightarrow L_2$$

This series converges to the limit $T = \pi/4 = 0.73589\ldots$, and this value does lie between the 10th partial sum, T_{10}, and the 11th partial sum, T_{11}, of the series, as shown below.

$$T_{10} = 0.76045\ldots \leq 0.73589\ldots \leq 0.80807\ldots = T_{11}$$

ACTIVITY SHEET 14.1

Question 1. The linear regression equation for this data is $y = -0.2883\ldots x + 627.2997\ldots$, which rounds to the nearest hundredth of a second as $y = -0.29x + 627.30$. The slope, approximately -0.29, is the decrease in seconds per year for the women's winning time. The Olympics takes place every four years, so the improvement from one Olympics to the next would be approximately four times this value, or $4*0.29 = 1.16$ seconds.

Question 2. This linear regression line intersects with the x axis at approximately $x = 2176$. If we used the linear regression equation on the data from 1912 to 1996 to predict this far into the future, the predicted women's winning time in this event in the year 2176 would be 0 seconds, an obvious impossibility.

Question 3. This answer shows a linear regression equation can give obviously false results for values too far away from the data on which it was developed. In this case the winning women's times would have to improve at a decreasing rate rather than at the same rate since you cannot have a winning time of 0 seconds.

ACTIVITY SHEET 14.2

Question 1. The linear regression equation for the men's times is $y = -0.17x + 391.92$, rounding both coefficients to the nearest hundredth. This line intersects the women's linear regression line at approximately $x = 2030$ and $y = 42.07$.

Question 2. This means that in the Olympics closest to the year 2030 the women's and the men's winning times will both be approximately 42.07 seconds.

Question 3. The year 2030 is nowhere near as far in the future as the year 2176 found in the answer to Question 2 in Activity Sheet 14.1. Therefore we could use the two linear regression equations to make an accurate prediction for $x = 2030$. The assumption, however, is that both the women's and the men's winning times decrease at a constant rate up to that date, which may not happen.

ACTIVITY SHEET 15.1

Question 1. $y = 1$ when $x = 0$, so we have $a = 1$. You go from any y value to the next by multiplying the first value by 5, so we have $b = 5$. Therefore the exponential function representing this situation is $y = 1*5^x$.

Question 2. Using a table of values we find that we first have a value of $y \geq 1{,}000{,}000$ when $x = 9$ (the actual value of y when $x = 9$ is 1,953,125).

Question 3. We need to enter this keystroke sequence 9 times to obtain a display value greater than 1,000,000. Each repetition of this keystroke sequence corresponds to the passage of one day, so 9 uses of the keystroke sequence ($x = 9$) display a value of $y = 1{,}953{,}125$. This answer agrees perfectly with our answer to Question 2.

ACTIVITY SHEET 15.2

Step 2. Theoretically, every time you pour the M&M's onto the plate, 50% of them should have the letter *M* on top. Therefore the population size should increase by 50% each time, giving a constant multiplier of 1.5 to go from one year to the next. A constant multiplier to go from one y value to the next is the basic requirement of an exponential equation, so such an equation would be appropriate here.

You began with $y = 8$ M&M's when $x = 0$, so you should have $a = 8$. And the constant multiplier for y is 1.5, so you should have $b = 1.5$. So, the exponential function that theoretically would model this situation is $y = 8*1.5^x$.

Step 3. When $x = 6$ we predict that the population size will be $y = 8*1.5^6 = 91.125$ or, rounding off, approximately 91 M&M's.

Steps 5 & 6. The answer here obviously depends on each group's data and the "Error of Prediction" value that this result leads to. If the Error of Prediction is in fact less than or equal to 0.05 then the result supports the conjecture; otherwise, it does not.

ACTIVITY SHEET 15.3

Step 2. Theoretically, half of the M&M's should have the letter *M* appearing on top each time you pour them out onto the plate. This means that each successive year the population size should be cut in half, or multiplied by 0.5. This situation is perfectly modeled by an exponential function with the population size at $x = 0$ serving as the value of a ($a = 80$) and the common multiplier as the value of b ($b = 0.5$). The exponential equation is therefore $y = 80*0.5^x$.

Step 3. When $x = 6$ we predict that $y = 80*0.5^6 = 1.25$ or about 1 M&M.

Step 4. The result here will depend on the actual data obtained from doing the experiment.

ACTIVITY SHEET 18.1

Question 1. No. In general, the inscribed figure will be an arbitrary quadrilateral, not a parallelogram.

Question 2. The ratio is now 1.60 and this result is invariant when dragging vertices or sides. This result holds for any quadrilateral, so it certainly holds for special quadrilaterals such as parallelograms, rhombuses, rectangles, and squares.

Question 3. In general, starting with a parallelogram, a rhombus, or a rectangle leads only to a parallelogram. Starting with a square, however, leads to another square.

ACTIVITY SHEET 19.1

Question 1. No, you do not get the same type of invariance. The sum of the lengths of the perpendicular line segments connecting an interior point to each side of an arbitrary triangle changes as you move the point around.

Question 2. Yes, you do get the same type of invariant sum. In fact, the sum of the segment lengths will always be equal to twice the length of the side of the square.

Question 3. No. As with the arbitrary triangle in Question 1, the sum of the segment lengths in an arbitrary quadrilateral will change as you move the point to different positions inside the quadrilateral.

Question 4.

> **Conjecture:** Given an *N*-sided ***regular** polygon* and a point inside this polygon, the **sum of the perpendicular line segments from the point to the sides of the polygon** will remain invariant as the point moves to any other position in the interior of the polygon.

ACTIVITY SHEET 21.1

Question 1. The ratio of the circumscribed circle's area to the inscribed circle's area for the equilateral triangle is 4.

Question 2. The ratio of the circumscribed circle's area to the inscribed circle's area for the square is 2.

Question 3. The area ratio decreased from 4 to 2 as we went from a three-sided regular polygon to a four-sided regular polygon. So, we can predict that the area ratio will continue to decrease as the number of sides of the regular polygon gets even larger.

ACTIVITY SHEET 22.1

The position of point A relative to the circle, and the value of the expression $AE*EC - BE*ED$, are related as follows.

- If point A remains outside the circle, the value of the expression will be positive.
- The value of the expression will decrease as point A is dragged closer to the circle.
- When point A is on the circle, the value of the expression will be 0.
- When point A is inside the circle, the value of the expression will be negative.

Index

abs(, 52
Activity sheets, solutions, 160–175
Algebra
  ancient Egyptian unit fractions, 4–8
  derivatives, 88–93
  Fibonacci sequence, 117–123
  fixed points and conveying sequences, 26–34
  infinite series, 94–101
  price increase/decreases, 19–25
  recursive functions, 9–18
  relationship between coefficients of first/second degree function, 81–87
  sum of infinite geometric series, 37–43
  trajectory of object in motion, 60–65
  visual discovery of trigonometric identities/formulas, 81–87
  visual inspection of real roots of polynomial function, 66–73
Alternating series, 96
Ancient Egyptian unit fraction rule, 4–8
Ancient Greeks, 5
Animate Point option, 145
Answers to activity sheets, 160–175
APPS, 53
Averaging, 28

Bonacci, Leonardo Pisano (Fibonacci), 117
Book of Shapes, 130. *See also* Geometry

Cabri Geometry, 125
"CabriWorld: The Third Cabri/Geometry International Conference," 125
CALC, 60, 74, 81
Calculator. *See* Graphing calculator; Scientific calculator
Calculator keys and features
  abs(, 52
  CALC, 60, 74, 81
  COS, 81
  cumSum, 37, 94
  ExpReg, 102, 110
  fix key, 9, 19, 26
  fPart, 44
  fraction key, 4
  fraction simplify key, 4
  GRAPH, 60, 66, 74, 81, 88, 102, 110
  Histogram, 44
  LinReg (ax + b), 102
  LIST, 37, 94, 102, 110
  max(, 52
  min(, 52
  operation keys, 9, 26
  percent key, 19
  PRGM, 44, 52
  PwrReg, 102
  repeated operation keys, 9, 26
  Seq(, 37, 94
  SIN, 81
  square root key, 26
  STAT, 44, 102, 110
  STAT PLOT, 102, 110
  TABLE, 60, 81, 88, 102, 110
  TBLSET, 60, 81, 88, 102, 110
  TRACE, 60, 81
  VARS, 88, 102, 110
  WINDOW, 60, 66, 74, 81, 88
  Y=, 66, 74, 81, 88
Chain letter, 112, 114
Converging sequences, 26–34
COS, 81
cumSum, 37, 94
Curve fitting, 102–109

Data analysis & probability
  curve fitting, 102–109
  exponential growth/exponential regression, 110–116
  probability–fairness, 52–59
  units digits of perfect squares, 44–51
Derivatives, 88–93
Dessart, Donald J., 2
Discrete math, 15
Divergent series, 41
Diverges to infinity, 96
Dr. Vogel's Gallery of Calculus Pathologies, 99
Dunham, Penelope H., 3, 36
Dynamic geometry software, 125–159
  activities. *See* Geometry
  background/overview, 125
  research, 126
"Dynamic Mathematics Visualization for Young Learners: Sketchpad in Grades 3–8," 125

"Effects of Hand-held Calculators in Precollege Mathematics Education: A Meta-Analysis" (Hembree/Dessart), 2
Ellington, Aimee J., 2–3
Entertainment Insiders web site, 105
Erdos-Mordell theorem, 139
Euclid's axiomatic geometry, 5
Evolution of a Graphing Calculator Course for Preserve Mathematics Teachers" (Mittag/Taylor), 36
Exponential growth/exponential regression, 110–116
Exponential regression equations, 104
ExpReg, 102, 110
Fermat points, 140
Fibonacci (Leonardo Pisano Bonacci), 117
Fibonacci sequence, 117–123
Fix key, 9, 19, 26
Fixed points and converging sequences, 26–34
Flash technology, 53
fPart, 44
Fraction key, 4
Fraction simplify key, 4

Geometer's Sketchpad, 125
Geometric Supposer, The, 125
Geometry, 127–159
  area relationships between inscribed/circumscribed circles, 147–151
  inscribed quadrilaterals, 132–136
  line segment–perimeter/area relationships, 142–146
  minimization problem, 155–159
  polygons–triangles, 137–141
  product of segments of intersecting chords in circle, 152–154
  properties of quadrilaterals *vs.* properties of their diagonals, 127–131
Golden mean, 122
Golden section, 121
Grades 6–8
  ancient Egyptian unit functions, 4–8
  fixed points and converging sequences, 26–34
  price increases/decreases, 19–25
  probability–fairness, 52–59
  recursive functions, 9–18
  units digits of perfect squares, 44–51
Grades 9–12
  curve fitting, 102–109
  derivatives, 88–93
  fixed points and converging sequences, 26–34
  geometry. *See* Geometry
  infinite series, 94–101
  probability–fairness, 52–59
  recursive functions, 9–18
  relationship between coefficients of first/second degree function, 81–87
  sum of infinite geometric series, 37–43
  trajectory of object in motion, 60–65
  units digits of perfect squares, 44–51
  visual discovery of trigonometric identities/formulas, 81–87
  visual inspection of real roots of polynomial function, 66–73
GRAPH, 60, 66, 74, 81, 88, 102, 110

Graphing calculator, 35–124. *See also* Scientific calculator
- ancient Egyptian unit fraction rule, 4–8
- converging sequences, 26–34
- curve fitting, 102–109
- derivatives, 88–93
- exponential growth/exponential regression, 110–116
- Fibonacci sequence, 117–123
- infinite series, 94–101
- keys/features. *See* Calculator keys and features
- linear regression–curve fitting, 102–109
- price increases/decreases, 22
- probability–fairness, 52–59
- recursive functions, 13
- relationship between coefficients of first/second degree function, 74–80
- research, 35–36
- sum of infinite geometric series, 37–43
- trajectory of object in motion, 60–65
- units digits of perfect squares, 44–51
- visual discovery of trigonometric identities/formulas, 81–87
- visual inspection of real roots of polynomial function, 66–73

Green Globs, 75
Green Globs and Graphing Equations, 75

"Handheld Graphing Technology at the Secondary Level: Research Findings and Implications for Classroom Practice," 35
Harmonic series, 100
Hembree, Ray, 2
HickokSports.com, 104, 105
Histogram, 44–51, 110–116

"Implications of Using Dynamic Geometry Technology for Teaching and Learning" (Olive), 126
Infinite series, 94–101
Inscribed quadrilaterals, 132–136
Invariants, 137
Iterative procedures
- converging sequences, 26–34
- recursive functions, 9–18

Jones, Keith, 126

Knott, Ron, 121

Line segment–perimeter/area relationships, 142–146
LinReg (ax + b), 102
LIST, 37, 94, 102, 110

max(, 52
"Meta-Analysis of the Effects of Calculators on Students' Achievement and Attitude Levels in Precollege Mathematics Classes" (Ellington), 2
min(, 52
Minimization problem, 155–159
Mittag, Kathleen Cage, 36
M&M's–exponential growth/regression, 115, 116
Motion Controller, 145

NCTM standards. *See* Algebra; Data analysis & probability; Geometry; Number & operations
Number & operations
- ancient Egyptian unit fractions, 4–8
- Fibonacci sequence, 117–123
- price increases/decreases, 19–25
- units digits of perfect squares, 44–51

"Number Spirals," 48

Olive, John, 126
Olympic data, 102–109
Operation keys, 9, 26

Parallel box plot, 44–51, 110–116
Parallelogram, 127–131, 132–136
Partial sums, 95
Percent key, 19
Polygons–triangles, 137–141
Pomerantz, Heidi, 1
Power regression equations, 104
PRGM, 44, 52
Price increases/decreases, 19–25
"Prime Spiral," 48
"Prime Village," 48
Probability–fairness, 52–59
PwrReg, 102
Pythagorean theorem, 134

Quadrilateral, 127–131, 132–136

Rectangle, 127–131, 132–136
Recursive functions, 9–18
Reflect option (Transform menu), 159
Relationship between coefficients of first/second degree function, 74–80
Relative frequency tables, 44–51
Repeated operation keys, 9, 26
Research
- dynamic geometry software, 126
- graphing calculator, 35–36
- scientific calculator, 2–3

"Research on the use of dynamic geometry software: implications for the classroom" (Jones), 126
Rhombus, 127–131, 132–136

Scatterplot, 44–51, 110–116
Scientific calculator, 1–34. *See also* Graphing calculator
- ancient Egyptian unit fraction rule, 4–8
- fixed points and converging sequences, 26–34
- keys/features. *See* Calculator keys and features
- price increases/decreases, 19–25
- recursive functions, 9–18
- research, 2–3

Scribes, 5
Seq(, 37, 94
SIN, 81
Sketchpad, 125. *See also* Geometry
Solutions to activity sheets, 160–175
Spreadsheet
- converging sequences, 29–30
- Fibonacci sequence, 120
- infinite series, 97–98
- recursive function, 14
- sum of infinite geometric series, 40
- trajectory of object in motion, 62
- visual inspection of real roots of polynomial function, 70

Square, 127–131, 132–136
Square root key, 26
Standards. *See* Algebra; Data analysis & probability; Geometry; Number & operations
STAT, 44, 102, 110
STAT PLOT, 102, 110
Sum of infinite geometric series, 37–43

TABLE, 60, 81, 88, 102, 110
Taylor, Sharon E., 36
TBLSET, 60, 81, 88, 102, 110
The Numbers, 105
TRACE, 60, 81
Trajectory of object in motion, 60–65
Transform menu–Reflect option, 159
Triangle, 132–136, 137–141

Unit fraction rule, 4–8
UNITS, 45–46
Units digits of perfect squares, 44–51

VARS, 88, 102, 110
Visual discovery of trigonometric identities/formulas, 81–87
Visual inspection of real roots of polynomial function, 66–73

WINDOW, 60, 66, 74, 81, 88

Y=, 66, 74, 81, 88

Zeno's Paradox, 95